IFIP Advances in Information and Communication Technology 389

IFIP – The International Federation for Information Processing

IFIP was founded in 1960 under the auspices of UNESCO, following the First World Computer Congress held in Paris the previous year. An umbrella organization for societies working in information processing, IFIP's aim is two-fold: to support information processing within its member countries and to encourage technology transfer to developing nations. As its mission statement clearly states,

> *IFIP's mission is to be the leading, truly international, apolitical organization which encourages and assists in the development, exploitation and application of information technology for the benefit of all people.*

IFIP is a non-profitmaking organization, run almost solely by 2500 volunteers. It operates through a number of technical committees, which organize events and publications. IFIP's events range from an international congress to local seminars, but the most important are:

- The IFIP World Computer Congress, held every second year;
- Open conferences;
- Working conferences.

The flagship event is the IFIP World Computer Congress, at which both invited and contributed papers are presented. Contributed papers are rigorously refereed and the rejection rate is high.

As with the Congress, participation in the open conferences is open to all and papers may be invited or submitted. Again, submitted papers are stringently refereed.

The working conferences are structured differently. They are usually run by a working group and attendance is small and by invitation only. Their purpose is to create an atmosphere conducive to innovation and development. Refereeing is also rigorous and papers are subjected to extensive group discussion.

Publications arising from IFIP events vary. The papers presented at the IFIP World Computer Congress and at open conferences are published as conference proceedings, while the results of the working conferences are often published as collections of selected and edited papers.

Any national society whose primary activity is about information processing may apply to become a full member of IFIP, although full membership is restricted to one society per country. Full members are entitled to vote at the annual General Assembly, National societies preferring a less committed involvement may apply for associate or corresponding membership. Associate members enjoy the same benefits as full members, but without voting rights. Corresponding members are not represented in IFIP bodies. Affiliated membership is open to non-national societies, and individual and honorary membership schemes are also offered.

Anol Bhattacherjee   Brian Fitzgerald (Eds.)

Shaping the Future of ICT Research

Methods and Approaches

IFIP WG 8.2 Working Conference
Tampa, FL, USA, December 13-14, 2012
Proceedings

 Springer

Volume Editors

Anol Bhattacherjee
University of South Florida
College of Business
4202 East Fowler Avenue, Tampa, FL 33620, USA
E-mail: abhatt@usf.edu

Brian Fitzgerald
University of Limerick, Lero
Limerick, Ireland
E-mail: brian.fitzgerald@lero.ie

ISSN 1868-4238   e-ISSN 1868-422X
ISBN 978-3-642-35141-9   e-ISBN 978-3-642-35142-6
DOI 10.1007/978-3-642-35142-6
Springer Heidelberg Dordrecht London New York

Library of Congress Control Number: 2012952163

CR Subject Classification (1998): K.4.3, K.6.0-4, J.0, H.0, H.4, H.1, K.4.1

Typesetting: Camera-ready by author, data conversion by Scientific Publishing Services, Chennai, India

Printed on acid-free paper

Springer is part of Springer Science+Business Media (www.springer.com)

Preface

Since the founding of the International Federation for Information Processing (IFIP) in 1960 as a non-profit organization dedicated to advancing the research and practice of information and communication technologies (ICT), we have experienced seismic changes in ICT. Organizational computing architectures have shifted from mainframe computing to client-server to distributed to cloud computing. Information technology has spawned new business models based on electronic commerce and service-oriented architecture. Communities and nations are relying on ICT to leapfrog into the future, and as the recent events in the Middle-East demonstrate, online social media has provided a new voice to a world-wide movement toward democracy. These changes present ICT researchers with new research opportunities, while also challenging them to find innovative approaches to conduct rigorous ICT studies.

In the context of this changing world, what are the key research problems that we, as ICT researchers, should be studying, and how should we be studying such problems? This conference seeks to present research designs and programs that have the potential to shape the future of ICT research. We sought research papers that explored new directions in the design, use, and impacts of ICT in our organizational and social lives, papers that explored new or integrated methods for studying issues relevant to ICT research, and papers that could provoke a healthy debate on the conduct of future ICT research. In particular, we sought ICT research papers that transcended boundaries between theories, methods, approaches, and disciplines.

This conference continues the tradition of spirited ICT research inquiry that characterized previous IFIP 8.2 conferences in Manchester (1984), Copenhagen (1990), Philadelphia (1997), and Manchester (2004). We want participants to help in forming a vision and agenda for the future of relevant and rigorous ICT research methods and approaches for the next decade. Our goal is to broaden this discussion beyond the information systems community to include researchers from many ICT-related disciplines.

We are very pleased to acknowledge the help and support of several people in delivering this conference. Firstly, conference general chairs, Al Hevner and Michael Myers, were always available to offer advice and provide feedback. Organizing chairs, Rosann Webb Collins and Joni Jones, helped plan and manage the logistics in order to ensure a successful conference experience for all participants. We also thank Lorraine Morgan for coordinating the publication of the conference proceedings with Springer. The program committee also did a wonderful job of thoughtful and timely reviewing for which we are extremely grateful. This committee consists of Richard Baskerville, Tom Butler, Kevin Crowston, Liz Davidson, Shirley Gregor, Helena Holmstrom-Olsson, Netta Iivari, James Jiang, Jahangir Karimi, Annette Mills, Abhay Nath Mishra, Eric Monteiro, Benjamin

Müller, Briony Oates, Carl-Magnus Olsson, Balaji Padmanabhan, Johan Per-
ols, Matti Rossi, Nancy Russo, Maha Shaikh, Jaeki Song, Arvind Tripathi, and
Youngjin Yoo.

Finally, the success of a conference really depends on the support and commitment of its participants. We thank you for your support and participation
and we look forward to a stimulating IFIP 8.2 conference.

October 2012   Anol Bhattacherjee
                                                          Brian Fitzgerald

Conference Chairs

General Chairs

Alan Hevner   University of South Florida, USA
Michael Myers   University of Auckland, New Zealand

Program Chairs

Anol Bhattacherjee   University of South Florida, USA
Brian Fitzgerald   University of Limerick, Ireland

Organizing Chairs

Rosann Webb Collins   University of South Florida, USA
Joni Jones   University of South Florida, USA

Program Committee

Richard Baskerville	Georgia State University, USA
Tom Butler	University of Cork, Ireland
Kevin Crowston	Syracuse University, USA
Liz Davidson	University of Hawaii, USA
Shirley Gregor	Australian National University, Australia
Netta Iivari	University of Oulu, Finland
James Jiang	Australian National University, Australia
Jahangir Karimi	University of Colorado at Denver, USA
Annette Mills	University of Canterbury, New Zealand
Abhay Nath Mishra	Georgia State University, USA
Eric Monteiro	NTNU, Norway
Benjamin Müller	University of Mannheim, Germany
Briony Oates	University of Teesside, UK
Helena Holmstrom Olsson	Malmö University, Sweden
Carl-Magnus Olsson	Malmö University, Sweden
Balaji Padmanabhan	University of South Florida, USA
Johan Perols	University of San Diego, USA
Matti Rossi	Aalto University, Finland
Nancy Russo	Northern Illinois University, USA
Maha Shaikh	University of Warwick, UK
Jaeki Song	Texas Tech University, USA
Arvind Tripathi	University of Auckland, New Zealand
Youngjin Yoo	Temple University, USA

Conference Sponsor

University of South Florida, USA

Table of Contents

Track I: New Methods in Design Science Research

Resolving Name Conflicts for Mobile Apps in Twitter Posts 3
  Sangaralingam Kajanan, Ahmed Shafeeq Bin Mohd Shariff,
  Kaushik Dutta, and Anindya Datta

Using Adjective Features from User Reviews to Generate Higher
Quality and Explainable Recommendations 18
  Xiaoying Xu, Anindya Datta, and Kaushik Dutta

Product Semantics in Design Research Practice 35
  Jonas Sjöström, Brian Donnellan, and Markus Helfert

Track II: Recent Developments in Inductive Research Methods

Action Design Ethnographic Research (ADER): Vested Interest
Networks and ICT Networks in Service Delivery of Land Records
in Bangladesh 51
  M. Shahanoor Alam, Laurence Brooks, and N.I. Khan

Grounded Analytic Research: Building Theory from a Body
of Research 68
  Bjørn Furuholt and Maung Kyaw Sein

Using Photo-Diary Interviews to Study Cyborgian Identity Performance
in Virtual Worlds 79
  Ulrike Schultze

Track III: Emerging Themes in Interpretive Case Study Research

Living in a Sociomaterial World 91
  Eric Monteiro, Petter Almklov, and Vidar Hepsø

Co-materialization: Digital Innovation Dynamics in the Offshore
Petroleum Industry 108
  Thomas Østerlie

Mutability and Becoming: Materializing of Public Sector Adoption
of Open Source Software 123
  Maha Shaikh

Track IV: New Ideas in Positivist Research

Moderating Effect of Environmental Factors on eHealth Development
and Health Outcomes: A Country-Level Analysis...................... 143
    Supunmali Ahangama and Danny Chiang Choon Poo

Social Networks and Communication Media for Generating Creative
Ideas 160
    Yi Wu and Klarissa Chang

Cultural Challenges in Information Systems Innovation: The Need
for Differentiation Studies 177
    Carl Lawrence and Markku Oivo

Track V: Innovative Trends in Information Systems Research

Digital Artifacts as Institutional Attractors: A Systems Biology
Perspective on Change in Organizational Routines 195
    SungYong Um, Youngjin Yoo, Nicholas Berente, and Kalle Lyytinen

Amazon Mechanical Turk: A Research Tool for Organizations
and Information Systems Scholars................................... 210
    Kevin Crowston

Customization of Product Software: Insight from an Extensive
IS Literature Review 222
    *Matthias Bertram, Mario Schaarschmidt, and
    Harald F.O. von Kortzfleisch*

Author Index... 237

Track I
New Methods
in Design Science Research

Resolving Name Conflicts
for Mobile Apps in Twitter Posts

Sangaralingam Kajanan, Ahmed Shafeeq Bin Mohd Shariff, Kaushik Dutta,
and Anindya Datta

School of Computing,
National University of Singapore, Singapore
skajanan@comp.nus.edu.sg, ahmedshafeeqm@gmail.com,
{dutta,datta}@comp.nus.edu.sg

Abstract. The Twitter platform has emerged as a leading medium of
conducting social commentary, where users remark upon all kinds of
entities, events and occurrences. As a result, organizations are starting to mine twitter posts to unearth the knowledge encoded in such
commentary. Mobile applications, commonly known as *mobile apps*, are
the fastest growing consumer product segment in the history of human
merchandizing, with over 600,000 apps on the Apple platform and over
350,000 on Android. A particularly interesting issue is to evaluate the
popularity of specific mobile apps by analyzing the social conversation
on them. Clearly, twitter posts related to apps are an important segment
of this conversation and have been a main area of research for us. In this
respect, one particularly important problem arises due to a name conflict
of mobile app names and the names that are used to refer the mobile
apps in twitter posts. In this paper, we present a strategy to reliably extract twitter posts that are related to specific apps, but discovering the
contextual clues that enable effective filtering of irrelevant twitter posts
is our concern. While our application is in the important space of mobile
apps, our techniques are completely general and may be applied to any
entity class. We have evaluated our approach against a popular Bayesian
classifier and a commercial solution. We have demonstrated that our approach is significantly more accurate than both of these. These results
as well as other theoretical and practical implications are discussed.

Keywords: Affinity, Microblogs, Twitter, Mobile Apps, Filter.

1 Introduction

The Twitter platform has emerged as a leading medium of conducting social
commentary, where users remark upon all kinds of entities, events and occurrences. As a result, organizations are starting to mine twitter posts to unearth
the knowledge encoded in such commentary. Applications that can benefit from
such knowledge discovery are many: trending topic discovery, sentiment analysis of consumer products and gauging public reaction to political campaigns to
name a few. A key requirement of a majority of such applications is the timely

A. Bhattacherjee and B. Fitzgerald (Eds.): Future of ICT Research, IFIP AICT 389, pp. 3–17, 2012.

identification of twitter posts related to specific entities of interest, like products, persons or events. Such identification is well understood to be difficult due to a number of reasons, including (a) real-time discovery of relevant twitter posts given their massive rate of generation [13,20], (b) handling multi-lingual posts and (c) interpreting highly cryptic tweets, driven by brevity constraints [7].

In this work, we will be exploring this problem, i.e., the real-time identification of microblog postings that contain references to pre-specified entities of interest. For example, we might wish to identify tweets that talk about the movie "Harry Potter and the Deathly Hallows: Part 2".

Two key problems that need to be addressed to perform such identification arise due to (a) the practice of *aliasing* entity names and (b) *naming conflicts* that arise between the entity of interest and other objects. *Aliasing*, driven by the need to conserve space, is the practice of using a subset of complete entity names (such as "Harry potter", for "Harry potter and the deathly hallows: Part 2") to refer to the entity. Clearly, if the identification system was unaware of such aliasing, it would perform poorly. The second problem, i.e., *naming conflicts* arise from semantic overloading of entity names, and is a common problem in the general search area. For instance, a film historian seeking information about the movie "ten commandments" (a phrase with wide connotations) will find that a simple search with just the movie title yields an enormous amount of information not related to the movie. However, adding contextual clues to the title (e.g., "ten commandments movie", "ten commandments de mille", "ten commandmentsheston") yield high quality results [11,24,6]. In most cases (such as in regular internet search), the user performing the search is aware of additional context clues (such as the fact Charlton Heston played the lead role in Ten Commandments) and can easily expand the search term.

In Twitter, the aliasing and entity name conflict problems assume special significance as the brevity of twitter posts precludes the usage of traditional context clues. While this problem arises while searching any entity type, we ran into this issue particularly often in the domain of mobile applications, as we explain below.

Mobile applications, commonly known as *mobile apps*, are the consumer software for smart-devices, such as those running on Google's Android [10] or Apple's iOS [3] platforms. They represent the fastest growing consumer product segment in the history of human merchandizing [30,17,16], with over 617,000 apps on the Apple platform and over 357,000 on Android. Their growth rate is astonishing, with nearly 3500 apps being added to the Android market and Apple app stores every day.

The importance of apps is underscored by the fact that the future of the mobile strategies of both Apple and Google are heavily dependent upon who wins the mobile app wars [34,21,32]. With this backdrop, there is tremendous academic as well as commercial interest in mobile apps.

An interesting feature about mobile apps is their virality - most successful apps (e.g., Angry Bird, Talking Tom, Flashlight etc.) gain popularity not by explicit outbound marketing, but rather, through viral word-of-mouth spread. Consequently, social media plays a significant role in the success of mobile apps.

Given this context, we have been trying to to evaluate the popularity spread of mobile apps by analyzing the social conversation on them. Twitter posts related to apps are an important segment of this conversation. However, when we tried to extract twitter posts related to specific apps we discovered that it was a difficult task, due, to the aliasing and name conflict problems. For instance when searching for tweets discussing the popular iPhone app titled "Movies by Flixster with Rotten Tomatoes - Free", we found that tweeters typically aliased this app simply as "Flixster". We then tried to simply search for tweets containing the term "Flixster". However, even this proved to be challenging as we discovered that "Flixster" is overloaded – it could refer to both the app or the website (`http://www.flixster.com/`) – its was not easy to discard the tweets referring to the website and retain those referring to the app. We found these issues to be common across many apps. Clearly, unless these issues are addressed meaningfully, it would be impossible to perform the core task, i.e., extracting tweets referring to apps.

In this paper, we present a strategy to reliably extract twitter posts that are related to specific apps, overcoming the aliasing and name conflict issues discussed above. While we were motivated by mobile apps, our techniques are completely general and may be applied to any entity class.

In the next section, we review related literature. In Section 3, we describe our solution approach. Section 4 experimentally demonstrates the efficacy of our techniques and in Section 6 we conclude the paper.

2   Related Work

The work related to this research may be classified as commercial or academic, and we discuss each in turn.

First let us address commercial solutions. *Tweet filter* [31] is a browser plugin that runs on top of `twitter.com`. Using *Tweet filter* we can filter tweets by matching usernames, keywords, phrases or source. *Filter Tweets* [9] is a browser based script for filtering tweets by a specific topic and it works only with the new Twitter version. One of the features in *Filter Tweets* is filtering tweets that contain a set of terms. *Social Mention* [26] is a social media search and analysis platform that aggregates user generated content from more than 100 social media web sites including: Twitter, Facebook, FriendFeed, YouTube, Digg, Google+ etc. It allows users to easily track and measure what people are saying about a person, company, product, or any topic across the web's social media landscape in real-time. Social Mention provides an API [27] to filter the user generated contents based on the given keywords from the popular social medias mentioned above.

All of the above-mentioned commercial solutions have similar characteristics. First, all of them work based on exact keyword match, however as described in the Section 1, mobile apps are seldom referred with the full name in the twitter posts, so it will be difficult, if not impossible, to find twitter posts related to mobile apps using any of three. In other words, these solutions do not address the aliasing or name conflict problems. We will demonstrate this experimentally in Section 4.

Let us now look at some academic research of relevance to our problem. Inherently, at the end, our aim is to classify each twitter post as whether it is related to a mobile app or not. Thus, at a high level our problem resembles a classification problem. In this respect the Bayesian classification technique is worth mentioning. The study titled "An Evaluation of Statistical Spam Filtering Techniques" [33] evaluates five supervised learning methods such as "Naive Bayes","Maximum Entropy model","Memory based learning", "Support vector machine"(SVM) and "Boosting" in the context of statistical spam filtering. They have studied the impact of different feature pruning methods and feature set sizes on each learner's performance using cost-sensitive measures. This study has observed that the significance of feature selection varies greatly from classifier to classifier. In particular,they found SVM, AdaBoost, and Maximum entropy model to be the top performers in this evaluation, sharing similar characteristics: not sensitive to feature selection strategy, easily scalable to very high feature dimension, and good performances across different data sets. In contrast, Naive Bayes [14,19], a commonly used classifier in spam filtering, is found to be sensitive to feature selection methods on small feature sets, and fails to function well in scenarios where false positives are penalized heavily. Many other studies [1,22,25] have studied the popularity of "Naive Bayes" [14,19] in anti spam research and found that it outperforms keyword based filtering, even with very small training corpora.

The paper "Short Text Classification in Twitter to Improve Information Filtering" by Sriram et al. [29] has proposed an intuitive approach to determine the class labels and set of features with a focus on *user intentions* on Twitter. Their work classifies incoming tweets into categories such as News (N), Events (E), Opinions (O), Deals (D), and Private Messages (PM) based on the author information and features within the tweets. Their work is based on sets of features which are selected using a greedy strategy. Sriram et al.'s work experimentally shows that their classification out-performs the traditional "Bag-Of-Words" strategy. Unlike this resarch, our approach does not rely on supervised learning , thus we do not have the overhead of feature selection and manual labeling. In addition, we can classify a tweet as referring to any mobile app out of an arbitarily sized set of apps, unlike Sriram et al, who need a predefined exact number of categories into which they perform the classification.

In addition to classification of short text messages, integrating messages with meta-information from other information sources such as Wikipedia and WordNet [4,12] are also relevant. Sankaranarayanan et al. [23] introduce TweetStand to classify tweets as news and non-news. Automatic text classification and hidden topic extraction [29,4] approaches perform well, when there is meta-information or the context of the short text is extended with knowledge extracted using large collections. This does not apply in our case.

Currently, there are about 1 millions mobile apps in the market [18]. To classify each twitter post as related to one or more of these apps, or not at all related to any of the mobile apps, will require equivalent number of classes, i.e. 1000,000 classes in the classification approach. Such a large number of classes are impossible to handle using existing machine learning and classification techniques such as SVM [5] and Artifical Neural Networks(ANN) [8]. Therefore, instead of applying a classification approach, in this paper, we address the problem at hand using corpus based data driven approach. In the next section, we first describe the intuition behind our approach and then explain the algorithm in detail.

3   Solution Approach

We will first provide the intuition behind our approach and then delve into details. A precise statement of our problem is as follows: **given app A, find twitter posts that refer to A**. Our approach has two steps namely "Alias Identification" and "Conflict Resolution".

1. First we need to discover what alias is commonly used by users to refer to app A as names are often abbreviated in the length-restricted twitter posts (140 characters). For instance, the popular iTunes app "Doodle Jump - BE WARNED: Insanely Addictive", is commonly referred to in twitter posts as "Doodle Jump". We call this step the *Alias Identification* step.
2. After alias identification, we need to resolve name conflicts, i.e.,make sure that the twitter posts we find refer to the app and not to other objects with the same name. One particularly ripe area for conflicts is between mobile apps and a regular web applications. To see this consider the popular iPhone app titled "Movies by Flixster with Rotten Tomatoes - Free". It turns out that this app is commonly referred to as "Flixster". However, a twitter post containing the term "Flixster" might be referring to the app, *or, to the highly popular sister website*. We are of course interested in the popularity of the app. Similar issues arise in the case of the Facebook app, or the Google Translate app. We refer to this phase as *Conflict Resolution*.

3.1   Intuition behind the Alias Identification Phase

To identify the appropriate alias of an app with name A, we find the sub phrase contained in A that is the most *meaningful* and *unique*. Such meaningfulness and uniqueness (described below) is judged in the context of a *Social Media Corpus* (SMC) we have constructed by lexical analysis of a vast amount of data gathered from Social Media Avenues such as Twitter, Facebook and the user comments awarded to apps in the native app stores.

Meaningfulness: Intuitively, meaningfulness refers to the semantic content of a phrase. For instance, in the context of the app title "Doodle Jump - BE WARNED: Insanely Addictive", the reader can easily see that the sub phrase "Doodle Jump" is more meaningful than, say "Be Warned", or "Insanely Addictive". From an information theoretic perspective, meaningful n-grams will exhibit higher collocation frequencies relative to individual occurrence frequencies of the constituent 1-grams. We describe this ratio as *Affinity*. Formally, we define the *Affinity* of a word phrase P as, $Affinity(P) = \frac{f(P)}{min_{\forall w_i \in P}(f(w_i))}$, where $f(P)$ is the frequency of phrase P in a corpus and $min(f(w_i))$ is the minimum frequency across the words in a phrase P in the SMC. For the app name "Doodle Jump - BE WARNED: Insanely Addictive!", Table 1 shows the frequencies and affinity measurement of word phrases, which formally identifies the word phrase "Doodle Jump" as more meaningful than others.Note that the table does not show all phrases whose affinities are measured for comparison. For a particular n ($n = 1 \ldots N$, where N is the number of words in the name of the application as the respective mobile app store), we take all n-grams from left to right beginning with the first word and stopping at the $(N - n + 1)^{\text{th}}$ word.

Table 1. Affinity Measure

Phrase	$f(P)$	Affinity
Doodle Jump	99	$99/1456 = 0.07$
Be Warned	8231	$8231/138408 = 0.06$
Insanely Addictive	18	$18/5315 = 0.003$

Uniqueness: The meaningfulness property, while useful, is by itself not adequate for our purposes. To see this consider the following. Let us hypothetically assume (perhaps due to sampling biases while corpus creation) that the sub phrase "insanely addictive" is as (or more) meaningful than "Doodle Jump". Our system, using meaningfulness alone, would then judge "insanely addictive" as the best alias for the app "Doodle Jump - BE WARNED: Insanely Addictive" – a patently bad choice (as "insanely addictive" might be used in the context of many other apps). The *uniqueness* property (used in tandem with meaningfulness) prevents this mis-judgment, by *ensuring that the selected alias is used often in the correct context, but rarely in alternate contexts*. Furthermore, affinity does not apply to 1-grams and we cannot compare affinity directly to the uniqueness property we shall define. As such, this step will help to choose between the most meaningful n-gram phrase and all other 1-grams such that the end result is both highly meaningful and unique. Thus, to quantify uniqueness, we make a slight modification to the well-known IR notion of *inverse document frequency (idf)* [28] for a word or word phrase. The traditional idf is defined as: $idf(P) = log_2 \frac{|D|}{1+df(P)}$, where $|D|$ is the total number of documents in the corpus and $df(P)$ is the document frequency of phrase P, namely the number of documents that contain phrase P in corpus. We have modified this expression to: $idf(P) = log_2 \frac{1}{1+tcount(P)}$, where $tcount(P)$ is the frequency of P as recorded by Twitter in the target time interval T and we have done away with $|D|$ because for all phrases, the number of documents in the corpus (in this case, number of tweets in Twitter's database) within the target time interval T will be the same. Since we're looking for the highest $idf(P)$ it does not matter what $|D|$ actually is. We retrieve phrase level $tcount(P)$ directly from Twitter. For instance, the *idf* of the phrase "Doodle Jump" in our corpus is 18.28 but the *idf* values of "Doodle" and "Jump" are 14.2 and 7.6 respectively. Therefore, "Doodle Jump" has more uniqueness and rarity than the individual terms "Doodle" and "Jump".

3.2   Intuition behind the Conflict Resolution Phase

The alias identification step ensures that the best alias is selected, but does not guarantee that this alias will not have conflicts with other object names, as the "Flixster" example above illustrated. In this phase we attempt to minimize this error. The core idea is as follows: Assume an alias, say S, is context-overloaded. Our objective is to identify the overloaded aliases and then rerun the core tweet search by using a new search term that consists of the alias and a few contextual terms that disambiguate the search(e.g., "flixster + iPhone"). The additional context raises the probability that the retrieved tweet is talking about the mobile app domain.

3.3   Details of Alias Identification Phase

As discussed in section 3.1, in this step we discover the alias A' of an app A, based on its meaningfulness and uniqueness values. This procedure is shown in Table 2 from steps 1-6. Here, step 1 extracts all sub phrases from A (using a parser [2]), and computes affinities of each sub phrase in step 2. Subsequently, in step 3 we extract the most meaningful (highest affinity) phrase. This phrase is then subjected to a uniqueness test in step 4 by comparing its *idf* to the *idf*s of all 1-grams derived from A. Based on this test, the selected alias A' is returned.

After alias identification, the tweets containing this alias are considered *Legitimate*, while disqualified posts are marked as *Spam*. The legitimate tweets are then subjected to the conflict resolution phase, described below, to ensure that these refer to the app, and not to other objects with similar labels.

3.4   Details of Conflict Resolution Phase

To ensure that legitimate tweets refer to mobile apps and not to alternate objects, we design a classification mechanism where we first identify dual purpose aliases (e.g., Flixster, Facebook) and then incorporate additional context. More specifically, we run the k-means clustering algorithm [15] on all the *idf* values of the aliases A' with $k = 2$, i.e. two clusters. The two initial mean points for each cluster are the lowest and the highest *idf* values across all aliases. This is shown in Table 2 in step 7. The result of the k-means classification will be two sets of aliases, a *high-idf* cluster and a *low-idf* cluster. An example follows.

After partitioning the top ranked Android apps based on the *idf* values of their aliases, we found "paper toss","pocket god", "words with friends","ebay mobile", "pandora radio" and "espn scorecenter" belonged to the high-*idf* cluster, indicating they exist only in mobile app domain. Conversely, "flixster", "google earth",

Table 2. Algorithm for retrieving exact query phrase to use on the tweet database to ensure high relevance

1. Generate set of all word phrases $\mathcal{C}$ of length 2, 3 or 4 of the app name A. For example, for the app name "Doodle Jump - BE WARNED: Insanely Addictive!", some of the collocates will be "Doodle Jump", "Be Warned" and "Insanely Addictive".
2. Compute $Affinity(C_i)$ for each word phrase $C_i \in \mathcal{C}$ as derived in Step 1. For example, $Affinity(\text{"Doodle Jump"}) = 0.07$, $Affinity(\text{"Doodle Jump Be"}) = 0.00068$ and $Affinity(\text{"Be Warned"}) = 0.06$.
3. Identify the word phrase C_i^{max} that has the highest value of $Affinity(C_i)$. In our example, the highest value is for $Affinity(\text{"Doodle Jump"}) = 0.07$, thus $C_i^{max} = $ "Doodle Jump".
4. Compute the idf for C_i^{max} and all one gram word of the name A. In our example, $idf(\text{"Doodle Jump"}) = 18.28$, $idf(\text{"Doodle"}) = 14.2$, $idf(\text{"Jump"}) = 7.6$, $idf(\text{"Warned"}) = 7.79$ and so on.
5. Identify the word phrase that has the highest idf as computed in step 4. In example, "Doodle Jump" has the highest idf.
6. Return the word phrase identified in Step 5 as the alternate app name A' of the app A.
7. After running steps 1-6 for all app names, we run k-means clustering on the idf values of the word phrases returned in step 6 with a k value of 2 and the initial means to be the highest idf and lowest idf values in the corpus respectively. This will yield two clusters, one that is high-idf and one that is low-idf.
8. For all word phrases that are part of the low-idf cluster, append extra context keywords before querying the tweet database. For all words phrases that are part of the high-idf cluster, we can use the word phrases "as is".

"skype" "facebook","kindle", "bible", "flashlight", "netflix", "backgrounds" and "translator" are aliases with low idf values, indicating these names are used both in mobile apps and in other domains, such as web applications.

For the aliases with higher idf, we accept their associated twitter posts, as there is a very high probability that the post is referring to the mobile app.

For the aliases with the low idf values, we incorporate additional filtering mechanisms, by adding additional keywords like "app","Android", "iPhone", "iPod", "Apple" and "iPad". Tweets containing any of these additional keywords are considered relevant(*Legitimate*), otherwise it is categorized as *Spam*.

4   Experimental Results

In this section we demonstrate the efficacy of our approach, which we will refer to as TApp. The idea is to evaluate the quality of the *legitimate tweets* produced – if a tweet refers to the appropriate mobile app, the result is correct, otherwise, for that particular tweet, our procedure has failed. Specifically, we need to test for both Type 1 and Type 2 errors, i.e., how well we retain and how well we avoid the rejection of good tweets. First, we do a comparison with Naïve Bayesian approach. Next, we compare with one of the commercial platform, Socialmention [26].

4.1   Comparison with Bayesian Approach

For a baseline comparison, we have used Naïve Bayes classifier [14,19], a popular method for document classification in anti-spam research [1,22,25]. It is widely used in text categorization task [19] and often serves as baseline method for comparison with other approaches [33]. In our implementation of Naïve Bayes (using the Laplacean prior to smooth the Bayesian estimation, as suggested in Nigam [19]) classification we extracted a set of keywords from every twitter post and used those as the feature set. Based on the key word occurrences in the twitter posts in the training data, probabilities are calculated. These probability values are used to classify the twitter posts.

Both the TApp and the Bayesian classification technique have been implemented using Java 1.6. We ran all the experiments using a Windows 7 machine with quad core processor of 2.33 GHz.

To compare TApp and the Bayesian classifier, we first selected a set of "apps of interest" – for this experiment, we chose the top 50 "hot" android apps using a popular mobile app search engine platform (http://www.appbrain.com/apps/hot/). To create our test bed for these 50 apps, we randomly selected tweets from our database of 14 million tweets and manually verified whether they contained references to these apps (*legitimate* tweets) or not (*spam*). In this fashion we manually identified 1000 posts from our database, consisting of 500 posts that refer to one of these 50 apps (*legitimate posts*) and 500 tweets that refer to mobile apps or internet web sites, but not any of the selected 50 mobile apps. We apply both the Bayesian classifier and the TApp approach on this test bed to classify these 1000 posts into *Legitimate* and *Spam*. In Figures 1 and 2, we plot the histogram distributions of accuracy of the two approach - Bayesian and TApp. As can be seen from Figure 1, the Bayesian classifier identifies 337 out of the 500 *Legitimate* posts (a recall rate of 67%), whereas the TApp approach demonstrates a recall of 97.2% by correctly classifying 486 of the 500 *Legitimate* posts. Similarly, as portrayed in Figure 2, the Bayesian classifier wrongly identified 174 of the 500 *Spam* posts as Legitimate, whereas TApp mis-identifies only 23 of 500. In Table 3, we have presented classical IR metrics such as precision, recall, true negative, accuracy and F-measure in both the cases. In all cases TApp significantly outperforms the Bayesian classifier (TApp scores above 90% in every case).

4.2   Comparison with SocialMention

SocialMention(SM) [26] is the leading social media search engine. To demonstrate the effectiveness of our approach, we decided to compare the accuracy of our results with those acquired from Socialmention. As discussed in the Section 2, the exact algorithms of Socialmention implementation is not known. However, by observing different search results we concluded Socialmention uses an exact keyword matching approach to identify the twitter posts that contains the given keywords. In this experiment, we used the same set of 50 apps used in the previous experiment in Section 4.1. For each app, we retrieved the tweeter

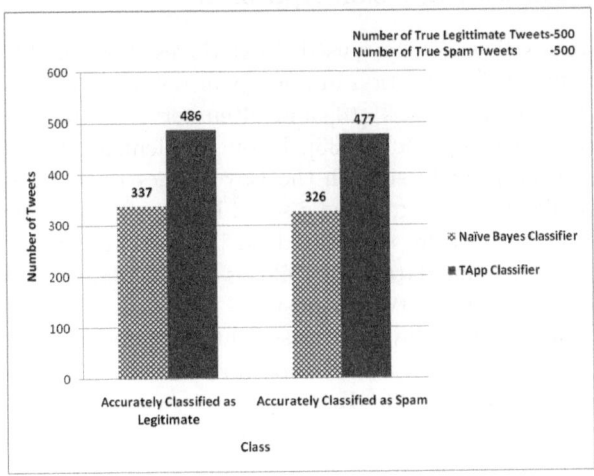

Fig. 1. Comparison of Accurate Classification

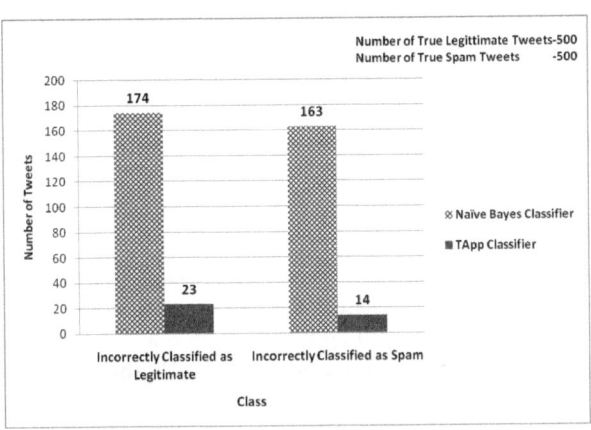

Fig. 2. Comparison of Incorrect Classification

Table 3. Comparison of IR metrics in Bayesian classifier vs. TApp

Matrix	Naïve Bayes classifier	TApp classifier
Precision	$100 * 337/(511) = 66\%$	$100 * 486/(509) = 95.6\%$
Recall	$100 * 337/(500) = 67\%$	$100 * 486/(500) = 97.2\%$
True Negative Rate	$100 * 326/(500) = 65.2\%$	$100 * 477/(500) = 95.4\%$
Accuracy	$100 * 663/(1000) = 66.3\%$	$100 * (963)/(1000) = 96.3\%$
F-measure	$(2 * 65.9 * 67.4)/(66 + 67) = 66.7\%$	$2 * 95.6 * 97.2/(95.6 + 97.2) = 96.4\%$

posts related to that app in the previous one month using both Socialmention API [27] and the TApp approach. The objective of our approach is to automate the Twitter post retrieval for large number of mobile apps. So, the input to both Socialmention and the TApp approach is app names as found in native app stores. The Socialmention uses these original app names to find the twitter posts. TApp approach applies name aliasing and name conflict resolution to retrieve the relevant tweets. However, the app names are chosen to be such that 22 out of 50 require either no aliasing and/or no name conflict resolution. This was done to access the effectiveness of the TApp technique in individually performing those 2 tasks.

To constrain the experimental data size, for each of the approach if the number of posts for an app is more than 50, we considered only the most recent 50 posts. Next, we passed the posts identified by both Socialmention and TApp along with the app names to two professional lexicographers. Each of the lexicographers has more than 5 years of experience of internet search optimization. They both worked together to arrive at an unanimous decision of which of these posts are "Valid" (i.e. the post is related to the respective app) and which of these are "invalid" (i.e. the post is not related to the respective app). We present the result in Table 4.

As can be seen from Table 4, for many apps, the Socialmention platform has retrieved tweets that are not related to that app. In total only 43.44% of the total tweets retrieved by Socialmention has been identified as "Valid" post by lexicographers. Whereas, for TApp approach, the absolute number of invalid posts for each app is much smaller compared to the Socialmention. Overall 95.45% of the twitter posts retrieved by TApp has been identified as "Valid" by lexicograpghers. The total number of valid tweets retrieved by TApp is 1584 compared to 769 by Socialmention. So both in terms of *accuracy* and the *coverage* of retrieval, TApp significantly outperformed Socialmention.

Additionally, we observe that Socialmention works well in cases when there no aliasing of the app names and when there is no naming conflicts between the entity of interest and other objects. In these cases, Socialmention achieved 82.93% accuracy. For example, the extracted tweets for the apps "Live Holdem Poker Pro", "Google Sky Map", "Handcent SMS" and "Lookout Mobile Security" in both Socialmention and TApp are highly relevant because these names are only used in mobile app domain and there is no aliasing by users. One should observe that, even in these simple cases, where there is no name conflict and aliasing, the accuracy in TApp case is higher than that of Socialmention. The exact approach followed in Socialmention is unknown, so we are not sure of the reason behind this improvement, however we anticipate that this is due to the generic keyword matching algorithms followed in Socialmention, vs. the phrase search using tweeter API followed in TApp.

In the second scenario, when the app names required aliasing, but no name conflict resolution, the Socialmention's accuracy in retrieving relevant tweeter posts was 52.97% compared to 94.57% in TApp approach. For example, the tweets extracted for the apps "SpeechSynthesis Data Installer", " Kid Mode:

Table 4. Comparison of Valid Tweets in Socialmention vs. TApp

Store App Name	Alias Name	Using SM		Using TApp	
		Valid	In-Valid	Valid	In-Valid
CardioTrainer	CardioTrainer	45	5	50	0
Endomondo Sports Tracker	Endomondo Sports Tracker	20	8	27	0
Flash Player 10.2	Flash Player 10.2	3	2	0	0
Google Sky Map	Google Sky Map	38	11	16	0
Handcent SMS	Handcent SMS	37	13	45	5
Instant Heart Rate	Instant Heart Rate	47	3	50	0
Live Holdem Poker Pro	Live Holdem Poker Pro	43	7	48	2
Lookout Mobile Security	Lookout Mobile Security	41	9	49	1
Stardunk	Stardunk	39	11	27	0
Total		313	69	312	8
Accuracy		81.93%		97.50%	
Calorie Counter by FatSecret	Calorie Counter	3	4	50	0
Documents To Go 3.0 Main App	Documents To Go	5	7	11	1
Funny Facts Free 8000+	Funny Facts	1	1	48	2
Bubble Blast 2	Bubble Blast	32	10	39	0
Kid Mode: Play + Learn	Kid Mode	4	24	40	10
Kids Connect the Dots Lite	Kids Connect The Dots	1	0	27	0
PicSay - Photo Editor	Picsay	4	0	50	0
Mango (manga reader) Free	Mango manga reader	10	3	43	6
Pandora internet radio	Pandora	5	1	17	5
SpeechSynthesis Data Installer	SpeechSynthesis	2	22	4	0
Talking Tom Cat Free	Talking Tom Cat	28	14	48	2
Vaulty Free Hides Pictures	Vaulty	1	0	26	0
Waze: Community GPS navigation	Waze	2	1	50	0
Total		98	87	453	26
Accuracy		52.97%		94.57%	
Adao File Manager	Adao File Manager	1	0	1	0
Advanced Task Killer	Advanced Task Killer	38	12	31	3
Angry Birds	Angry Birds	30	20	46	4
Backgrounds	Backgrounds	3	47	38	0
Barcode Scanner	Barcode Scanner	6	44	48	2
Bible	Bible	0	50	13	5
Craigslist	Craigslist	0	50	2	2
Drag Racing	Drag Racing	11	39	49	1
Epocrates	Epocrates	33	17	50	0
ES Task Manager	ES Task Manager	2	5	8	0
ESPN ScoreCenter	ESPN Scorecenter	34	16	43	6
Facebook for Android	Facebook	18	32	42	0
FxCamera	FxCamera	18	5	17	0
Google Maps	Google Maps	2	48	26	6
Horoscope	Horoscope	3	47	15	0
KakaoTalk	KakaoTalk	9	41	48	2
LauncherPro	LauncherPro	31	19	50	0
Mobile Banking	Mobile Banking	6	44	47	3
Mouse Trap	Mouse Trap	2	48	9	0
My Tracks	My Tracks	0	49	4	0
NFL Mobile	NFL Mobile	19	31	50	0
Ringdroid	Ringdroid	26	17	18	0
Tap Fish	Tap Fish	22	28	47	3
The Weather Channel	Weather Channel	3	47	45	5
Tiny Flashlight + LED	Tiny Flashlight	24	26	47	3
Total		358	845	819	41
Accuracy		29.75%		95.23%	
Total		769	1001	1584	75
Accuracy		43.44%		95.45%	

(Left margin category labels: "No aliasing & name conflict", "Aliasing required, but no name conflict", "Both aliasing and name conflict required")

Play + Learn" and "Vaulty Free Hides" are mostly irrelevant or unfound because of aliasing practice of users when they post their tweets. These apps are typically referred to as "SpeechSynthesis" ,"Kid Mode" and "Vaulty" in most of the tweets.

To show the effectiveness of TApp's entity name conflict handling, we focus on the third category of app names, where both aliasing and name conflict resolution are required. If we look at the valid tweet count for the apps "Drag Racing","Mouse Trap","Mobile Banking" and "My Tracks" in case of Socialmention, they are very low compared to the invalid tweet count. These app names are used outside the mobile application domain as well and so required name conflict resolution in TApp approach, which is clearly not done in Socialmention. For these type of app names, Socialmention had a pretty low accuracy of just 29.75% in retrieving relevant tweets compared to 95.23% accuracy in TApp case.

This demonstrates the importance and effectiveness of both the aliasing and name conflict resolution steps in TApp.

5 Discussion

In this section we discuss the broader implications of our TApp approach. Our research falls in the design science research paradigm of Information Systems [35]. We have developed an artifact that can successfully resolve name conflicts of app names in twitter posts. We have demonstrated the artifact through experimental study and a comparison with a manual method. Our two step approach out performs the benchmark Naïve Bayes classifier and a commercial implementation (Socialmention [26]) both on true negative and false positive errors.

Identifying social media mentions related to most popular products in general and mobile apps in particular has important implications for marketers as well as for product owners. Being able to predict the social media popularity of items have tremendous value to not only service providers but also marketers who would bid for ad-space on items with high potential popularity in order to maximize the exposure. TApp approach can be used to identify user generated contents across social media, which in turn can be used to measure product's popularity. Our approach can be utilized in many ICT research domains such as, identifying twitter posts related to brand monitoring in e-commerce, identifying the public opinions of e-participation, e-services and general e-government implementations by using the social media mentions, identifying students opinions of e-learning systems and analyzing the public views on digitizing the medical records of patients(Electronic Medical Records: EMR). Thus our approach is generalizable and broadly applicable across wide range of ICT research domains in general.

6 Conclusion

In this paper we have addressed the problem of reliably identifying tweets related to mobile apps. In the process we have addressed the *aliasing* and *name conflict* problems inherent in the task. We have compared the accuracy of our approach to Naïve Baysian approach and a commercial implementation (socialmention). Our approach outperformed in all measures of accuracy compared to Baysian approach and the socialmention. While our application is in the area of mobile apps, our techniques are generally applicable.

References

1. Androutsopoulos, I., Koutsias, J., Chandrinos, K.V., Ch, K.V., Paliouras, G., Spyropoulos, C.D.: An evaluation of naive bayesian anti-spam filtering, 9–17 (2000)
2. Apache, Open nlp, http://opennlp.sourceforge.net/projects.html (last accessed July, 2012)
3. AppleiOS. Apple-ios, http://www.apple.com/ios/ (last accessed on July 14, 2011)
4. Banerjee, S.: Clustering short texts using wikipedia. In: Proceedings of the 30th Annual International ACM SIGIR Conference (2007)
5. Chang, C.C., Lin, C.J.: LIBSVM: a library for support vector machines (2001)
6. Cui, H., Wen, J.-R., Nie, J.-Y., Ma, W.-Y.: Query expansion by mining user logs. IEEE Transactions on Knowledge and Data Engineering 15(4), 829–839 (2003)
7. Dent, K., Paul, S.: Through the twitter glass: Detecting questions in micro-text. In: Proceedings of AAAI 2011 Workshop on Analyzing Microtext (2011)
8. Fausett, L. (ed.): Fundamentals of neural networks: architectures, algorithms, and applications. Prentice-Hall, Inc., Upper Saddle River (1994)
9. Filtertweets, Filter tweets for greasemonkey, http://userscripts.org/scripts/show/87289 (last accessed June 27, 2012)
10. Google Inc. Android developers, http://developer.android.com/index.html (last accessed on July 14, 2011)
11. Google Inc. Google search appliance help center, http://code.google.com/apis/searchappliance/documentation/46/help_gsa/serve_synonym.html (last accessed on May 13, 2011)
12. Hu, X., Sun, N., Zhang, C., Chua, T.-S.: Exploiting internal and external semantics for the clustering of short texts using world knowledge. In: CIKM 2009: Proceeding of the 18th ACM Conference on Information and Knowledge Management, pp. 919–928. ACM, New York (2009)
13. Jansen, B.J., Liu, Z., Weaver, C., Campbell, G., Gregg, M.: Real time search on the web: Queries, topics, and economic value. Inf. Process. Manage. 47, 491–506 (2011)
14. Lewis, D.D.: Naive (bayes) at forty: The independence assumption in information retrieval, pp. 4–15. Springer (1998)
15. MacQueen, J.B.: Some methods for classification and analysis of multivariate observations. In: Cam, L.M.L., Neyman, J. (eds.) Proc. of the fifth Berkeley Symposium on Mathematical Statistics and Probability, vol. 1, pp. 281–297. University of California Press (1967)
16. Markets & Markets. World mobile applications market - advanced technologies, global forecast (2010-2015), http://www.marketsandmarkets.com/Market-Reports/mobile-applications-228.html (last accessed on May 13, 2011)
17. Mashable. Mobile app market to surge to $17.5 billion by 2012, http://mashable.com/2010/03/17/mobile-app-market-17-5-billion/ (last accessed on May 13, 2011)

18. Mobilewalla. Mobilewalla-an app search engine, `http://mobilewalla.com/` (last accessed on May 13, 2012)

19. Nigam, K.: Using maximum entropy for text classification. In: IJCAI 1999 Workshop on Machine Learning for Information Filtering, pp. 61–67 (1999)

20. One Riot. The inner workings of a realtime search engine (2009)

21. PC World. It's android vs. apple: Will you switch sides?, `http://www.pcworld.com/article/199109/its_android_vs_apple_will_you_switch_sides.html` (last accessed on May 13, 2011)

22. Sahami, M., Dumais, S., Heckerman, D., Horvitz, E.: A bayesian approach to filtering junk E-mail. In: Learning for Text Categorization: Papers from the 1998 Workshop, Madison, Wisconsin, AAAI Technical Report WS-98-05 (1998)

23. Sankaranarayanan, J., Samet, H., Teitler, B.E., Lieberman, M.D., Sperling, J.: Twitterstand: news in tweets. In: Proceedings of the 17th ACM SIGSPATIAL International Conference on Advances in Geographic Information Systems, GIS 2009, pp. 42–51. ACM, New York (2009)

24. Sarkas, N., Bansal, N., Das, G., Koudas, N.: Measure-driven keyword-query expansion. Proceedings of the Vldb Endowment 2, 121–132 (2009)

25. Schneider, K.-M.: A comparison of event models for naive bayes anti-spam e-mail filtering. In: Proceedings of the 11th Conference of the European Chapter of the Association for Computational Linguistics (EACL 2003), pp. 307–314 (2003)

26. SocialMention. Social mention, `http://socialmention.com` (last accessed on November 5, 2011)

27. SocialMention. Social mention api, `http://socialmention.com/api/` (last accessed on November 5, 201)

28. Spärck Jones, K.: A statistical interpretation of term specificity and its application in retrieval. Journal of Documentation 28(1), 11–21 (1972)

29. Sriram, B., Fuhry, D., Demir, E., Ferhatosmanoglu, H., Demirbas, M.: Short text classification in twitter to improve information filtering. In: Proceeding of the 33rd International ACM SIGIR Conference on Research and Development in Information Retrieval, SIGIR 2010, pp. 841–842. ACM, New York (2010)

30. Techcrunch. Report: Mobile app market will be worth $25 billion by 2015 apple ios share: 20%, `http://techcrunch.com/2011/01/18/report-mobile-app-market-will-be-worth-25-billion-by-2015-apples-share-20` (last accessed on May 13, 2011)

31. TweetFilter. Tweetfilter for greasemonkey, `http://userscripts.org/scripts/show/49905` (last accessed June 26, 2012)

32. Venture Beat. Why apple can not beat android, `http://venturebeat.com/2010/11/05/why-apple-cant-beat-android` (last accessed on May 13, 2011)

33. Zhang, L., Zhu, J., Yao, T.: An evaluation of statistical spam filtering techniques. ACM Transactions on Asian Language Information Processing (TALIP) 3 (2004)

34. Znet. Android vs. apple: The 2011 cage match, `http://www.zdnet.com/blog/btl/android-vs-apple-the-2011-cage-match/43682` (last accessed on May 13, 2011)

35. Hevner, A.R., March, S.T., Park, J., Ram, S.: Design science in information systems research. MIS Quarterly 28(1), 75–105 (2004)

Using Adjective Features from User Reviews to Generate Higher Quality and Explainable Recommendations

Xiaoying Xu, Anindya Datta, and Kaushik Dutta

Department of Information Systems, School of Computing, National University of Singapore
{xu1987,datta,dutta}@comp.nus.edu.sg

Abstract. Recommender systems have played a significant role in alleviating the "information overload" problem. Existing Collaborative Filtering approaches face the data sparsity problem and transparency problem, and the content-based approaches suffer the problem of insufficient attributes. In this paper, we show that abundant adjective features embedded in user reviews can be used to characterize movies as well as users' taste. We extend the standard TF-IDF term weighting scheme by introducing cluster frequency (CLF) to automatically extract high quality adjective features from user reviews for recommendation. We also develop a movie recommendation framework incorporating adjective features to generated highly accurate rating prediction and high quality recommendation explanation. The results of experiments performed on a real world dataset show that our proposed method outperforms the state-of-the-art techniques.

Keywords: Recommender systems, User reviews, Adjective Features, Sparsity, Transparency.

1   Introduction

Recommender systems (*RS*) have been widely applied to alleviate the well-known "information overload" problem observed on e-commerce portals, and have experienced wide deployment at major technology companies like Amazon[1], TiVo[2] and Netflix[3]. Two broad flavors RS (and hybrids thereof) are employed in practice.

1. *Collaborative Filtering* (*CF*) *RS*, whose basic idea is to find a group of similar users who share the same tastes with the target user, and then recommend the items they like to the target user [1]. This is the most common form of RS used in practice.
2. *Content-based RS*, which tries to exploit descriptive attributes of items (such as directors of movies or authors of books) to perform recommendations [2].

---

[1] http://www.amazon.com

[2] http://www.tivo.com

[3] http://www.netflix.com

A. Bhattacherjee and B. Fitzgerald (Eds.): Future of ICT Research, IFIP AICT 389, pp. 18–34, 2012.

While CF has been used successfully, there are well known shortcomings. One of the major drawbacks of CF techniques is the problem that they heavily depend on user ratings. Unfortunately, in most domains studied (movies, books, restaurants etc.) a majority of items turn out to be unrated, resulting in *sparse* ratings matrices, which adversely impact the quality of recommendations [3, 4].

A second well-known, and equally significant, drawback of virtually all CF techniques is the lack of *transparency* [5]. These methods work as black boxes without offering the users much insight into the system logic or justification for the recommendation, which typically lower the users' trust on the recommendation produced [5, 6]. As has been demonstrated conclusively, trust is the most important attribute, which impacts users' willingness to act upon recommendations [7].

In a promising recent development, researchers are attempting to accommodate additional meta-content generated by users into the recommendation process. Driven by the popularity of social media, a bulk of this work factors in *user generated tags*, which are, typically, arbitrary words and short phrases provided by the users to label items in the system [8]. Compared to descriptive attributes typically used in content-based CF, tags cover more features of the items and are more comprehended by users. However, since tags are voluntarily and freely provided by the users, problems such as unwillingness to tag and diverging vocabulary can easily arise [2]. Recall that the sparsity of ratings is a challenge of rating-based recommendation, it turns out that the problem of sparsity is even worse in the tag space. Based on the extensive experiments we conducted, we can cover only 3.45% of items (movies, in our case) if we only use the tags to infer users' preference. Using ratings, coverage increases significantly. Clearly, while user generated meta-content shows promise, there exists substantial opportunity for further improvements.

The work reported in this paper is part of a project to create more effective recommender systems using user generated meta-content. The objective of this project was to design recommendation techniques that are (a) *substantially better in produced quality* and (b) *explainable*. We started off by exploring possible content to incorporate and immediately noticed an interesting phenomenon: a readily available source of "opinion" information for many consumer products (movies, books, hotels, electronic products, mobile apps) are user reviews and such reviews have been widely used for a variety of tasks in many application areas of data mining and information retrieval. Yet, the use of textual reviews in designing recommender systems has received scant attention from scientists. There do exist a few papers reporting the incorporation of free-text user reviews to perform recommendations, almost all of which employ opinion mining and summarization techniques to factorize user reviews and then to infer user preferences [9-11]. There is no reported work, in the recommendation area, that attempts to extract meta-information in addition to user ratings from reviews.

We note however, that a wealth of information is available from reviews that could possibly be used to enhance the recommendation process. In this paper we focus on one specific kind of information from user reviews, namely *adjective features*. While the intent is to incorporate various other types of data from reviews in future work, adjectives represent a particularly attractive feature to use in recommendations. At its core, recommendation engines suggest items that the user should *like* (and, clearly, not *dislike*). When asked to reveal why people like or dislike something, they often use adjectives to explain their preference. For instance, when asked why she likes the movie *Titanic*, a user's answer often use words such as "romantic", "moving", "astounding", "beautiful" and "sad" – all adjectives. These features can be found in abundance in user reviews and remain unexplored in recommendation research.

Therefore, in this paper, we design a recommendation framework that incorporates adjective features extracted from external user reviews in addition to ratings to generate more accurate and more explainable movie recommendation, without the requirement for users to provide any tags. To automatically extract adjective features from user reviews, we employ well understood POS tagging methods. However, we quickly discover that a lot of adjectives are not helpful in discriminating tastes, i.e., they are too general to be adequately representative of users' tastes, e.g., "good", while some adjectives are too specific to capture the users' general taste aspects, e.g., "unsinkable" in the reviews of *Titanic*. To handle these problems, we extend traditional TF-IDF term weighting to TF-IDF-CLF by introducing another term weighting measure, called *cluster frequency* (CLF), to balance the *representativeness* and *generalizability* of the extracted features. Moreover, we adapt the concept of Regularized Singular Value Decomposition (RSVD) to construct item feature vectors and user feature vectors to generate more accurate rating prediction and more explainable recommendation by listing additional personalized item features.

The result of our work is a recommendation technique that makes substantial advances over extant techniques, like CF approaches and tag based systems. In particular, CF-based approaches achieve high coverage (almost 100%) at the cost of high prediction error (MAE is 0.69 - 0.75), whereas tag-based approaches achieve low prediction error (MAE is 0.67), they have extremely low coverage (9%). Our proposed method not only reduces the prediction error of the state-of-art CF algorithm and the state-of-art tag-based method by 11.27% and 8.77% respectively, but also achieves almost 100% coverage similar to CF-based approaches. Moreover, our approach provides high quality personalized recommendation explanation.

We believe this work to be important for four reasons.

1. Firstly, to the best of our knowledge, this is the first work to incorporate adjective features extracted from textual user reviews in recommendation.
2. Secondly, we extract better adjective features for the purpose of recommendation by introducing the notion of *Cluster frequency* (CLF), balancing the *representativeness* and *generalizability* of the extracted features, which has not been addressed by existing research, and contributes to higher prediction accuracy.
3. Thirdly, by using the abundant adjective features extracted from external user reviews, we relieve the tag sparsity problem and diverging vocabulary problem which have not been well solved in existing tag-based approaches.
4. Finally, we are one of the first recommendation techniques that provide full *transparency*. By decomposing the users' ratings into multi-dimensional vectors characterized by adjective features, we not only address the data sparsity problem, but also highlight the transparency of recommendation that is ignored by existing CF approaches.

The rest of this paper is organized as follows. Firstly we present our proposed recommendation framework including the detail description of each component. The remainder of the paper then presents the experiment and results. We review some related work before the conclusion and finally, we conclude by summarizing the paper, including the contribution, limitation and implication for future research.

2   Recommendation Framework

We now describe our proposed approach, starting off with the intuition behind it, and then proceeding to describe its details. While our approach is general and can be used to recommend any consumer item, we find that it is easier to explain ideas if we choose a specific example domain. Given that the most studied consumer domain in the recommendation context is movies, and the most results are available from the movie domain (to use in assessing the effectiveness of our approach), we will, henceforth, use the movie domain to present our technique. In other words, we will present our method, from this point forward, as a method to recommend movies to users.

2.1   Intuition and Overview

We are interested in predicting ratings for the movies that are new to the users, and recommending those movies with highest predicted ratings to them, together with reasonable and personalized explanations to improve the transparency of the recommendation logic. Noting that the limited number of descriptive attributes which are commonly used in content-based movie recommendation (e.g., actor, director) are not sufficient, we automatically extract adjective features from external user reviews (available in abundance in systems like IMDb[4], and Rotten Tomatoes[5]) to define distinguishing aspects of items and of the users' tastes, which are able to truly reflect the users' perception towards the movies in a higher and more abstract level. For example, the adjective features extracted from the user reviews of *Titanic* can be "romantic", "sad", "astounding". We predict the rating of *Titanic* for a user by estimating to what extent *Titanic* is romantic, is sad and is astounding, and how much this user likes romantic movies, sad movies and astounding movies.

2.2   Movie Recommendation Framework

The overview our movie recommendation framework is shown in Figure 1, where the shaded rectangles represent the components we have designed and implemented to realize our recommendation engine. There are five such components: review crawler, POS tagger, feature extractor, vector generator and recommender. More details of each component will be introduced in the ensuing sections of the paper.

Review Crawler. We obtain user reviews of the movies from a reputed external source, i.e. IMDb (the *Internet Movie Database*). IMDb is one of the most popular online databases of movie information, with over 100 million unique users each

---

[4] http://www.imdb.com
[5] http://www.rottentomatoes.com

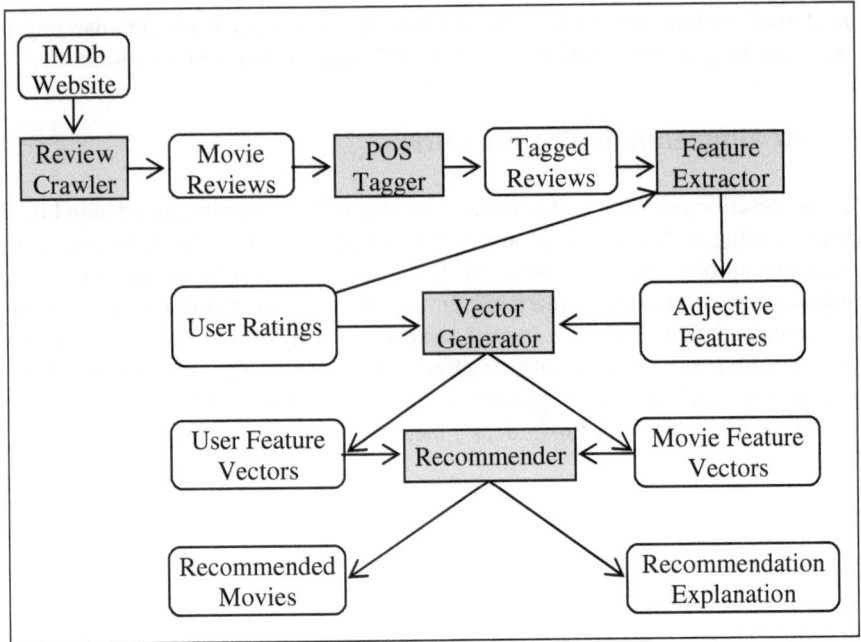

Fig. 1. Movie Recommendation Framework

month. IMDb also offers a platform for users to review movies, and allows other users to indicate whether they find certain review is useful. Figure 2 shows one user review of *Titanic* on IMDb website.

To obtain the reviews contents, we use a web crawler to collect the first 4 pages of user reviews (10 reviews per page) for each movie from the IMDb website, ranked by their usefulness, and then we extract the review contents from the webpages.

POS Tagger. After getting the user reviews for each movie, we employ the Stanford POS tagger [12] to assign parts of speech to each word in the reviews, such as noun, verb, adjective, etc. Since we intend to extract adjective features, we only keep the adjectives in the reviews. Taking the first paragraph of review in Figure 2 as an example, after the POS tagging, only the following words remain:

different good great boring cliché beautiful sad

Feature Extractor. This component extracts adjective features from the tagged user reviews. Firstly, we need to assign a weight for each adjective term in the reviews. In the domain of information retrieval, term weighting is a measure of how important a word is in a document. The TF-IDF term weighting, which is a very commonly used term weighting scheme, for term t in document d is given by:

$$tf\text{-}idf_{t,d} = tf_{t,d} \times idf_t .$$ (1)

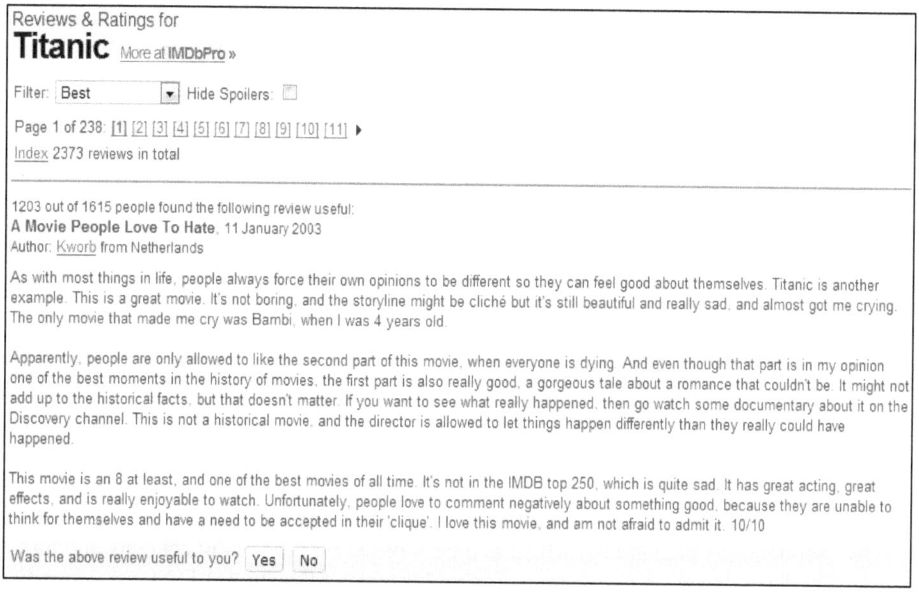

Reviews & Ratings for
Titanic   More at IMDbPro »

Filter: Best   ▼   Hide Spoilers: ☐

Page 1 of 238: [1] [2] [3] [4] [5] [6] [7] [8] [9] [10] [11] ▶
Index 2373 reviews in total

1203 out of 1615 people found the following review useful:
A Movie People Love To Hate, 11 January 2003
Author: Kworb from Netherlands

As with most things in life, people always force their own opinions to be different so they can feel good about themselves. Titanic is another example. This is a great movie. It's not boring, and the storyline might be cliché but it's still beautiful and really sad, and almost got me crying. The only movie that made me cry was Bambi, when I was 4 years old.

Apparently, people are only allowed to like the second part of this movie, when everyone is dying. And even though that part is in my opinion one of the best moments in the history of movies, the first part is also really good, a gorgeous tale about a romance that couldn't be. It might not add up to the historical facts, but that doesn't matter. If you want to see what really happened, then go watch some documentary about it on the Discovery channel. This is not a historical movie, and the director is allowed to let things happen differently than they really could have happened.

This movie is an 8 at least, and one of the best movies of all time. It's not in the IMDB top 250, which is quite sad. It has great acting, great effects, and is really enjoyable to watch. Unfortunately, people love to comment negatively about something good, because they are unable to think for themselves and have a need to be accepted in their 'clique'. I love this movie, and am not afraid to admit it. 10/10

Was the above review useful to you? Yes   No

Fig. 2. IMDb User Review Page

where $tf_{t,d}$ is the frequency of term t in document d, and idf_t is the inverse document frequency of a term t, which indicates the term's discrimination power.

We regard the collection of all reviews of a movie as a document. The TF-IDF weighting for every word in the reviews can be easily obtained. While features extracted by TF-IDF weighting are able to represent movie characteristics, they are often tainted by two issues: (a) they may be too specific and might not serve as a generalizable, or common characteristic across similar movies, e.g. the word "unsinkable", which has very high TF-IDF scores in the reviews of *Titanic*, is too specific since we are unlikely to find other movies related to "unsinkable", thus it is not highly suitable to be used for representing the users' taste; and (b) they may not be able to extract some general features which are good for exposing users' taste aspects, e.g. when we are extracting features from the reviews of *Titanic*, the word "sad" may have high TF scores but low IDF scores therefore resulting in relatively low TF-IDF scores, however "sad" is a good feature since it accurately reflects a key perception of users towards this movie. In addition to *generalizability*, discussed above, the *representativeness* of the extracted features is also important, e.g. the word "good" is too general so that we cannot use it to represent the users' preference. In order to balance the *representativeness* and *generalizability*, we introduce another term weighting measure into TF-IDF, i.e. cluster frequency (CLF), to measure how common a word is among a cluster of documents which are similar to a particular document. We get a cluster of similar movies for a given movie, and accordingly, all reviews of the movies in the cluster will be used for calculating the CLF.

If we find a cluster of similar movies for *Titanic*, they may share some common characteristics of tragedy and the word "sad" would have high frequency among the reviews of this cluster. By introducing CLF, the term weighing of the word "sad" is higher and it is more likely to be extracted. Since we also give weight to TF-IDF weighting, those words that are too general (e.g. "good") will be filtered out.

Clearly, to realize the CLF idea, we need to group movies by "similarity". The similarity between movies can be computed by either of the following two approaches. First, we can adopt the idea of Amazon's item-based CF and use cosine similarity to compute the distance between two movies based on the users' co-rating patterns:

$$\cos(\vec{r_i}, \vec{r_j}) = \frac{\vec{r_i} \times \vec{r_j}}{\left\| \vec{r_i} \right\| \left\| \vec{r_j} \right\|} = \frac{\sum_{u \in U_{i,j}} r_{u,i} r_{u,j}}{\sqrt{\sum_{u \in U_i} r_{u,i}^2 \sum_{v \in U_j} r_{v,j}^2}} \ . \tag{2}$$

where $U_{i,j}$ denotes the set of users rating both movie i and movie j, U_i denotes the set of users rating movie i and U_j denotes the set of users rating movie j. For each movie i, we select top M movies having highest cosine similarity scores as a group of similar movies.

Second, noticing that the item-based CF approach heavily depends on the user ratings that may not have good performance if the ratings are sparse, we also employ the Topic Modeling approach [13] which is purely based on the review contents and eliminates the dependency on user ratings. Latent Dirichlet Allocation (LDA) is a generative probabilistic model for collections of discrete data such as text corpora. Since we regard the collection of all reviews of a movie as a document, by applying LDA, each document corresponding to each movie can be represented as a multinomial distribution over latent topics, where each topic is characterized by a distribution over words. We apply Kullback–Leibler (KL) divergence, which is a non-symmetric measure of the difference between two probability distributions, to calculate the divergence from movie i's topic distribution, i.e. P_i, to movie j's topic distribution, i.e. P_j:

$$D_{KL}(P_i \| P_j) = \sum_{l \in LatentTopics} P_i(l) \ln \frac{P_i(l)}{P_j(l)} \ . \tag{3}$$

where $P_i(l)$ denotes the probability that movie i belongs to the latent topic l. For each movie i, we select top M movies having smallest KL divergence as a cluster of similar movies.

After getting the cluster of similar movies for movie i, CLF weighting of term t in the reviews of i can be computed by counting how many movies in the cluster whose reviews contain term t. Finally, the integrated TF-IDF-CLF term weighting scheme is given by:

$$tf\text{-}idf\text{-}clf_{t,i} = tf_{t,i} \times idf_t \times clf_{t,i}^{\lambda_1} \ . \tag{4}$$

where λ_1 is a parameter indicating how much weight is put in the CLF weighting. For each movie, the adjective features are extracted from its reviews by selecting the top K adjectives having the highest TF-IDF-CLF weightings, and then are passed to the vector generator.

Vector Generator. After getting the extracted features of each movie, we represent each movie as well as each user in the form of feature vector. Specifically, each movie i is represented as a vector Q_i, in which each element is associated with one of its features. The values of the elements measure the extent to which movie i possesses those features. Similarly, each user u is represented as a vector P_u and the elements are associated with the features of all movies. The values of the elements measure the extent to which user u likes those features. For example, let's assume that we have only two movies in the system, i.e. *Titanic* and *Spider-man*, and for each movie we extract 3 features from the user reviews, the movie feature vectors and the user feature vectors for two system users are as following:

Table 1. Movie Featrue Vector of *Titanic*

Feature	romantic	sad	astounding
Value	0.5	0.4	0.1

Table 2. Movie Feature Vector of *Spider-man*

Feature	romantic	spectacular	scary
Value	0.2	0.3	0.5

Table 3. User Feature Vectors

	romantic	sad	astounding	spectacular	scary
User A	0.4	0.5	-0.2	0.3	-0.1
User B	-0.1	0.1	0.5	0.3	0.4

The same as the latent factor model, we include the baseline predictors to estimate the non-interaction effects from users and movies respectively (i.e. $udev_u$ and $idev_i$). A predicted rating of movie i for user u is given by:

$$\hat{r}_{u,i} = \mu + udev_u + idev_i + \sum_{f \in F(i)} e_{u,f} e_{i,f} . \tag{5}$$

μ denotes the overall average rating, $udev_u$ and $idev_i$ indicate the observed deviations of user u and item i respectively from the average. $F(i)$ denotes the set of features belonging to movie i. $e_{u,f}$ is the value of feature f in user u's feature vector P_u, and $e_{i,f}$ is the value of feature f in movie i's feature vector Q_i.

We employ a stochastic gradient descent optimization adapted from RSVD, which was proposed by [14] and has been successfully applied by many others, to estimate the values of the elements for both movie feature vectors and user feature vectors, as well as the baseline predictors. We iterate through the training data set until the prediction errors in the validation dataset are minimum.

Recommender. With the movie feature vectors and user feature vectors, we can easily predict a rating for a particular user given a movie that is new to him using formula (5). In order to recommend movies to a user, we can predict the ratings of all movies that are new to him, then rank these movies according to the predicted ratings, and recommend him the top N movies with highest predicted ratings.

One of the key features of our method is that in addition to providing recommendations, we provide explanation. We do this by explicitly listing features that caused an item to occur in the list of recommendations. For each movie i in user u's recommended list, the product of two feature values $e_{u,f} \cdot e_{i,f}$ is the partial interaction effect regarding feature f, and measures the extent to which feature f contributes to cause movie i being recommended to user u. Therefore, we rank all the features in $F(i)$ according to the partial interaction effect, and provide the top K features having highest products in addition to the recommended movie i, as an explanation of recommendation. Using the above-mentioned example, if the movie *Spider-man* is recommended to user B, then we can get the partial interaction effect regarding each feature of *Spider-man*, as following:

Table 4. Partial Interaction Effect

	romantic	spectacular	scary
$e_{B,f}$	-0.1	0.3	0.4
$e_{Spider-man,f}$	0.2	0.3	0.5
$e_{B,f} \times e_{Spider-man,f}$	-0.02	0.09	0.2

If we only provide the top one feature as the explanation to user B for recommending this movie, the feature "scary" having the highest partial interaction effect is selected.

Since the values of features are different in different users' feature vectors depending on their preference on these features, even we recommend the same movie to two different users, the explanation should be different. Thus, *our explanation of recommendation is personalized, truly reflecting the users' tastes.*

3   Experiment and Results

All recommender systems largely rely on their *prediction engines*, which are able to predict users' preference over items. There is a basic assumption that users prefer recommender system that provides "accurate predictions"[15]. Therefore, most research in recommender systems, seek to develop algorithms that provide better prediction, and evaluate recommender systems by measuring their prediction accuracies. In line with this, we use the *Mean Absolute Error* (MAE) metric that is commonly used in recommendation research to evaluate the accuracy of rating prediction. MAE is defined as:

$$MAE = \frac{\sum_{r_{u,i} \in TestingSet} \left| r_{u,i} - \hat{r}_{u,i} \right|}{|TestingSet|}. \tag{6}$$

where $r_{u,i}$ is the rating given by user u to item i in the testing dataset, $\hat{r}_{u,i}$ is the predicted rating and $|TestingSet|$ is the size of testing dataset.

While accurate prediction is crucial, it still does not address one key goal of good recommender systems, to be able to cover a wide range of items. In other words, an algorithm may have high prediction power, but if it is only able to work over a small portion of items it is not a desirable situation. Accordingly, researchers also measure the *coverage* of recommender systems, which refers to the proportion of items that the system can recommend, indicating the ability of exploring diverse items. We use the percentage of items in the testing set of which users' preference can be inferred, in terms of either probabilities or predicted ratings:

$$Coverage = \frac{\#Predicatble\ Items\ in\ TestingSet}{|TestingSet|} \times 100\% \ . \qquad (7)$$

In our experiment, we will evaluate our proposed method in terms of both rating prediction accuracy and item space coverage. We will also provide the qualitative results of recommendation explanation.

3.1 Experiment Setup

We use two kinds of data in our experiment. Firstly, we use the publicly available Movielens 10M version dataset which consists of 10 million ratings and 95580 tags applied to 10681 movies by 71567 users of the online movie recommender service MovieLens. The user ratings are on a scale of 1 to 5, with 1 being bad and 5 being excellent. In the original dataset, only 4009 (5.60%) users provide tags to movies, and only 7601 (71.16%) movies receive tags from users. We preprocess the data to generate a tag-dense subset exactly the same as the one used by Wei, et al. [8] for the purpose of comparing results. In the subset, every user gives at least one tag to movies, and every movie receives at least one tag from users. Let <user,movie,tag,rating> denote a tuple. The subset has 1112 tuples with 201 users, 501 movies and 404 tags. Secondly, we crawl the first 40 user reviews from IMDb website for each movie in the dataset, ranked by the number of users who indicate that the review is useful. 99.61% of the movies in the dataset have user reviews in IMDb.

To evaluate the performance of our proposed method, we will compare both the rating prediction accuracy and the item space coverage among the following methods:

1. **User-based CF (UCF)** [1]. This method uses the traditional user-based collaborative filtering.
2. **Item-based CF (ICF)** [16]. This method is the Amazon's item-based collaborative filtering.
3. **Tag Bayesian Network (TBN)**. This method generates recommendation based on the ternary relationship among users-items-tags using Bayesian Network.
4. **Probabilistic Matrix Factorization (PMF)** [17]. This is a state-of-art rating-based collaborative filtering algorithm that utilizes the relationship among users, items and ratings.
5. **Quaternary Sematic Analysis (QSA)** [8]. This method represents the state-of-art tag-based approaches. It models the quaternary relationship of users-items-tags-ratings as 4-order tensor and performs the multi-way latent semantic analysis.
6. **Adjective Feature Vector (AFV).** This is our proposed method using adjective features extracted from external user reviews. Since we use two approaches to get the cluster of similar movies, our method has two variants: *AFV using rating-based similarity* (AFV-R) and *AFV using review-topic-based similarity* (AFV-T).

3.2   Results of Item Rating Prediction

We first evaluate the item rating prediction performance of our proposed AFV-R and AFV-T methods. We randomly split the dataset into five subsets and each time use one subset as testing set and the remaining subsets as training set (aka. five-fold validation), and compute the MAE for different methods except for TBN, since this method estimates the probability that a user will like a particular item instead of predicting rating. We vary the parameters of our method to find the settings that give the best performance. This occurs when cluster size $M=20$, feature number $K=110$, $=2$, $=25$, $=10$, $=0.02$, $lrate=0.005$, $s=0.1$, and the times of iteration are 200. The results are shown in Figure 3.

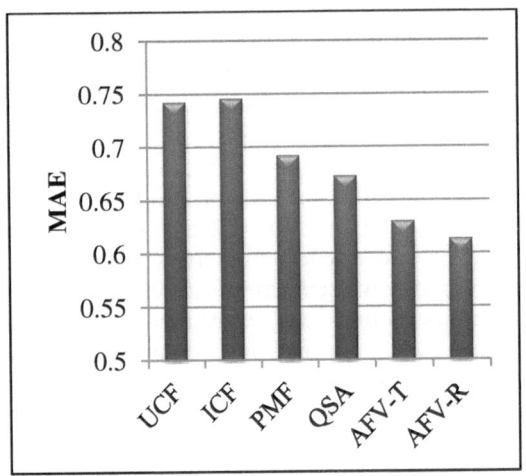

Fig. 3. Rating Prediction Accuracy (Lower MAE indicates higher accuracy)

To analyze the statistical significance of the results, we conduct a one tail t-test. Table 5 shows the p-value of comparing the results of AFV-T and AFV-R with other methods respectively. The results indicate that both of our AFV-T and AFV-R methods significantly outperform the existing methods. Specifically, AFV-T reduces the prediction error of the state-of-art CF algorithm and the state-of-art tag-based method by 8.90% and 6.33% respectively, and AFV-R reduces the prediction error of the two state-of-art algorithms by 11.27% and 8.77% respectively.

Table 5. P-value of Accuracy Significance Test

	P-value(AFV-T)	P-value(AFV-R)
BCF	0.0000	0.0000
ICF	0.0000	0.0000
PMF	0.0010	0.0005
QSA	0.0040	0.0010

3.3   Results of Recommendation Coverage

In addition to item rating prediction accuracy, we also compare the coverage of our methods with other methods. The results on the tag-dense subset are shown in Figure 4. PMF, QSA, and AFV-T achieve 100% coverage and the two traditional CF approaches also achieve high coverage. Since we apply ICF in AFV-R, the coverage of AFV-R is the same as ICF. However, coverage of TBN, which is purely based on tags, is only 58%, even if the data subset is tag-dense. Although the QSA method achieves 100% coverage, it is not the case in reality, since it requires every user provides tags and every movie receives tags. Actually, in the original dataset, only 5.60% of users provide tags to movies, and only 71.16% of movies receive tags from users.

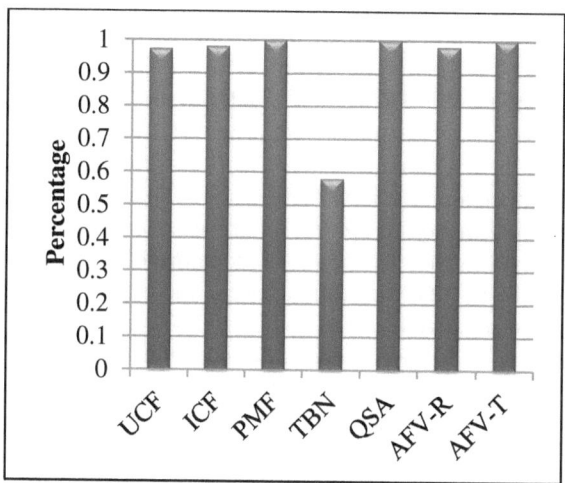

Fig. 4. Coverage on Tag-dense Subset

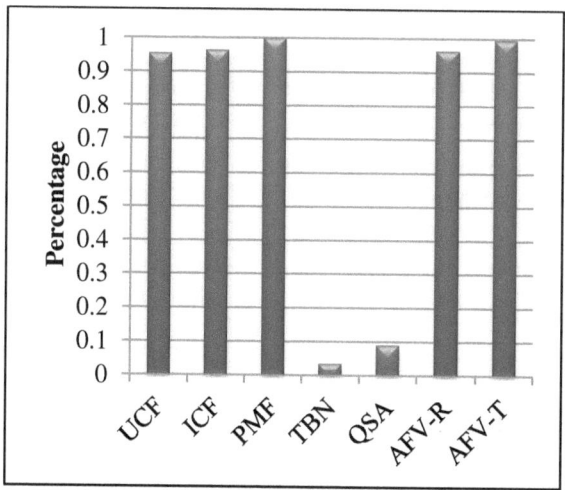

Fig. 5. Coverage on Full Dataset

We also evaluate the coverage of different methods in the full dataset, and the results are shown in Figure 5. In the full dataset, QSA only achieves 9.07% coverage and TBN is even worse, which is only 3.45%. Since the proposed AFV-T and AFV-R methods use the external reviews and do not require any tags from user, they achieve high coverage. Specifically, the coverage of AFV-R is the same as ICF, which is 96.4%, and the coverage of AFV-T is independent of user ratings but is determined by the proportion of movies having user reviews, which is close to 100%.

3.4   Results of Recommendation Explanation

The transparency of recommender system is often ignored by most CF approaches, while our method is able to provide explanation of recommendation for the system users. We are going to show the qualitative results of recommendation explanation using our method.

Applying the proposed AFV-R method which has the highest prediction accuracy, we recommend 5 movies for each user. We arbitrarily select three users who have 2 common movies in their recommendation list to illustrate the qualitative results of recommendation explanation given by our method. The two common movies are *My Neighbor Totoro* and *Grave of the Fireflies*. For each user, Table 6 shows the 8 listed features for each movie, as the explanation of recommending this movie to him.

As is shown by the results, for different users, the explanation of recommending the same movie is personalized, taking both the movie features and the users' tastes on each feature into consideration. In addition to providing the recommended movie, the explanation gains the users more insights into the recommendation mechanism, and therefore makes the recommendation more trustful and more acceptable to the users.

Table 6. Recommendation Explanation

	My Neighbor Totoro	*Grave of the Fireflies*
User A	curious, suitable, imaginative, warm, magical, friendly, sentimental, sweet	magical, suitable, cold, gorgeous, sentimental, beautiful, happy, extraordinary
User B	endearing, suitable, imaginative, giant, cute, poetic, boundless, fantastical	giant, astonished, live, engrossing, animated, suitable, poetic, gentle
User C	lovely, delightful, happy, gentle, spectacular, engaged, curious, magic	lovely, gentle, happy, magical, afraid, heartfelt, cold, engrossing

4   Related Work

There have been a large amount of recommendation research, most of which belongs to two main streams, i.e. CF approach and content-based approach. Our proposed method adopts the concept of SVD from CF approach into content-based approach to address the data sparsity problem and transparency problem. We also extend the existing automatic tag generation methods to extract adjective features from external user reviews for the purpose of recommendation. In the following, we review the related work to our proposed method.

4.1   Collaborative Filtering (CF) Recommendation

Neighborhood Models. Owing to its compelling simplicity and good quality of recommendations, CF has been deeply explored in the last ten years and represents the most commonly used recommendation technique. The most common approaches to CF are based on neighborhood models. Typically, these approaches can be classified into two types, i.e. user-based [1] and item-based [16]. Both the user-based and item-based CF works on the same basic principal. First a distance (typically cosine distance) is measured between users or items based on which user liked which item. Next, this distance is used to measure the similarity between two items or two users.

Latent Factor Models. Latent factor models such as probabilistic matrix factorization (PMF) provide an alternative approach to CF by mapping both items and users to the same latent factor space, which is automatically inferred from user feedback and tries to explain ratings by characterizing both users and items on the latent factors. Singular Value Decomposition (SVD) [18] is a well-known method for matrix factorization that provides the best lower rank approximations of the original matrix.

Transparency in Recommender Systems. According to a rule stem from psychology, people are generally more comfortable with what they are familiar with and understand [7]. However, most of the collaborative filtering techniques seem to completely ignore this important rule and work as the black boxes. HCI research on recommender systems highlights the role that transparency plays in recommendation. Rashmi et al. [5] showed that both mean liking and mean confidence were significantly increased in a recommender system which was more transparent. They argued that from the users' perspective, a good algorithm that generates accurate recommendations is not enough to constitute a useful system. The system also needs to convey its inner logic and why a particular recommendation is suitable to the user. Henriette et al. [6] conducted an experiment and the results also showed that acceptance of the recommendations was increased by explaining to the user why a recommendation was made. To summarize, transparency in recommender systems is an important issue that cannot be ignored. To address the shortcoming of the black box approaches, our proposed approach incorporates the characteristics of content-based recommendation to offer explanation for recommendation.

4.2   Content-Based Recommendation

The intuition of content-based recommendation is to learn to recommend items that are similar to the ones that the user liked in the past. The similarity between items is calculated based on the features associated with the compared items. For example, if a user has positively rated a movie that belongs to the comedy genre, then the system can learn to recommend other movies from this genre. Content-based techniques have a natural limit in the number and type of features that are associated with the items that these systems recommend.

Recently, due to the popularity of social tagging systems, tags as a specific kind of user-generated contents have drawn attention from researchers. Tags are generated by users who collaboratively annotate and categorize resources of interests with freely chosen keywords [19]. Compared to descriptive attributes, tags cover more features of the items and are more comprehended by the users. Wei et al. [8] proposed a unified framework for recommendation by modeling the quaternary relationship among users, items, tags and ratings as a 4-order tensor and performed a multi-way latent semantic analysis, representing the state-of-the-art.

4.3   Automatic Tag Generation

Researches on automatic tag generation stem from information retrieval and text mining. There are two streams of such researches. The first stream tries to suggest relevant tags for new document based on existing tags (aka. tag assignment). In practice, tags are chosen from a controlled vocabulary of terms, and documents are classified according to their content into classes that correspond to elements of the vocabulary. Tags generated by these approaches have high generalizability and they can well identify the common features of the similar documents. However, the representativeness of these tags may be weak so that it is hard to differentiate the documents.

Another stream of work aims at automatically extracting tags from textual documents on the basis of properties such as frequency, without any predefined vocabulary (aka. tag extraction). Many approaches can be used in tag extraction, like term frequency, TF-IDF, etc. Tags given by extraction methods are able to highly represent the associated documents; however, they face the problem of diverging vocabulary and have difficulty in exposing the common features among similar documents. For the purpose of recommendation, it is important to balance the representativeness and generalizability of the extracted features, which is addressed in our approach.

5   Conclusion

In this work, we have shown that adjective features embedded in user reviews can be used to characterize movies as well as users' taste. We employ POS tagging and propose introducing cluster frequency into traditional TF-IDF term weight scheme to extract adjective features from external user reviews, alleviating the problem diverging vocabulary, and balancing the representativeness and generalizability of the extracted features. We also propose a novel method which adapts stochastic gradient descent optimization from RSVD to construct item feature vectors and user feature vectors. The experiment results show that the proposed method outperforms the state-of-art CF algorithm and state-of-art tag-based method in terms of rating prediction accuracy. Specifically, our proposed R-AFV method reduces the prediction error of the state-of-art CF algorithm and the state-of-art tag-based method by 11.27% and 8.77% respectively. Our proposed method does not require any tags from users. On the one hand, it relieves the users' efforts to provide tags; on the other hand, it can always achieve high coverage of recommendation while the coverage of tag-based methods is extremely low when the tags are sparse, which is always the case in reality. Moreover, the proposed method is able to provide personalized explanation of recommendation for the users, increasing the users' trust on the recommendation.

There are some limitations of our work. Firstly, we only consider the adjective features and ignore other descriptive attributes of movies. Our method can be extended to incorporate other descriptive attributes to generate more accurate recommendation and higher quality of explanation. Secondly, we do not consider the semantic relationship between the adjective features. Future work can focus on the semantic analysis of the adjective features.

Although our recommendation framework focuses on the movie domain, it can be easily applied in other domains where user reviews are available. Since our method captures the users' taste in a higher and more abstract level, it can be also applied in cross-domain recommendation.

References

1. Resnick, P., Iacovou, N., Suchak, M., Bergstorm, P., Riedl, J.: GroupLens: An Open Architecture for Collaborative Filtering of Netnews. In: Proceedings of ACM 1994 Conference on Computer Supported Cooperative Work, pp. 175–186. ACM (1994)
2. Lops, P., Gemmis, M., Semeraro, G.: Content-based Recommender Systems: State of the Art and Trends. In: Ricci, F., Rokach, L., Shapira, B. (eds.) Recommender Systems Handbook, pp. 73–105. Springer (2011)
3. Su, X., Khoshgoftaar, T.M.: A survey of collaborative filtering techniques. Advances in Artificial Intelligence 4 (2009)
4. Adomavicius, G., Tuzhilin, A.: Toward the next generation of recommender systems: A survey of the state-of-the-art and possible extensions. IEEE Transactions on Knowledge and Data Engineering 17, 734–749 (2005)
5. Sinha, R., Swearingen, K.: The role of transparency in recommender systems. In: CHI 2002: Extended Abstracts on Human Factors in Computing Systems, pp. 830–831. ACM (2002)
6. Cramer, H., Evers, V., Ramlal, S., van Someren, M., Rutledge, L., Stash, N., Aroyo, L., Wielinga, B.: The effects of transparency on trust in and acceptance of a content-based art recommender. User Modeling and User-Adapted Interaction 18, 455–496 (2008)
7. Massa, P., Avesani, P.: Trust Metrics in Recommender Systems. In: Karat, J., Vanderdonckt, J., Golbeck, J. (eds.) Computing with Social Trust, pp. 259–285. Springer, London (2009)
8. Wei, C., Hsu, W., Lee, M.: A unified framework for recommendations based on quaternary semantic analysis. In: Proceedings of the 34th International ACM SIGIR Conference on Research and Development in Information Retrieval, pp. 1023–1032. ACM (2011)

9. Jakob, N., Weber, S.-H., Müller, M.-C., Gurevych, I.: Beyond the stars: exploiting free-text user reviews to improve the accuracy of movie recommendations. In: Proceedings of the 1st International CIKM Workshop on Topic-Sentiment Analysis for Mass Opinion, pp. 57–64. ACM, Hong Kong (2009)

10. Faridani, S.: Using canonical correlation analysis for generalized sentiment analysis, product recommendation and search. In: Proceedings of the Fifth ACM Conference on Recommender Systems, pp. 355–358. ACM (2011)

11. Leung, C.W.K., Chan, S.C.F., Chung, F.: Integrating Collaborative Filtering and Sentiment Analysis: A Rating Inference Approach. In: Proceedings of The ECAI 2006 Workshop on Recommender Systems, pp. 62–66 (2006)

12. Toutanova, K., Klein, D., Manning, C.D., Singer, Y.: Feature-rich part-of-speech tagging with a cyclic dependency network. In: Proceedings of the 2003 Conference of the North American Chapter of the Association for Computational Linguistics on Human Language Technology, vol. 1, pp. 173–180. Association for Computational Linguistics, Edmonton (2003)

13. Blei, D., Ng, A., Jordan, M.: Latent Dirichlet Allocation. Journal of Machine Learning Research 3, 993–1022 (2003)

14. http://sifter.org/simon/journal/20061211.html

15. Shani, G., Gunawardana, A.: Evaluating Recommendation Systems. In: Ricci, F., Rokach, L., Shapira, B. (eds.) Recommender Systems Handbook, pp. 73–105. Springer (2011)

16. Sarwar, B., Karypis, G., Konstan, J., Reidl, J.: Item-based collaborative filtering recommendation algorithms. In: World Wide Web, pp. 285–295 (2001)

17. Salakhutdinov, R., Mnih, A.: Probabilistic matrix factorization. Advances in Neural Information Processing Systems 20, 1257–1264 (2008)

18. Takács, G., Pilászy, I., Németh, B., Tikk, D.: Matrix factorization and neighbor based algorithms for the netflix prize problem. In: Proceedings of the 2008 ACM Conference on Recommender Systems, pp. 267–274. ACM, Lausanne (2008)

19. de Gemmis, M., Lops, P., Semeraro, G., Basile, P.: Integrating tags in a semantic content-based recommender. In: Proceedings of the 2008 ACM Conference on Recommender Systems, pp. 163–170. ACM (2008)

Product Semantics in Design Research Practice

Jonas Sjöström[1], Brian Donnellan[2], and Markus Helfert[3]

[1] Department of Informatics & Media and Department of Public Health and Caring Sciences,
Uppsala University, Sweden
jonas.sjostrom@im.uu.se
[2] National University of Ireland Maynooth Ireland and the Innovation Value Institute
brian.donnellan@nuim.ie
[3] Dublin City University, Ireland
markus.helfert@computing.dcu.ie

Abstract. The concept of product semantics and its focus on meaning is used to interpret design research as design. It is argued that we may conceive of design research as design in two realms: The practical and the academic. In doing design research, there is a reciprocal shaping of artifacts: Better artifacts (contributions to practice) through appropriation of knowledge and methods from the academic realm, and better knowledge artifacts (contributions to academia) by drawing relevance and experiences of appropriation from the practical realm. We adopt a product semantics view to discuss research as design. Product semantics highlights the meaning of artifacts with respect to their (i) stakeholders, (ii) artifacts-in-use, (iii) artifacts-in-language, (iv) artifact lifecycle, and (v) ecology. Based on this interpretation, we propose activities that should characterize the practice of doing design research. Finally we provide an example of Design Research Practice in action.

Keywords: Design, research, practice, meaning, artifact.

1 Introduction

The IS field has paid an increased interest in design research (DR) over the last two decades. Design research is becoming recognized as equally important to behavioural information systems (IS) research [1,2]. Design is depicted as 'fundamental' to the IS discipline [3]. DR is manifested through special issues in leading journals, conference tracks, and dedicated conferences for design science research in IS. Purao et al [4] and Baskerville et al [5] provide a rich account of the development of DR in the IS field.

There is an on-going discussion about the norms that should govern DR, including both (i) what type of knowledge we can expect as a result of research, and (ii) how to accomplish rigor in the design process in order to substantiate claims. This corresponds to the *process* of research and the *product* (outcomes) of research. In design science research [1,2] knowledge outcome is defined as design science artifacts, i.e. constructs, models, methods and instantiations. Hevner et al [6] also propose that design science research may lead to new evaluation techniques. The idea

A. Bhattacherjee and B. Fitzgerald (Eds.): Future of ICT Research, IFIP AICT 389, pp. 35–48, 2012.

of building design theory has been proposed [7,8], while action design research (ADR) suggests that the minimum requirement of the ADR approach is to formulate design principles that are applicable to design solutions for a class of problem [9]. The ambition in ADR initiatives should be to contribute to theory [9]. 'Scholarly contributions' are endorsed by major journals [10]. Orlikowski & Iacono [11] identify five views of the IT artifact; (i) Tool view – functions and capabilities to perform tasks, substitute for labour, or improve productivity, (ii) Proxy view – perceptions as something to use and of value, (iii) Ensemble view – embedded relationship within social, organisational, and economic context, (iv) Computational view – computational capabilities including processing and representational model and (v) Nominal view – abstract, non-specific, collective view. A very inclusive definition of IT artifacts is provided by Gill & Hevner [12]: "IT artifacts are broadly defined as constructs (vocabulary and symbols), models (abstractions and representations), methods (algorithms and practices), and instantiations (implemented and prototype systems). More generally, artifacts can be viewed as the symbolic representation or physical instantiation of design concepts. Even within a discipline such as MIS, they are not necessarily limited to information systems. Rather, MIS artifacts include organizational designs, process designs, and other intentionally constructed entities relating to information systems."

Our interpretation of the discourse summarized above is that there are co-existing ideas about what the outcome of DR should be (models, methods, instantiations, constructs, new evaluation techniques, design principles, or design theory). Here, for the sake of our argument, we speak of design research as *design of knowledge artifacts*.

While this meta-theoretical development of DR in the IS field emerges, there has still been little effort to factor in other design traditions into the IS field. Although some IS research has promoted design thinking (e.g. [13,14]), it has not yet had considerable impact on the design research discourse in IS. Design thinking (e.g. [15,16]) and its notion of *product semantics* highlight stakeholders in design and their sense-making of artifacts. Product semantics stresses contextual approaches that focus on the meaning of artifacts in use and typically consider the design of affordances, constraints, feedback, coherence, learnability, multi-sensory redundancy, variability, robustness, and so forth as experienced by different stakeholders. Some recent IS publications incorporate concepts from design thinking (e.g. [10,12,17]). Interestingly, there has been little or no discussion about how DR can be conceived from a design perspective. Baskerville et al [10] show that lessons learned in design studies prove useful to further the meta-theoretical models in the IS field. Baskerville et al [10] employ the works of Cross [15] to distinguish conceptually between design and research in DR. In this paper, we make a similar contribution. We challenge the supposed distinction between design and research, claiming that design researchers in essence are designers of knowledge artifacts. A practice perspective is adopted to characterize design research as practice.

We employ ideas from product semantics to factor in fundamentals of design thinking into IS design research [16]. We explore design research as practice; and the multiple realms in which design research operates (section 2). The notion of product semantics, and the axiomaticity of meaning in design is elaborated (section 3), and used to elaborate on a case of design research practice as design (section 4). In section 5, implications for design research practice are discussed.

2   Realms of Design Research

Sociologists have elaborated the concept of *practice* for a long time, and there is no 'unified' view of what it means [18]. Schatski [19] explains practice as "embodied materially mediated arrays of human activity centrally organized around shared practical understanding". The use of artifacts ("materially mediated") in action is recognized, while at the same time human action is acknowledged as part of a social context. Schatski's account of practice theory resonates well with the idea of a reciprocal shaping of action and structure, as proposed by Giddens [20]. Orlikowski [21] elaborates on Giddens' ideas through her notion of a duality of technology (as begin shaped by, and shaping, human action). In this paper, we adopt the view that design and appropriation of technology is strongly 'fused' with human action.

A key proposition in design research is that research results should be relevant and useful for practice [6]. At the same time, IS researchers are expected to contribute to the academic knowledge base (e.g. [7]). Goldkuhl [22] articulates a distinction between contributions to *local* practice (e.g. through a DR effort within a specific company) and contributions to *general* practice through re-usable knowledge (e.g. workshops and practitioner-oriented text books). Apart from contributing to both practice and academia, design researchers should draw rigor from the knowledge base and draw relevance from practice [6]. Design researchers thus operate in at least two different (but interdependent) social structures. We refer to these here as the *practical realm* and the *academic realm* (Figure 1). Each realm may be broken down into more specific practices, such as a single company in the practical realm or a specific sub-community (e.g. a journal or a conference) in the academic realm.

Figure 1 illustrates our view of design research as practice. The framework is clearly influenced by the IS design science research framework [1,6]. The realms of practice and academia can be recognized from Baskerville et al [10]. Our adaptation of the IS DSR framework is based on the notion that the DR practice interacts with other practices, either in the practical realm or in the academic realm. This corresponds with the ideals of relevant and useful research outputs from a practice point of view, while at the same time adhering to academic ideals. We acknowledge that ideals in practice and academia may partially overlap. In contrast to Hevner et al. [6], we seek to explicitly view the relation between the DR practice and the academic realm as action, governed by the ideals emerging in interplay with relevant stakeholder communities in the two realms. This way, ideals are situated rather than fixed, instead we highlight that any DR practice needs to be based on a process both to monitor and influence the discourse in the two realms. Research in IS and other disciplines is characterized by ideals that emerge through social interaction within the research community. An example of this is expressed by DeSanctis [23]: "Scholarly publication is a jointly constructed process, reflective of dialogue among researchers, reviewers, editors, and readers." Within a community, ideals emerge and evolve.

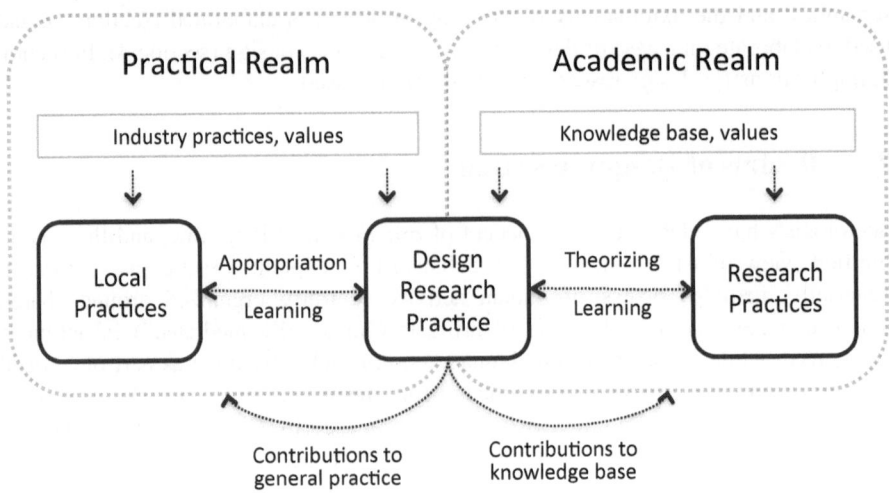

Fig. 1. The Multiple Realms of Design Research

Within the practical realm, we find local practices (e.g. public and commercial organizations). Practices in the academic realm may include research communities (such as AIS and ACM), governed by emergent value systems that are applied in the assessment of proposed contributions to the knowledge base. Practices in both realms may also be more narrowly defined, e.g. non-profit organizations in the practical realm or specific journals or communities in the academic realm.

In design research, learning occurs through moral inquiry [24]; i.e. an attempt to improve a situation. Evaluation is a core activity in DR, and there are several ideas about how to approach evaluation (what to evaluate, when to evaluate and how to evaluate). Arguably, the DSR approach [3] is biased towards a positivistic tradition of evaluation, while the ADR approach [9] emphasizes an interpretive approach to assessing artifacts when appropriated in practice. Similarly, Venable [25] suggests that we should distinguish between artificial versus naturalistic evaluation of artifacts. Artificial evaluation is conducted through experimental or analytical techniques (evaluating the artifact-as-such), while naturalistic evaluation concerns use qualities and emergent phenomena that cannot be assessed without an actual appropriation of the artifact in a 'real' empirical setting. Through appropriate evaluation efforts, design researchers can demonstrate the qualities of their artifacts. Gregor and Hevner [26] elaborate further on the relation between artificial and naturalistic evaluation and its relation to design science vs. behavioural science.

For design researchers, the ideal is to design artifacts that are highly valued, having an impact in both the practical realm and in the academic realm. An underlying DR assumption is that a DR practice will be able to design better artifacts by drawing from both realms. The practical realm ingrains design with relevance and allows us to perform naturalistic evaluations of artifacts, while the academic realm provides a knowledge base for design and evaluation, both with respect to the process and the product of research. Further, we are expected to contribute to both realms, and to communicate our results to multiple audiences [6].

3   Adopting Product Semantics to Characterize Realms

Krippendorff defines product semantics as "a vocabulary and methodology for designing artifacts in view of the meanings they could acquire for their users and the communities of their stakeholders". Although Krippendorff uses the term product *semantics*, we agree with Ehn [33] that it is in fact more appropriate to refer to Krippendorff's ideas as a *pragmatic* view of design. That being said, the notion of *meaning* and its impact on design is still at the core of product semantics. Krippendorff [16, p. 47] explains that meaning has a central role in design thinking: "Humans do not see and act on the physical qualities of things, but on what they mean to them." He refers to this as the 'axiomaticity of meaning' and argues: "There is no escape from the axiom. It states an undeniable truth that is so strong that one might as well embrace it fully for the strengths it provides for the design discourse. Without realizing its strength, designers are doomed to chase the ghosts of other discourses." [16 p. 50].

The notion of meaning is recognized in the social sciences. Krippendorff's notion of meaning resonates well with Peirce's *semiosis*, Bühler's *symbolic interactionism*, Polanyi's *sense-reading* and *sense-giving*, as well as Weick's *sense-making*, to mention a few. Polanyi [34 p. 181] states: "Both the way we endow our own utterances with meaning and our attribution of meaning to the utterances of others are acts of tacit knowing. They represent sense-giving and sense-reading within the structure of tacit knowing". As humans, we continually make sense of the world around us on the basis of our cumulated experiences. The interpretive view of the world is well recognized in IS research [35,36]. Krippendorff [16] emphasizes that designers need to seek a 2nd order understanding – i.e. employ design methods that allow them to gain some degree of understanding of the meaning different stakeholders ascribe to artifacts. Krippendorff suggests that designers increase their chances to design successful artifacts by taking into account four different perspectives on how individuals attribute meaning to artifacts: (i) The meaning of *artifacts in use*, (ii) the meaning of *artifacts in language*, (iii) the meaning of a *lifecycle of artifacts*, and (iv) the meaning of an *ecology of artifacts*.

The success of an artifact depends on the meaning ascribed to them by stakeholders in each realm. We do not claim that every practice within each realm is identical, but that practices that belong to the same realm share similarities, and that there are notable differences between practices in the academic and the practical realm.

4   IT-CMF: An Illustration of Design Research as Practice

In this section, we introduce the design research practice *Innovation Value Institute (IVI)* and their *IT-Capability Maturity Model (IT-CMF)*. We include the case to illustrate the explanatory power of product semantics in design research. IT-CMF is a high-level process capability maturity framework for managing the IT function within an organization. The framework identifies a number of critical IT processes, and describes an approach to designing maturity frameworks for each process.

Table 1. Five aspects to consider in design

Aspect	Description
Stakeholders	Individuals and/or organizations that are affected by the artifact(s); or that have influence over the dissemination of artifact(s).
Artifacts in use	The way that stakeholders appropriate artifacts; and the way they make sense of some them through their appropriation experiences. Understood as the interplay between appropriation of artifacts (materiality) and the social structure.
Artifacts in language	How stakeholders speak of artifacts. Especially adjectives that signal how stakeholders assess the quality of artifact(s).
Lifecycle of artifacts	The way that stakeholders conceive of the 'status' of some artifact(s) within the realm – the way it has been appropriated and its projected future role within the realm.
Ecology of artifacts	Other artifacts in this realm (competing, supporting) that affect the way that stakeholders attach meaning to the artifact(s) in focus.

The IT-CMF is a novel approach to managing IT resources due to its structured Design Science-based methodology [28]. The *IT-CMF Content Development and Review Process* is implemented by the IT-CMF development community of stakeholders in the Innovation Value Institute (www.ivi.ie). The IT-CMF is comprised by a set of interrelated artifacts. In terms of design science research [6] it consists of constructs, models, methods and instantiations. The IT-CMF *constructs* are basic definitions and templates to describe various IT managemens issues. IT-CMF *models* include, among other things, critical process definitions and models to compare frameworks. IT-CMF *methods* include descriptions on how to assess maturity, and steps in the transition to new maturity levels. Finally, there are *instantiations*; software tools that are based on and facilitate the use of the IT-CMF constructs, models, and methods. In the case of the IT-CMF we see that both practical contributions and theoretical contributions are artifacts (products of design). Stakeholders from practice and academia interpret the idea of 'use', 'language', 'lifecycle' and 'ecology' differently.

In the remainder of this section, we appropriate Krippendorff's [16] notion of meaning to characterize IVI as a design research practice, and scrutinized the potential meanings of the IT-CMF using aspects of meaning derived from product semantics (as characterized in table 1).

4.1 Stakeholders

Krippendorff [16] emphasizes that "no artifact can be realized within a culture without being meaningful to those who can move it through its various definitions." Product semantics consequentially advocates a design process with a strong focus on – and participation of – stakeholders.

In the practical realm, stakeholders may be understood as *local* practitioners, such as companies or government agencies. In addition, *general* practice may benefit from practical theory/design science artifacts/design principles to improve their organizations. Further, R&D organizations benefit from commercialization of DR outcome/innovation/patents.

In the academic realm, stakeholders include (but are not limited to) individual researchers, the DR practice as such, and the institution(s) to which the DR belongs, funding agencies/organizations *et cetera*. However, stakeholders also include other researchers (reviewers, editors, other scholars).

The IVI community is comprised of university-based academic researchers and industry-based practitioner-researchers drawn from over 80 companies located throughout the world. Researchers collaborate with practitioners and subject matter experts within research teams to learn from key domain experts. Catering for constraints often faced when working in collaboration with practitioners, and individual expertise a design science oriented research process has emerged within the community. A key role of IVI – which we conceive of as a design research practice – is to facilitate guided emergence [9] of the IT-CMF in the IVI web of stakeholders.

IT-CMF design is divided into four phases separated by stage reviews with key deliverables at each stage. At phase 1, details relating to the artifacts are consulted and expanded with input from group of key opinion leaders, subject matter experts, industry, and academic literature. At phase 2 comparisons are made with artefacts in industry frameworks and industry best practices. At phase 3 the artefacts are reviewed with 3-5 external organisations and key opinion leaders. At phase 4 the artefacts are exercised through field experiments in at least three organisations.

4.2   The Meaning of Artifacts-in-Use

In terms of DR outcomes in the practical realm, the aim of design is (arguably) to develop knowledge oriented towards change in a socio-material assemblage. Krippendorff [16] emphasizes the meaning of artifacts in use. The phenomena of 'design in use' has been discussed by IS researchers in terms of, for example, drift [38], tailoring [37], reinvention [31] and appropriation (e.g. [37,38]. There has been a lot of interest put into how artifacts, e.g. IT systems, are appropriated in the practical realm. In addition, appropriation is a pre-requisite to 'naturalistic' evaluation [25] of our artifacts.

The phased design approach in IVI leads to a step-wise refinement of artifacts, from ideas to actual appropriation by local practices. IT-CMF has also been appropriated by several of the industrial stakeholders, in some cases through researcher-practitioner collaboration based on action research, in some cases using other evaluation techniques appropriated at different implementation stages [29].

Experiences from the development of the IT-CMF show that the everyday engagement in an information process "shows unexpected consequences: events, behaviors, and features of systems and the people who use them fall outside the scope of the original specifications" [32, p 44]. Use patterns are irregular, often contradictory, untidy, and subject to approximation. Current design science literature tends to separate the design of the artifact from the teleological goal of the artifact (i.e. its use in on-going but changing information processes) while at the same time declaring that these two aspects are inseparable. Our position is that it is impossible to completely specify an information process *ex ante*. The information manipulated by an actor engaged with an information system is intended to be consumed by human actors in some fashion, rather than to satisfy the whims of a technology or an *a priori* design.

In a similar manner, knowledge artifacts are actually evaluated based on their 'appropriation' in the academic realm. Local and international workshops, special interest communities, and conferences provide opportunities to 'prototype' artifacts in the academic realm. However, true 'appropriation' of knowledge artifacts will only occur when the artifacts are adopted in new design situations, by their own DR practice or by other researchers who incorporate knowledge artifacts in their own studies. By appropriation in new situations, we will be able to perform 'naturalistic' evaluations of these knowledge artifacts in a new design setting. A DR practice can exploit this opportunity, as a means to evaluate and further improve their work.

4.3   The Meaning of Artifacts-in-Language

Krippendorff claims that an important role of a designer is to interpret the discourse among stakeholders, stating "The fate of all artifacts is decided in language". Communication between designers and other stakeholders is a core issue. Several approaches to improving sense-making have been proposed over the years, such as various types of user-centered approaches, e.g. prototyping in interaction design, and arenas and concepts for customer-developer interaction in agile development. They all share the idea that designers need to promote communication and learning between stakeholders. In product semantics [16], the importance of language is manifested in several ways, e.g. through user-centered design processes and through questionnaires that are used to assess how stakeholders perceive the artifact and its potential usefulness during the design process.

The IT-CMF stage reviews provide a communicative arena where stakeholders assess artifacts-in-use and new design proposals. In addition, the academic arena is considered important to scrutinize artifacts in terms of (for example) conceptual coherence, rigor and theoretical justification. By exposing 'scholarly adapted' representations of the IT-CMF – i.e. research papers that address certain aspects of the framework and the design research process - peers from the academic community provide constructive criticism that support the development of artifacts further.

The peer review mechanism provides a feedback loop between the practical and the academic realm, where the practical realm feeds design researchers with relevance and appropriation experiences, while the academic realm supports assessment of 'scholarly' oriented qualities of artifacts. Thus, different representations of the IT-CMF artifacts reside in multiple discourses, and design researchers shift focus between these. A challenge for an institute like IVI is to strategically appropriate the publication process as a type of 'scholarly evaluation' of artifacts. Clearly, there are career incentives for academic scholars to relate to academic norms (otherwise they do not get published). Other stakeholders will not support the scholarly work if there is no evident value for their industrial practices.

In the academic realm, the difference between 'use of artifacts' and 'artifacts in language' becomes somewhat fuzzy. If the artifact is a concept, we may conceive of it as being appropriated when it becomes part of a discourse. Indeed, Krippendorff [16] characterizes discourse as a type of complex and human-centered artifact. Use of knowledge artifacts may consist of how we interpret those artifacts, represent them in our own discourses and appropriate them into our own research. However, researchers attempt to sensitize themselves to how their knowledge artifacts are interpreted and assessed by other researchers in the scholarly discourse (e.g. what reviewers express and how their work is cited). This is a type of feedback, both with respect to the way knowledge artifacts are appropriated and how they are framed in language by others. Academic ideals, especially in DR, promote communication to different audiences (e.g. [6]). We emphasize here that the way others speak of our artifacts (both in the practical and the academic realm) is valuable for improvement of knowledge artifacts.

4.4   The Meaning of a Lifecycle of Artifacts

Krippendorff 's emphasis on the lifecycle perspective suggests that designers should focus on the "before" the project, the "procurement" process of aligning actants in a design project and how the object of a design becomes this specific design object. This view has been discussed in the DR discourse. The socio-material notion of emergence resonates well with the idea of *mutability* of artifacts ([7], [12]). Although artifact mutability has been elaborated ([10]; [7]), it is still peripheral in the DR discourse. The idea of mutability, however, is clearly a basis for Gill & Hevner's [12] utility-fitness model, which proposes that we focus on (i) the ability of an artifact to prove useful in a specific situation, and (ii) that the artifact proves useful over time in various situations in its socio-material context, (iii) in competition with other artifacts that address the same class of problems. Gill & Hevner's model thus introduces a perspective on the value of artifacts that is similar to Krippendorff's [16] emphasis on understanding the meaning of artifacts from a lifecycle perspective as well as an ecological perspective (next section).

The lifecycle perspective may also prove useful for the design of 'knowledge artifacts'. If the ultimate goal of DR is to make a difference, it is imperative to consider artifacts from a lifecycle perspective. This can be done both with respect to the practical realm and the academic realm.

Figure 2 illustrates our view on the emergent contributions that DR practices can make into the two realms. In the practical realm, artifacts 'advance' in steps, such as formative design workshops with prototypes, appropriation into local practices and subsequent evaluation of the results, dissemination to general practice, and sometimes 'success' in general practice. In those cases, artifacts become an integrated part of the ecology of artifacts (e.g. the relational database model and its implementations in database management technologies). In the academic realm, ideas are initially discussed within the design practice or in smaller workshops in institutions or networks. After that, results are exposed through workshops and conferences, followed by attempts to publish in journals. Finally, the artifacts may be adopted, cited, and part of the cumulative research within the academic realm.

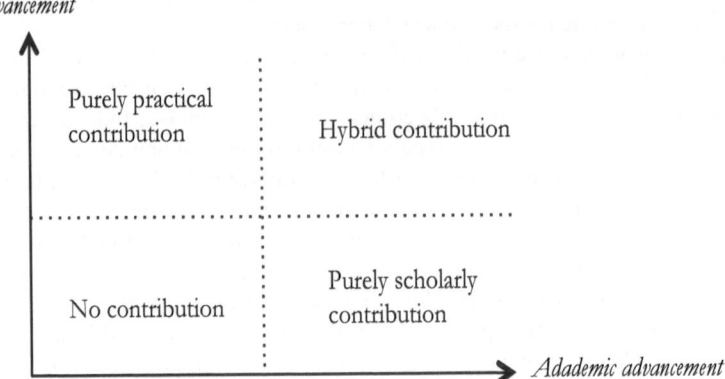

Fig. 2. Artifact advancement in the two realms of DR

In practice, we attempt to build IT artifacts that are mutable to fit into the emerging social world. In academia, we attempt to generalize artifacts beyond limited contexts and specific technologies. The lifecycle perspective is also highly political: A designer (design researcher) needs to plan ahead and manage the needs of multiple stakeholders to promote continued resources for design and future success of an artifact.

At some point, advancements in both realms may become obsolete or fade away due to a changed world or new artifacts that outcompete the old ones.

The establishment of IVI is the result of a shared interest among stakeholders to develop artifacts that are valuable in a long-term perspective. Various versions of the IT-CMF are currently appropriated (to different degrees) in companies in the IVI community. Experiences from cases of situated appropriation feed re-design of the framework on the generic level. Revised versions of IT-CMF may be adopted by the local practices. The idea is that the DR practice supports improvements – thus the survival – of the IT-CMF over time.

The lifecycle of artifacts in the two realms may be out of phase. In the IVI context, the main progress has taken place in the practical realm, rather than in the academic realm. There is not necessarily a correlation between success in the two realms. However, a fundamental idea in design research appears to be that the interplay between practice and academia promotes the quality of artifacts. Following this idea, artifacts that are reviewed in accordance with ideals from both realms should be more likely to be valuable in a long-term perspective.

It is not unlikely that a heavily used artifact in the practical realm will be subject to more scholarly attention. Conversely, artifacts that are successful in academia, such as balanced scorecards [27], may lead to practical design solutions.

4.5   The Meaning of an Ecology of Artifacts

Krippendorff's [16] perspective on ecology, influenced by Bateson [30], proposes that designers need to recognize the meaning of an ecology of artifacts, stating that

"Designers who can handle the ecological meaning of their proposals have a better chance of keeping their designs alive." People attach meaning to artifacts in relation to other artifacts. This relationship can span a number of dimensions e.g. cooperation, competition, interdependence, reproduction and retirement of artifacts in specific contexts. An example from a technical perspective is that artifacts depend on infrastructure. There are other relations in an ecology of artifacts, such as competing artifacts, or artifacts that 'thrive' through the existence of other artifacts [12]. From the perspective of technical stakeholders, the ecology looks different. IT strategists / architects would try to see how a specific IT artifact 'fits in' and contributes to an existing IT infrastructure. When it comes to models and methods, those would be assessed against the current methods and models in use in a particular organization.

In the academic realm, our artifacts are similarly connected to an ecology of knowledge artifacts. We are expected to draw from the knowledge base e.g. [6] and strive for a cumulative tradition [7]. When designing a new artifact (i.e. producing knowledge) designers/researchers need to build upon existing artifacts and clearly relate their new artifacts to the knowledge base. Further, for design researchers, there is a need to build artifacts targeting the practical realm in order to meet the ideals of relevance and utility.

The IT-CMF is comprised of different but inter-dependant critical capabilities that grow and develop in relation to each to each other. It is a system of artifacts in its own. However, for its stakeholders, it will also be made sense of in relation to their existing base of artifacts (and other available governance-related concepts). For instance, several companies in the IVI community are using parts of the IT-CMF, adapted to fit in with other governance frameworks such as ITIL. The second phase in the IVI design process provides a structure to reflect about the 'ecology' and its implications for the continued design of the IT-CMF. For design research practice, this implies a need to identify activities to support the evolution of design artifacts over time (lifecycle perspective) to make them part of the 'ecology' of artifacts.

The qualities of an artifact alone cannot explain its survival in a competitive world. Organizational development and decision-making is a political process. Thus, any artifact that is not supported actively by stakeholders become a "prey" to other artifacts – "predators" that are more extensively promoted, e.g. for commercial reasons. When it comes to academic promotion of ideas, publications in high impact journals increase the readership as well as the likelihood of citations. Furthermore, researchers may engage in various activities to expose their ideas to others in academia. Commercial organizations have strong incentives to promote their products. An implication for a DR practice like IVI is that they also need to reflect about the promotion of their artifacts, either through commercial strategies or through other mechanisms. Consequently, any DR practice aiming for innovation needs to actively monitor the appropriate 'ecology' of artifacts and promote their own artifacts within this ecology.

5   Concluding Discussion

The product semantic perspective provides a lens to make sense of design research practice, as illustrated by the IT-CMF case. The development of the IT-CMF illustrates a situation where both practical contributions and theoretical contributions are artifacts. Although stakeholders from industry and academia may interpret the idea of 'use', 'language', 'lifecycle' and 'ecology' differently, nevertheless the community is able to obtain a second order understanding of stakeholder views within the two realms, and promote the success of artifacts in both realms.

We have addressed a number of issues faced in design research practice, issues not previously in focus in the DR discourse. The outcome of DR practice should be valuable for other practices that are governed by their own set of values and history (knowledge base). In contrast to previous research we do not presume that *any specific values* – such as rigor and relevance – are in focus. We conclude that an important activity in a DR practice is to continually investigate the ideals that need be met in *both* realms, and also to try to affect those ideals. We recognize the emergent characteristics of the realms, and the reciprocal shaping of values between any practice and its environment. Even though some values may be rather stable over time (such as relevance and rigor in IS research), they are indeed dynamic and context-specific. A conclusion from this is that continuous interpretation and active participation in the discourse on ideals are important activities in DR practice. The way that we conduct research and succeed in publishing reinforces and/or weakens ideals in the research community.

The idea of emergent and reciprocally shaped ideals may prove useful in further conceptualizing DR evaluation. Evaluation takes place formatively to improve design, but also as a means to demonstrate artifact qualities to stakeholders. As stated by Krippendorff [16]: "No artifact can be realized within a culture without being meaningful to those who can move it through its various definitions". Evaluation needs to be understood from the political perspective as well as the formative perspective. Exposure of an artifact, whether in the practical realm or in the academic realm, is multi-functional. As a design researcher, academic publication as well as appropriation of artifacts in practice, needs to be conceived of as interwoven yet analytically distinguishable activities. The very reason to operate as design researchers is based on the assumption that the quality of the emerging compound of artifacts is increased through the interplay between evaluation in the academic realm and evaluation in the practical realm. We conceive of the exposure of an artifact into *either* realm as a form of 'naturalistic evaluation'. In addition to this, DR practices may conduct artificial evaluation 'in-house', e.g. through qualified discourse within the DR team and simulations. This leads us to a more elaborate concept of evaluation in design research, which occurs in many forms: (1) artificial evaluation; through evaluation measures taking place within the DR practice, (2) naturalistic evaluation; through appropriation of ideas in local practices, and through feedback from those practices to the DR practice, and (3) scholarly evaluation; through the discourse that takes place within the academic realm through peer-review and other forms of interaction between researchers.

The proposed product semantics perspective on DR practice harmonizes with 'the practice turn' in organizational research. By addressing DR as design, we recognize the politics and value-ladenness of design research. As stated by Gherardi [18, p. 124]: "[..] practice as epistemology articulates knowledge in and about organizing as practical accomplishment, rather than as a transcendental account of a decontextualized reality done by a genderless and disembodied researcher."

Acknowledgements. This work has been partially funded by the Swedish Research School of Management and Information Technology (MIT).

References

1. Hevner, A.R.: A three-cycle view of design science research. Scandinavian Journal of Information Systems 19(2), 87–92 (2007)
2. Iivari, J.: A paradigmatic analysis of information systems as a design science. Scandinavian Journal of Information Systems 19(2), 39–64 (2007)
3. March, S.T., Smith, G.F.: Design and natural-science research on information technology. Decision Support Systems 15(4), 251–266 (1995)
4. Purao, S., Baldwin, C.Y., Hevner, A., Story, V.C., Pries-Heje, J., Smith, B., Zhu, Y.: The Sciences of Design: Observations on an Emerging Field. Working paper. Harvard Business School (2008)
5. Baskerville, R., Lyytinen, K., Sambamurthy, V., Straub, D.: A response to the design-oriented information systems research memorandum. European Journal of Information Systems 20, 11–15 (2011a)
6. Hevner, A.R., March, S.T., Park, J., Ram, S.: Design Science in Information Systems Research. MIS Quarterly 1(28), 75–105 (2004)
7. Gregor, S., Jones, D.: The Anatomy of a Design Theory. Journal of the Association for Information Systems 8(5), 312–335 (2007)
8. Kuechler, B., Vaishnavi, V.: On theory development in design science research: anatomy of a research project. European Journal of Information Systems 17(5), 489–504 (2008)
9. Sein, M.K., Henfridsson, O., Purao, S., Rossi, M., Lindgren, R.: Action Design Research. MIS Quarterly 35(1), 37–56 (2011)
10. Baskerville, R., Kaul, M., Storey, V.: Unpacking the Duality of Design Science. In: ICIS 2011 Proceedings. Paper 10 (2011b)
11. Orlikowski, W., Iacono, C.: Research commentary: desperately seeking the "IT" in IT research-A call to theorizing the IT artifact. Information Systems Research 12(2), 121–134 (2001)
12. Gill, T.G., Hevner, A.R.: A Fitness-Utility Model for Design Science Research. In: Jain, H., Sinha, A.P., Vitharana, P. (eds.) DESRIST 2011. LNCS, vol. 6629, pp. 237–252. Springer, Heidelberg (2011)
13. Winograd, T., Flores, F.: Understanding Computers and Cognition: A New Foundation for Design. Ablex, Norwood (1986)
14. Ehn, P.: The Art and Science of Designing Computer Artefacts. Scandinavian Journal of Information Systems 1(1), Art. 3 (1989)
15. Cross, N.: Designerly ways of knowing: Design discipline versus de sign science. Design Issues 17(3), 49–55 (2001)
16. Krippendorff, K.: The Semantic Turn: A New Foundation for Design. CRC Press (2006)
17. Sjöström, J.: Designing Information System – A pragmatic account. Doctoral Dissertation, Uppsala University, Sweden (2010) ISBN 978-91-506-2149-5
18. Gherardi, S.: Introduction: The Critical Power of the 'Practice Lens'. Management Learning 40(2), 115–128 (2009)

19. Schatski, T.R.: Introduction: Practice theory. In: Schatzki, T.R., Knorr, C.K., von Savigny, E. (eds.) The Practice Turn in Contemporary Theory. Routledge, London (2001)
20. Giddens, A.: The Constitution of Society: Outline of the Theory of Structuration. Polity, Cambridge (1984)
21. Orlikowski, W.: The duality of technology: Rethinking the concept of technology in organizations. Organization Science 3(3), 398–427 (1992)
22. Goldkuhl, G.: Design theories in information systems-a need for multi- grounding. Journal of Information Technology Theory and Application 6(2), 59–72 (2004)
23. DeSanctis, G.: The Social Life of Information Systems Research - A Response to Benbasat and Zmud's Call for Returning to the IT Artifact. Journal of the Association for Information Systems 4(7), 360–376 (2003)
24. Dewey, J.: Logic: The theory of inquiry. Henry Holt and Company, New York (1938)
25. Venable, J.: A framework for Design Science research activities. In: Khosrow-Pour, M. (ed.) 2006 Information Resources Management Association International Conference, May 21, pp. 184–187. Idea Group Publishing, Washington, DC (2006)
26. Gregor, S., Hevner, A.: Positioning and Presenting Design Science Research for Maximum Impact. Paper Currently Under Journal Review (in press)
27. Kaplan, R.S., Norton, D.P.: The Balanced Scorecard: measures that drive performance. Harvard Business Review, 71–80 (January- February 1992)
28. Helfert, M., Costello, G., Donnellan, B.: The Case for Design Science Utility -Evaluation of Design Science Artefacts within the IT Capability Maturity Framework. In: Artifact Design and Workplace Intervention (ADWI) Workshop, Barcelona, June 10 (2012)
29. Donnellan, B., Helfert, M.: The IT-CMF: A Practical Application of Design Science. In: Winter, R., Zhao, J.L., Aier, S. (eds.) DESRIST 2010. LNCS, vol. 6105, pp. 550–553. Springer, Heidelberg (2010)
30. Bateson, G.: Steps to an Ecology of Mind: Collected Essays in Anthropology, Psychiatry, Evolution, and Epistemology. University of Chicago Press (1972) ISBN 0-226-03905-6
31. Orlikowski, W.: Using technology and constituting structures: a practice lens for studying technology in organizations. Organization Science 11(4), 404–428 (2000)
32. Ågerfalk, P.J.: Investigating Actability Dimensions: A language/action perspective on criteria for information systems evaluation. Interacting with Computers 16(5), 957–988 (2004)
33. Ehn, P.: Review of The Semantic Turn: A New Foundation for Design. Artifact 1(1), 59–63 (2007)
34. Polanyi, M.: The Tacit Dimension. Doubleday & Co. Inc., New York (1966)
35. Walsham, G.: The emergence of interpretivism in IS research. Information Systems Research 6(4), 376–394 (1995)
36. Klein, H.K., Myers, M.D.: A set of principles for conducting and evaluating interpretive field studies in information systems. MIS Quarterly 23(1), 67–93 (1999)
37. De Sanctis, G., Poole, M.S.: Capturing the complexity in advanced technology use: adaptive structuration theory. Organization Science 5(2), 121–147 (1994)
38. Trigg, R., Bødker, S.: From implementation to design: Tailoring and the emergence of systematization. In: Proceedings CSCW 1994, Chapel Hill, NC (1994)

Track II

Recent Developments
in Inductive Research Methods

Action Design Ethnographic Research (ADER): Vested Interest Networks and ICT Networks in Service Delivery of Land Records in Bangladesh

M. Shahanoor Alam[1], Laurence Brooks[1,*], and N.I. Khan[2]

[1] Department of Information Systems and Computing, Brunel University,
London, UB8 3PH, UK
[2] National Project Director, Access to Information (A2I), Office of the Prime Minister,
Tejgaon, Dhaka, & Secretary, Ministry of ICT, Bangladesh
{Muhammad.Alam,Laurence.Brooks}@brunel.ac.uk

Abstract. Identifying rigorous and relevant research methods has for a long time been a challenge in IS research. This is amplified in developing countries, where understanding the context is key. This paper presents an Action Design Research based approach, incorporating ethnography, which aims to provide a more authentic and relevant analysis. The Action Design Ethnographic Research (ADER) method is illustrated through the case of ICTs and land records management in Bangladesh. The findings show that where ICTs have been introduced so far, they do not clearly relate to the specific organizational context and service delivery processes. Furthermore, they fail to recognize the role of what is termed here 'vested interest networks', which sit outside the formal processes, but are key to their effective functioning. This paper suggests ADER has the potential to enable the development of more contextually contingent, authentic and hence useful ICTs, especially in the developing countries context.

Keywords: Action Research, Design Research, Action Design Research, Action Design Ethnographic Research, land records management, Bangladesh.

1 Introduction

Studying ICTs in developing countries, a complex sub-field of IS discipline, requires rigorous research methods because usual quantitative analyses and descriptive methods fail to capture sufficient insights and therefore to solve current problems [1-3]. Empirical and interventional methods notably Action Research (AR), Design Research (DR) and Action Design Research (ADR) have the potential to ensure rigorous research through unfolding insights and solving immediate problems. Amongst these, ADR is the youngest and most promising method, developed within the IS discipline in order to achieve rigor and relevance. ADR aims to solve immediate problems through concurrent and authentic evaluation. Thus, ADR unfolds

---

* Corresponding author.

A. Bhattacherjee and B. Fitzgerald (Eds.): Future of ICT Research, IFIP AICT 389, pp. 51–67, 2012.

significant features as a rigorous research method for studying ICTs in developing countries. However, it has been developed in the context of developed countries; consequently ADR says little about how to reach insights in the study of ICTs in the context of developing countries. Thus, studying ICTs in complex contexts of developing countries requires an additional lens alongside ADR to uncover the subtle contexts and to conduct objective and concurrent evaluation. Therefore, the ethnographic perspective, a basket of research tools looks to have potential value in IS research for eliciting insights and conducting objective evaluations [4, 5]. Consistent with these, this paper intends to apply ADR in the context of developing countries along with ethnographic perspectives that can be termed as Action Design Ethnographic Research (ADER), an extended variant of ADR.

The diverse interests and multi-disciplinary nature of Information Systems (IS) research has generated a longstanding need for rigorous research methods to study organization and human actors who shape ICTs [6]. To this end, attempts have been made by IS professionals and practitioners [7, 8]. Recently, ADR has brought DR and AR under one umbrella through framing DR [7] with the essence of AR [8] to ensure rigor and relevance and to avoid overlapping [9]. Uniquely, ADR does not separate design and evaluation sequentially like the 'stage-gate sequential model' [9].

However, implementation of ICTs has been shaped by formal and informal as well as hidden subtle contexts in developing countries [1, 3]. The ethnographic perspective is reputed to be able to apply its basket of tools and techniques to elicit insights into contexts under study. This pioneer study applies ADR in a complex context i.e., service delivery of land records in Bangladesh where informal and hidden practices strongly prevail; we incorporate ethnographic perspectives into the ADR framework. This does not require any extra steps, but helps to uncover hidden contexts and contribute to the ADR process. Therefore, this paper presents ADER as an extended variant of ADR.

Due to over population, land is an extremely scarce resource in Bangladesh. It has a total of 14.4 million hectares of land for its 160 million people; 60% of the total labour force is deployed in agriculture, which contributes 55% of the total GDP [10]. Land records are inevitably needed for legal, financial and welfare services, development planning, transfer of land ownership, determination of ownership and size of land parcels and resolution of land litigations. Thus, land records are a basic service delivery.

Bangladesh gained independence in 1971, following both British India rule (1757-1947) and Pakistan rule (1947-1971). Its land records system was originally developed by the Colonial government in the 1920s, revised in the 1950s (under the Pakistan administration) and finally another version has been produced since the 1970s. Therefore, a land parcel has three versions of land records and legally all these are functioning. It makes the land records system archaic dilapidated and complex. Furthermore, service delivery of land records follows a rigid bureaucratic process. All parties involved have developed rampant corruption and rent seeking practices in this type of service delivery in Bangladesh, termed as 'vested interests' [11]. Consequently this service has been ranked top for corruption and become a major source of litigation and public suffering. To address these problems, the incumbent government has launched the project 'Access to Information' (A2I). A2I aims to develop ICT networks to bring this service delivery to the citizens' doorstep. It has established a total 4501 telecentres, known as Union Information Service Centres (UISC) in the rural areas and a web portal and an e-service centre in each district throughout the country, from November 2010. Since its inception, A2I has been facing problems with implementing ICT networks in this service area. Thus, since December 2011, the research team, collaborating with A2I, has been working to address the problems in implementing ICT networks in land records management, using ADER.

2   Methodology

The ADER team comprises three members combining IS professionals and practitioners. The first author played a dual role: formerly an employee in this service delivery and currently a doctoral student. The second author/academic researcher coordinates the practitioners and professionals. The third author is a practitioner involved in A2I management and served in land records related services for a total of ten years. Initially, the team chose ADR to address the problems in implementing ICT networks in this service delivery process, instead of AR or DR. Since the team has the opportunity to work with the A2I service delivery provider and telecentres, there is the opportunity to build and redesign this service delivery processing ADER. Further, it provides concurrent and objective evaluation of both the initially designed and ADER designed ICTs networks.

ADR outlines two streams of building, intervention and evaluation. One is ICT dominant and the other is organisation dominant [9]. The study has chosen an organisation dominant stream of ADR because in this service delivery process the role of ICT is minimal compared with the role of the organization as an ensemble artefact. While conducting ADR, the study faced difficulties with identifying the reasons for failure in implementing ICT networks using only the usual questionnaire survey, observation and interviews; instead it adopted an ethnographic perspective to investigate the underlying causes. Ethnographic perspectives rely on a number tools and techniques whereby the insider and outsider view are prominent. The ADER team applies an insider (native) point-of-view from the perspectives of service delivery staff and citizens through participating in the real contexts via participant observation, role playing, building rapport, applying storytelling and life history techniques. It applies an outsider view (researcher) to build rationalistic achievable processes and networks based on the practices, contexts and capacities from all the stages of ADR. The heterogeneity of the ADER team as native and non-native professionals and practitioners has given the opportunity to employ ethnographic perspectives in the ADR process.

ADR's focus is on situated learning. Therefore, this study focuses on a project in a district of Bangladesh called Shopnapur (not its real name) and its sub-district Rooppur (not its real name). The sample includes the Deputy Commissioner's Office, the e-Service Centre, the District Records Room (DRR) located in the district headquarters and the five UISCs of the sub-district. Since both ADR and ethnographic perspectives require long term commitment and involvement, the study involved long term involvement with the service providers, service delivery staff, citizens and many other actors in the ICT networks and vested interest networks. Consequently, a wide range of methods, techniques and tools have been used for data collection; these include observation, participant observation, ethnographic interviews, document analysis and focus group discussions. Data is interpreted is via thematic analysis within an interpretive perspective using an Actor Network Theory (ANT) theoretical lens.

3   Literature

IS studies in developing countries (DCs) focus on development, implementation and use of ICT artefacts and tracing the roots of the obstacle behaviour and processes of implementing ICTs [1, 6, 12]. Since ICTs alone do not change the existing organizational practices, network and settings there is a need for studies to examine ICTs in organisational contexts [5]. Users do not accept ICTs as it is designed, they reshape it through practices and contexts. Thus, understanding the implementation of ICTs in service delivery is challenging for its complex interrelationships with socio-economic contexts. Moreover, implementation of ICTs in service delivery of land records is difficult because of the existence of various interests [13]. It is influenced by social, cultural and bureaucratic practices and ICT fails if its design ignores them [14]. Similarly, Sahay and Avgerou [15] identified the domination of existing networks as a bar to implementing ICTs in DCs. Thus, implementation of ICTs in service delivery of land records is not merely a technical issue but also rests on organizational contexts, actors and networks.

ICTs can be used to improve service delivery [16], but it involves many phases, processes, actors, roles and practices. As a potential theoretical framework to support this, ANT is a powerful lens that focuses on technology and actors' complex relationships through examining networks between people, machines and non-corporeal artefacts collectively [17]. Further, it seeks intertwined relationships between human actors, agency and ICTs for better understanding the embedded rules, resources, behaviours and human actors [18].

ANT explains the world as the sum of networks which include humans, things, ideas, and concepts as 'actors' in the networks [19, 20]. It provides a substantial realistic framework to reveal organizational learning in broadly four steps – problematisation, interessement, enrolment and mobilisation all achieved through translation. Problematisation develops ideas or artefacts to address a specific problem by focal actor(s) and makes it indispensable to the other actors through rhetorical means in terms of resources and capacities. This activity is called an obligatory passage point (OPP) [21]. Afterwards, the actors bargain with their interests (interessement), and make alliances through these interests and via concessions (enrolment). Actor-networks are the consequence of an alignment of diverse interests and the basis of enrolment of different actors into the network. Finally, actors become spokespersons in the networks and mobilise them [22].

This paper employs ANT as an analytical tool for understanding the actors and contexts relating to the ICT network with a view to guiding ADER (rather than contributing to the theory).

4   Action Design Research

Organizational contexts inscribe development and use of IT artefacts that bring intended and unintended consequences [5, 9]. A complementarity between AR and DR is significant to design artefacts and redesign it through on-going use and evaluation. It helps to guide initial design and capture ensemble artefacts that emerge through use and redesign [9]. Consistent with these, ADR has been developed as a research method in which AR has a complimentary role in the DR process.

ADR aims to study ensemble artefacts in organisational contexts to "generate prescriptive design knowledge through building and evaluating ensemble IT artefacts in organizational settings" [9]. An ensemble IT artefact includes material and organizational features that are socially recognized as bundles of hardware and/or software [23]. Thus, designing an ensemble artefact requires interactions between technological and organizational dimensions [24] while organizational contexts, structures and networks play significant roles. Consequently, ensemble IT artefacts emerge from design, use and on-going refinement.

ADR is guided by theoretical precursors including the researcher's intent, the influence of users, as well as the context of on-going use [9]. ADR comprises four stages: 1) problem formulation, 2) building intervention and evaluation, 3) reflection and learning and 4) formalization of learning. These steps are guided by seven principles, shown in fig. 1:

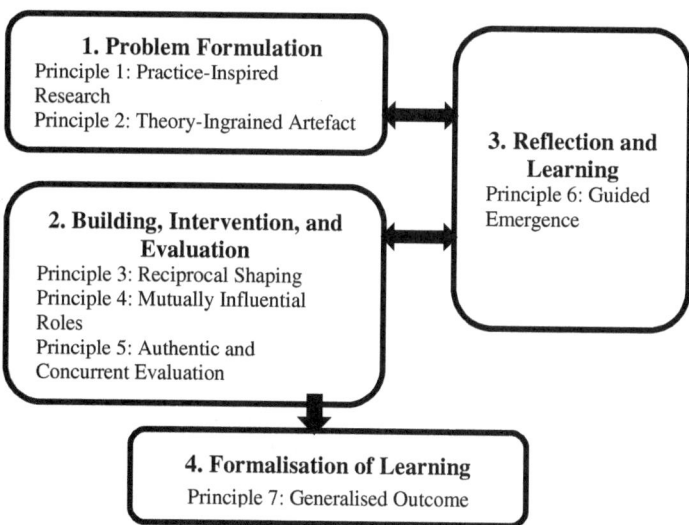

Fig. 1. Action Design Research (adopted from Sein et al., 2011)

4.1   Problem Formulation

ADR formulates problems in organizational contexts drawing from empirical cases or anticipated by researchers from practitioners, end-users, existing technologies and/or previous research [9]. It is shaped by research opportunities based on existing theories and technologies; involvement and commitment; research questions, and setting up roles and responsibilities. [9]. Thus, this stage follows two principles: practice-inspired research for contextualizing problems and solving a class problem; and theory-ingrained research focusing on ensemble artefacts that are informed by theories [9].

4.2   Building, Intervention and Evaluation (BIE)

This stage iteratively interweaves three core activities i.e., building IT artefacts; intervening organizational settings and evaluating it concurrently and objectively [9]. BIE has two distinct streams, IT dominant and organization dominant. Technological innovation requires IT dominant BIE where initially the role of practitioner is limited. On the other hand, organization dominant BIE is effective where the role of artefact is minimal and innovation relies on organizational intervention where practitioner and users play a potential role [9]. This stage includes three principles: reciprocal shaping between artefact and organizational contexts; mutual learning between researcher and practitioners and applying on-going authentic and concurrent evaluation [9].

4.3   Reflection and Learning

Reflection and learning refers to formulated problems, theoretical premises and emerged solution that contribute towards research process and knowledge [9]. It applies 'guided emergence' a principle containing two contrasting views 'guided' and 'emergence'. The former implies an external perspective i.e., guided intervention. The latter displays a sense of organic evolution which can be seen as an insider's perspective [9]. Both the perspectives help to reshape the designed artefact through on-going use in organizational context that derives from authentic and concurrent evaluation [25].

4.4   Formalization of Learning

This stage aims to formalize learning through generalizing the 'situated learning' [26]. The situated nature of ADR outcomes includes organizational change and implementation of an artefact. Thus, the researcher outlines accomplishments and describes organizational outcomes to formalize learning. It suggests three levels of outcomes: the problem instance; generalization from solution instances and derivation of design principles.

4.5   ADER – A Need for an Ethnographic Perspective in ADR

Ethnography refers to a sub-field of anthropology, a methodology, research perspectives that study human behaviour from social and cultural contexts. It is one of the most in-depth research methods and has contributed to the design and implementation of technology, informed by social and organizational contexts [27].

The ethnographic perspective employs a number tools i.e., living in the research field, inductive and participant observation, open ended interviews, emic (insider/native) and etic (outsider) views etc. Further, it applies inter-subjective ways of knowing through the 'reflexivity of actor' – the inquiring of researcher self and 'reflexivity of accounts' – ways of knowing the sense of clients or users which is beyond the self [28]. Moreover, it interprets the meaning of contexts rather than just description. Thus, ethnographic perspectives add potential value in empirical and interventional studies aimed at research problems, intervening process, evaluating objectively and generating knowledge.

Ethnographic perspectives play a pivotal role in the process of formulating problems through eliciting insights into the contexts, applying its tools and techniques. Further, insider and outsider perspectives help to develop a broader understanding of organizational intervention and building models and processes. Moreover, it helps reduce bias and tainted accounts through extensive observation and thick description for objective evaluation [29, 30]. Both ethnographic perspectives and thick description are interrelated, with thick description emerging from ethnographic techniques. Consequently, ethnographic perspectives can be seen as complementary to the ADR process. This study seeks to build a framework which incorporates ethnographic perspectives into ADR (see fig. 2).

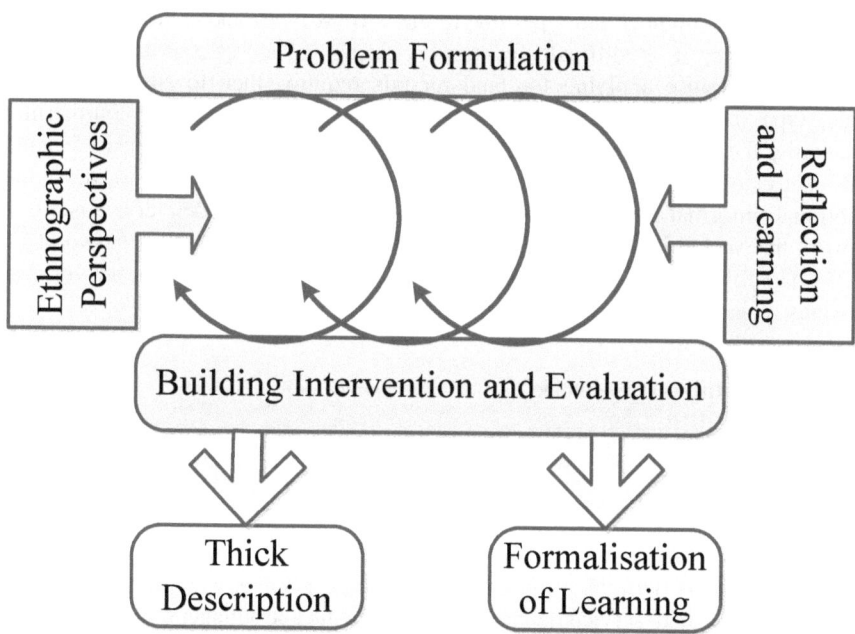

Fig. 2. Action Design Ethnographic Research (ADER) (adapted from Sein et al., 2011)

The proposed Action Design Ethnographic Research (ADER) framework aims to contribute to ADR in the following ways:

1. Applying an ethnographic perspective bridge between stages. It reflects an iterative relationship from problem formulation to formalization of learning.
2. It helps to ensure objective evaluation and enhance authenticity through applying both insiders' and outsiders' perspectives.
3. It applies a number of perspectives, tools and techniques from ethnography known as thick description. Thus the ADER framework shows its potential to contribute to practice and knowledge

5   Initial Design of ICT Networks in Organizational Contexts

In Bangladesh, land records denote Records of Right (RoR) that contain land information - name of owner(s), parcel size, type, taxes and geographic boundary. RoR is recorded through a land cadastral[1] survey. Usually land plots owned by a family are grouped into a RoR and a few hundred RoRs in a geographic area form a block. Service delivery of land records refer to issuing certified copies of RoR from the District Record Room (DRR) of the Deputy Commissioner's office.

The family based aggregated RoR system is complicated. For instance, a RoR contains names of land owners, ratios of ownership and land plots. Further, there are three types of RoRs that have been developed during three regimes (Colonial, Pakistan and Bangladesh). Consequently, land owners do not know accurately their RoR and Plot ID number and types due to the various types and aggregated nature of RoR. Therefore, it is difficult for most citizens to access service delivery by themselves, because applying for land records requires then to specify the block name, type of land record, RoR ID number and owner's name(s). Furthermore, calculating fee-stamps and folios is complicated and citizens cannot easily calculate this. Thus, over time, various networks have been developed: local, hidden, traditional, informal and organizational to mediate this service delivery. Since every network has vested interests, this paper treated them as vested interest networks (see fig. 3). The following section discusses the nature of the vested interest networks and how they reshaped the initial ICT network design.

5.1   Vested Interest Networks

A number of categories of actors and networks belong to the vested interest networks in this service delivery:

5.1.1 Local Networks
These include *Deed-writers, Muhuris and Mobile Middlemen* who are visible in rural localities and mediate service delivery for their clients and villagers. Deed-writers are practitioners writing land registration deeds. A land record is inevitably needed for the land registration deed, so they are involved in mediating this service delivery of their

---

[1] An official register containing information on the value, extent, and ownership of land for the purposes of taxation (Encarta dictionary).

clients and villagers. *'Muhuris'* are assistants to lawyers. Since 90% of the suits/cases relate to land records, *Muhuris* mediate and process land records for their clients and local citizens. Mobile Middleman is a hybrid of *'Muhuris'* and 'Deed-writers'. They mediate this service delivery through mobile phone networks with the DRR staff that receive information from them by mobile phone and submit applications using the Web-portal and process their delivery. This network is preferable for rural citizens, as it avoids complex processes and significant travel.

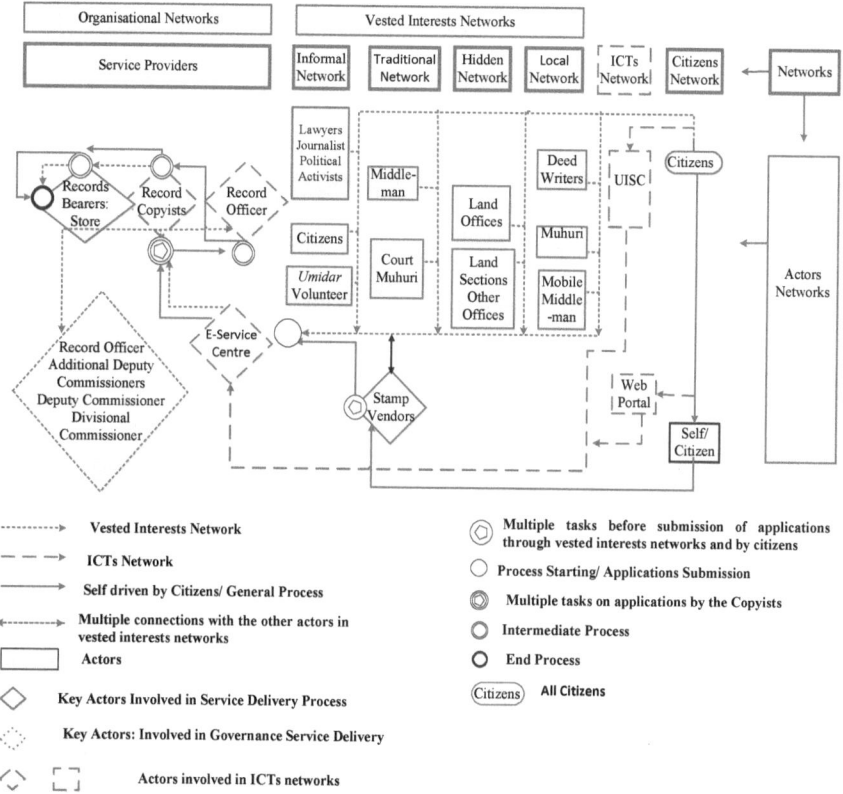

Fig. 3. The initial design of ICT networks and vested interest networks

5.1.2 Hidden Networks

Staff serving in land related section offices and other staff surrounding the DRR maintain hidden networks to mediate this service delivery. They are not visible on the spot. Citizens need land records to receive service delivery e.g., updating land records, collecting payment for land acquired and paying taxes. These networks mediate speedy and secure service delivery for their clients.

5.1.3 Traditional Networks

Stamp-vendors, *Court-muhuris* and middlemen are traditional networks because they do this as a profession. Stamp-vendors are licensed to sell stamps and are required to pay fees for this service delivery. *Court-muhuris*, a sect of *muhuris*, who are licensed lawyers' assistants but work full-time to mediate this service delivery. Middlemen are either connected with political networks or staff networks. Their location is in front of the DRR. They have forms, stamps and folios for filing applications for this service delivery. Citizens who come to DRR for this service go them to complete the application process. If any record is damaged they know how to reproduce it, either legally or fraudulently.

5.1.4 Informal Networks

Lawyers, journalists and political activists are powerful actors in these networks. They use their professional identity to mediate this service delivery. The staff is also loyal to them because they are able to harm the vested interests of the staff. *Umidar*, the unpaid volunteers at DRR, mediate vested interests between the traditional networks and the staff. Therefore, every actor in the vested interested networks has their own vested interests and they are connected with the organizational networks

5.2   Organizational Networks and Vested Interest Networks

5.2.1 DRR Staff Networks: Horizontal Interface

The DRR staff includes Record Bearers, Copyists and Record Keepers. The Bearers sort and carry the land record registers from Store to Copyists. Copyists and Keepers both create certified copies of records. The Record Officer finally attests the processed records. The staff is horizontally connected with the vested interest networks.

Bearers maintain the closest network to records because they sort and carry them. The DRR has 10,000 record registers and they are stored about 300 feet away from the Copyists' Room. Bearers sort and carry daily about 200 registers. Since they have access to all records, they are connected with the vested interest networks which expedite sorting, carrying and supplying information about the availability of records.

The dilapidated condition of the records and the manual copying process creates a need for the Copyists-record network. About 35% of records are damaged, but there is no list of them. Thus, it is at the Copyist's discretion as to whether he will process the certified copy or reject it on the grounds of damaged records. Thus, DRR staff ensures faster delivery through vested interest networks, while applying a high rate of rejection and delays in the case of ICT based applications.

5.2.2 Service Delivery Staff Networks: Vertical Interface

The DRR staff is vertically connected within organizational networks with the Officers involved in managing this service delivery (see fig. 3). Thus, staff distributes the benefits of vested interests to upper level officers, to secure their position. Thus, keeping the existing vested interest networks is a higher priority in the organizational networks than implementing the ICT networks.

5.2.3 Service Delivery Process and Vested Interest Networks

Filing an application for land records requires an application form, stamp-fees and folio-papers, which belong to the vested interest networks. Further, filling in an application form for land records is complicated. Thus, citizens are bound to enter into the vested interest networks. Further, since this service delivery works faster through vested interest networks, possibly within one or two working days, depending on networks and interests, whereas it takes several weeks through the ICT networks. Thus, the citizens already distrust the ICTs networks.

5.3   The Initial Designs of ICT Networks and Underlying Contexts

The A2I aims to bring service delivery of land records to the citizen's doorstep through ICT networks. IT artefacts were designed: three access points UISC, e-Service Centres and Web-portals and connecting them with the DRR to enable citizens' access to this service delivery. UISC is designed to submit online applications to DRR, but the organizational networks mandates that it also needs to submit a printed copy of the online submitted application via the postal service along with fee and folios. Their argument is that every application needs fee-stamps pasting on it and folio-papers. Since there is no option to submit fee-stamps and folio-papers with online applications, UISCs need to a send a printed copy of the online submitted application along with fee-stamps and folio papers. Consequently, it has created twice the tasks taking 15 days for an online application to reach the end of the process and another 15 days for this service to return to citizens (see fig.3). Thus, the ICT networks increases steps and processes. Further, the staff does not find vested interests in ICT networks thus there are a high number of rejections of applications coming from ICT networks.

The e-Service Centre is designed for the submission of online applications by citizens who are living in the district headquarters or coming to the DRR. The vested interest networks and the organizational networks reshaped this as a place for receiving paper-based application from vested interests networks; while the online entry is for the satisfaction of A2I, nothing else. As a result, the e-Service Centre created opportunities for the vested interest networks to prevail.

The Web-portal is designed to submit online applications for land records. Since only 0.35% of the population have Internet access this is unrealistic. However, it is also harnessed by the vested interest network. Since the copyists have good Internet connections and printers, they use it as an opportunity for submitting online applications via the Web-portal on behalf of vested interest networks. Further, it develops Mobile Middleman. Using the web-portal, the staff mediates service delivery of Mobile Middlemen networks.

Though the initial design of ICT networks aimed to enhance citizens' access to this service delivery, it was overtaken by other actors i.e., the vested interest networks and organizational networks. Consequently, the ICT networks have been reshaped.

6   ICT Networks in the ADER Context

6.1   Problem Formulation

ADER brings forth insights into the context in implementing the initial design of ICT networks. During the design of the ICT networks by A2I, organizational contexts were not taken into account. Moreover, it was sequentially separated into building artefacts and implementation. As a result, the role of IT artefacts has been over emphasised while ignoring the contexts, capacities and role of the organisation. For instance, A2I designed three access points - UISC, e-Service Centre and Web-portal without contextualizing their role in local contexts and capacities. As a result, ICTs networks have neither achieved their goal nor addressed the underlying problems in this service delivery.

ADER formulates problems in the organizational contexts i.e., the prevailing vested interests networks; the relationships between vested interests networks and organizational networks and process of service delivery (see 5.1 & 5.2). Further, the existing legal infrastructure does not permit online payments. Moreover, the Internet users rarely require this service but it is essential to rural citizens.

ADER finds that with these contexts the initial IT dominant artefact (i.e., multiple access points in ICT networks) were not inscribed by the organization but appropriated by the vested interest networks. Further, the multiple access points and contexts do not allow for an obligatory passage point (OPP) and intervention. As a result, the ICT networks have been reshaped by the vested interest networks.

Therefore, ADER recognizes that it requires guided intervention to bridge the gap between the ICT networks and the organizational networks to set an OPP. Thus, with the view of guided interventions and setting OPP, ADER sees UISCs as a single access point and only allows online applications; no printed copy to prevent vested interest networks. Consequently, it has developed networks between citizens, UISCs, the DRR and the postal service through setting this OPP (See Fig.4).

To elicit these insights and formulate problems required setting long term interventions, building rapport with DRR staff and relevant actors, getting acquainted with the processes and the interests and seeing these from the local points of view (DRR staff, citizens and other actors).

6.2   Building Intervention and Evaluation (BIE)

Based on the problem formulations, ADER designed an ensemble IT artefact bringing ICTs and organizational contexts as mutually interdependent networks (See Fig.4).

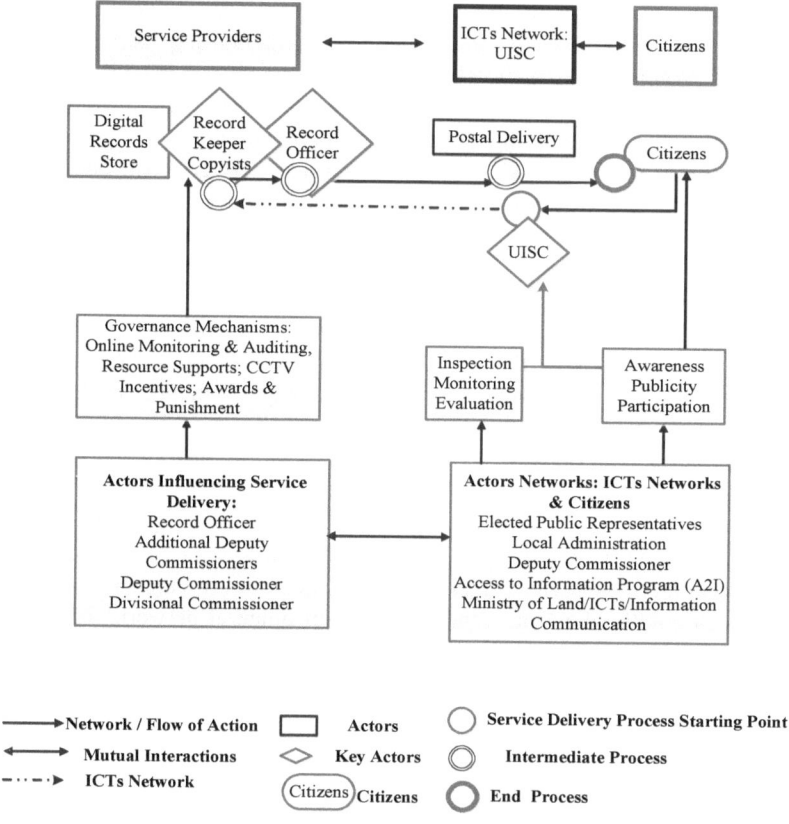

Fig. 4. ADER designed ICTs Networks

To inscribe the ICT networks within the organizational networks, ADER provide guidance for interventions with the existing capacities and technology. The DRR requires fee-stamps, folio-papers for each application and accounts for auditing. BIE seeks organizational capacities and practices, to address them. A guided intervention builds a bilateral network between UISCs and the DRR. Within this network, each UISC deposits fees and folios in advance for about 20 applications to the DRR. Upon receiving online applications from UISCs, the DRR deducts an amount of fees and folios. Further, the ADER team develops a register containing information for auditing fee-stamps including the application number, applicant name, name of UISC, amount of fee-stamp and folios, receiving date, copyist name and delivery date for each application. This makes it easy to track the applications and service delivery information for verification and evaluation.

The ADER designed ICT networks have been implementing in one Sub-district and it redesign is on-going. Evaluating the system after two months shows that a total of 30 applications have been received from five UISCs. Findings revealed that service delivery time has reduced from 20-30 days to 3-4 days at ⅔ the cost of the previous process. Moreover, based on these results and on-going evaluation, this ADER designed ICT networks have been transferred to its neighbouring district.

Building organizational networks with ICT networks provides a common interessement between the actors of the ICT networks, DRR staff, citizens and UISC. Citizens benefitted from receiving the service without entering into any vested interest networks, UISCs benefitted with increased service delivery. The staff does not directly benefit. However, since they do not have options to provide service delivery to vested interest networks, they do serve the vested interests of organizational networks. Thus, three key actors are enrolled in the ICT networks.

Further, to avoid anticipated vested interest networks threats between UISC and the staff, the Postal Service has been enrolled to provide home delivery of this service to the recipients. Consequently, the vested interest networks find no way to access the ICT networks. Further, the mobilization process engages a number of organizational actors to support the ICTs networks through monitoring, coordinating and building citizens awareness (see Fig.4). The Ministry of Land has provided A2I with a 500 million Bangladeshi Taka (about $6.1 million) fund to computerize all existing records. This would further support the success of the ADER designed ICT networks.

The ethnographic perspectives play a potential role as a link between formulated problems and BIE. Applying outsiders' view i.e., the researchers' perspectives, knowledge and skills, they intervene and develop bilateral networks between DRR and UISC to overcome the problem of sending printed copies of the online submitted application, and reduce steps and time for providing this service delivery through ICT networks.

6.3   Critical Reflection and Learning

This case shows how the complex organizational contexts, organizational networks and vested interests networks collectively reshaped the IT artefacts. The initially artefact designs were IT dominant and incompatible with the organizational context, and failed to achieve its goal. Moreover, it has been inscribed by the vested interested networks. This ADER approach has redesigned the artefacts with a guided intervention contextualizing the legal, organizational and social infrastructures.

The insiders' view is used to understand the organic, emerging and on-going use of initial artefacts. It is worth noting that the staff developed mobile-middleman networks using the web-portal. Thus applying insiders' view gives valuable insights and learning about how the initial artefacts have been reshaped by on-going use. These help to design guided intervention.

Using the ADER allowed for redesigning the artefact from the researchers point view i.e., outsiders' view. It has identified various contexts; the IT artefacts' role (less important) and organization's role (more important). In such contexts, ADER provides guided intervention to inscribe the artefact into the organizational contexts. For instance, ADER built bilateral networks between the DRR and UISCs to implement ICT networks in this service. Further, it helped with mobilizing ICT networks through incorporating the organizational actors.

Notably, the staff are low paid thus without appropriate incentives it would be difficult to make the ICT networks sustainable. Akbar (pseudonym), a records bearer confessed, "My salary is insufficient for food and clothes for my four member family. Besides, I need to pay tuition for my two children studying at college". This reflects how he joined the vested interest networks for survival (note that not all staff are in this position and some quite 'well off').

6.4 Formalization of Learning

The ADER enabled learning for both the organization and the researchers. The organization realized that it needs to understand the role of staff, organizational networks and vested interest networks that reshape ICT networks. Further, guided intervention is significant for continuous redesign of the artefacts. Since, ADER develops situated learning; the A2I has replicated them into a neighbouring district of Shopnapur. Further, it disseminated ADER learning to the relevant actors through presentations, workshops and discussions.

Moreover, A2I has outlined ADER learning at its Annual Conference for the Deputy Commissioners' of the country with a view to implementing them countrywide. A2I is expecting to implement the ADER designed ICT networks at the end of 2012. Finally, A2I, the Ministry of Land and the Ministry of Law have been working on amending the legal infrastructures, the obstacles for ICT networks have been identified by ADER.

Furthermore, the study derives learning for the researchers that DR need to build artefacts in organizational contexts. Since typically the DR framework does not include organizational contexts, ADR provides significant opportunity to build artefacts within organizational contexts and redesign organizational intervention. Finally, the study illustrated that incorporating ethnographic perspectives within ADR has the potential to elicit complex underlying contexts of developing countries and aid in redesigning the artefacts.

6.5 Thick Description

It has been said that ethnography is by definition "thick description" (where "thin description" is the activity and "thick description" refers to the meaning behind it, as well as its symbolic importance in society [30]) integral to ADER as reflected in the findings derived from the study. Incorporating an ethnographic perspective give a distinct nature to ADR, bringing together its insiders' and outsiders' views, along with a number of tools. This allows ADER to elicit valuable insights and underlying contexts that make the findings more informative, objective and authentic. Further, thick description seeks to add value to the ADER findings for practitioners and disciplines.

7   Conclusion

Applying ADER in land records service delivery in Bangladesh can show a significant impact through redesigning the on-going ICT project. Since, service delivery is a highly complex field in developing countries, using an ethnographic perspective helps the ADER team to elicit insights to understand the processes, actors and networks. Eliciting the ethnographic perspective is not always easy because it requires spending time in the field and having a high level of analytical skills. This ADER team exploits the advantages through putting practitioners and professional together.

Therefore, ADER can be seen as a potential research method for studying ICTs in developing countries where the usual quantitative and descriptive analyses are not sufficient to reach into the insights of the organizational contexts and contribute to addressing practitioners' problems.

Acknowledgement. The authors express their sincere thanks to three anonymous reviewers for their valuable comments and directions on the first draft of this paper.

References

1. Avgerou, C., Walsham, G. (eds.): Information Technology in Context: Studies from the Perspective of Developing Countries. Ashgate, London (2000)
2. Unwin, T.: Context: The place of information and communication technologies for development. In: Unwin, T. (ed.) ICT4D Information and Communication Technologies for Development, pp. 1–51. Cambridge University Press, Cambridge (2009), http://www.gg.rhul.ac.uk/ict4d/Chapter1.pdf (accessed June 15, 2012)
3. Heeks, R.: Policy Arena: Do Information Communication Technologies (ICTS) Contribute to Development? Journal of International Development 22, 625–640 (2010)
4. Walsham, G.: Interpretive case studies in IS research: nature and method. European Journal of Information Systems 4, 74–81 (1995)
5. Orlikowski, W.J.: The duality of technology: Rethinking the concept of technology in organizations. Organization Science 3, 398–427 (1992)
6. Avgerou, C., Madon, S.: Framing IS studies. London School of Economics and Political Sciences, London (2002)
7. Hevner, R., March, S.T., Park, J., Ram, S.: Design science in information systems research. MIS Quarterly 28(1), 75–105 (2004)
8. Baskerville, R.: Action research for information systems. In: AMCIS 1999 Proceedings, Paper 288 (1999)
9. Sein, M.K., Henfridsson, O., Purao, S., Rossi, M., Lindgren, R.: Action Design Research. MIS Quarterly 35(3), 37–56 (2011)
10. Moore, B.H.: Land Reform: From Failed Expectations to Renewed Opportunity. Land Agenda First 1, 2 (2008), http://www.alrd.org/pdf/enl/Newsletter%201.pdf
11. Imran, A., Gregor, S.: Vested interests obstructing information systems use: Land administration in a least developed country in SIG GlobDev. In: Fourth Annual Workshop, Shanghai, China, December 3, pp. 1–24 (2011)

12. Walsham, G.: Making a World of Difference: IT in a Global Context. John Wiley, Chichester (2001)
13. Sinha, S.: Computerisation of land records. Economic and Political Weekly 38(35), 3739–3740 (2003)
14. Acharya, R.B.: Adopting geo-ICT for land administration: Problems and solutions. Presented at 7th FIG Conference, Spatial Data Serving People: Land Governance and the Environment – Building the Capacity (2009)
15. Sahay, S., Avgerou, C.: Introducing the special issue on information and communication technologies in developing countries. Inf. Soc. 18(2), 73–76 (2002)
16. Thomas, P.: Bhoomi, Gyan Ganga, e-governance and the right to information: ICTs and development in India. Telematics Inf. 26(1), 20–31 (2009)
17. Hassard, J., Law, J., Lee, N.: Themed section: Actor-Network theory and managerialism. Organisational Studies 6, 385–390 (1999)
18. Atkinson, C.J., Brooks, L.S.: StructurANTion: A theoretical framework for integrating human and IS research and development. In: AMCIS 2003 Proceedings. Paper 378, pp. 2895–2902 (2003)
19. Law, J.: Notes on the theory of the Actor-Network: Ordering, strategy, and heterogeneity. Systems Practice 5, 379–393 (1992)
20. Latour, B.: Reassembling the Social: An Introduction to Actor-Network-Theory. Oxford University Press, Oxford (2005)
21. Callon, M.: Some elements of a sociology of translation: Domestication of the scallops and the fishermen of St Brieuc Bay. In: Law, J. (ed.) Power, Action and Belief: A New Sociology of Knowledge?, pp. 196–233. Routledge & Kegan Paul, London (1986)
22. Silva, L.: Epistemological and theoretical challenges for studying power and politics in information systems. Information Systems Journal 17(2), 165–183 (2007)
23. Orlikowski, W.J., Iacono, C.S.: Research Commentary: Desperately Seeking the 'IT' in IT Research–A Call to Theorizing the IT Artifact. Information Systems Research 12(2), 121–134 (2001)
24. Gregor, S., Jones, D.: The anatomy of a design theory. Journal of the Association for Information Systems 8, 312–335 (2007)
25. Garud, R., Jain, S., Tuertscher, P.: Incomplete by design and designing for incompleteness. Organization Studies 29(3), 351–371 (2008)
26. van Aken, J.E.: Management research based on the paradigm of the design sciences: The quest for field-tested and grounded technological rules. Journal of Management Studies 41(2), 219–246 (2004)
27. Myers, M.D.: Investigating information systems with ethnographic research. Communications of the Association for Information Systems 2, 1–20 (1999)
28. Crabtree, M.R., Tolmie, P.: Doing Design Ethnography. Springer, London (2012)
29. Geertz: From the native's point of view: On the nature of anthropological understanding. In: Geertz, C. (ed.) Local Knowledge, pp. 55–70 (1983)
30. Geertz: Thick Description: Toward an Interpretive Theory of Culture. Basic Book Inc., New York (1973)

Grounded Analytic Research: Building Theory from a Body of Research

Bjørn Furuholt and Maung Kyaw Sein

Department of Information Systems
University of Agder, 4604 Kristiansand, Norway
{Bjorn.Furuholt,Maung.K.Sein}@uia.no

Abstract. In this paper, we present Grounded Analytic Research (GAR) as a method to build theory by synthesizing empirical findings from multiple studies that has been conducted by a single researcher. GAR incorporates concepts from grounded theory, analytic research and systematic literature review. The method was applied in a doctoral dissertation work to build the theoretical concept of *Demand Sustainability* of public Internet access in the context of bridging the digital divide. We describe GAR and compare it with existing theory building methods that are similar to it in epistemology and ontology.

Keywords: Theory building, analytical research, grounded theory, digital divide, demand, sustainability, ICT for development.

1   Introduction

The call for theory building in the Information Systems (IS) discipline has been a sustained one. Successive editors-in-chief of *MIS Quarterly*, the prime journal in IS, have stressed the need for developing theories indigenous to the field [1, 2]. In its wake, came encouragements and inducements to develop new and innovative methods for theory building. A concrete example is the expansion of the journal's "Theory and Review" department in 2007. In an impassioned plea for theory development the incumbent editor-in-chief and the department senior editor called for submissions that, among others, were [3:iv]:

- *Comprehensive syntheses (using qualitative, grounded theory, meta-analytic, set-theoretic, or text mining methods) of previously published research with strong theoretical implications, and,*
- *Pure theory papers with strong grounding in prior empirical research and/or practice*

"Highly valued characteristics" of such submissions included [3:v]

- *Theoretical statements enriched by relevant findings from previously published qualitative and quantitative research*
- *Research syntheses that consider relevant qualitative, as well as quantitative, studies*
- *Research syntheses that employ set-theoretic or text mining methods as well as those that employ qualitative or meta-analytic techniques*

A. Bhattacherjee and B. Fitzgerald (Eds.): Future of ICT Research, IFIP AICT 389, pp. 68–78, 2012.

Clearly, the message was to develop theory through synthesizing prior work and building on it. Specific methods and approaches were mentioned. This has helped IS researchers in their quest of theory [4]. Yet, there are instances where no existing method is exactly appropriate to capture the nuances and the context of the data collected in a research endeavour which subsequently affected the process of theory building. The only alternative left is to develop a completely new method either from scratch or by tweaking and integrating existing methods.

Such was the case with the challenge we faced in developing a theory in the context of Information and Communication Technologies for Development (ICT4D) on the sustainability of public internet access points (PIAPs) as a way to bridge the so-called Digital Divide. The research was the doctoral dissertation work of the first author (FA). Our search for an appropriate method resulted in an innovative method which we term Grounded Analytic Research (GAR).

In the rest of the paper, we will first narrate the story that led to GAR through a confessional account of FA's dissertation work. Since the topic of the dissertation is inextricably intertwined with the search, this account also briefly describes the state of the art in the literature of the topic. We then move on to describe how our search led to GAR. Throughout, we use the dissertation as illustration. We end the paper by discussing GAR vis-à-vis existing methods and by reflecting on its implications.

2   The Background Story

Like in many cases, GAR was born out of necessity. FA was working on his dissertation under the supervision of the second author (SA) at a Scandinavian university. [1] The thesis was to be "paper-based": comprised of a series of published articles, tied together in a "kappa" or an extended report (typically 70 to 100 pages). The kappa is not a summary. It presents the core of the intellectual and theoretical contribution to knowledge that determines whether the work deserves a PhD degree. The papers provide the support and the evidence for such theorizing.

Typically, a PhD candidate conducts his/her research under a planned and structured program. The research questions are first articulated in the thesis proposal, then refined as the dissertation work progresses. Data collection and the writing of the individual articles follow a pre-defined plan and route although deviations and detours are not uncommon.

Our case, however, was not typical. FA had been conducting research in the ICT for development (ICT4D) area under the overarching theme of "Bridging the Digital Divide" with a specific focus on "Public Internet Access Points (PIAP)". He was not a doctoral student, nor was he planning to be one. Other than staying within the overarching theme, the ten papers from this body of work had little in common at first glance. After a decade or so of this work, FA was encouraged by colleagues and peers (the co-supervisors among them) to leverage his work into a doctoral degree. After all, such a lengthy body of work ought to have created new knowledge and made enough contribution to the field to be worthy of a PhD.

---

[1] There was also a co-supervisor who contributed valuable insights to the dissertation work but was less involved in the development of GAR.

Suitably enthused, FA entered a doctoral program and dove with much gusto into the process of working towards a PhD. When he got down to the daunting task of writing the "kappa", he ran into a hurdle. He did not have a predefined research question for the kappa because his individual papers had their own research questions He had to essentially come up with his contribution to knowledge in the form of a theory or a theoretical concept to add to the body of knowledge. Over several discussions with his co-supervisors, such a concept emerged. It was *"Demand Sustainability".* [2]

PIAPs have been the traditional mode for bridging the digital divide in developing countries through physical access. A model for their sustainability had remained elusive. The vast majority of the ICT4D literature had focussed on the supply side of internet access while relegating the demand side to appropriate noises in the "Discussion" and "Conclusion" segments of articles. Ironically, the need to look at the demand side had been a major refrain of researchers and practitioners in ICT4D. Opinions such as "the demand is driving the whole thing" or "sustainability could only be demand-driven" were actually heard at conferences and gatherings.

A more basic question was: "What is sustainability?" While several conceptualizations exist in the literature (such as financial social, organizational), none could adequately explain why some form of PIAPs survive while others fade away. It gradually dawned on us that sustaining demand itself could lead to viability of PIAPs. So, above all forms of sustainability, the core concept is Demand Sustainability.

The conceptualization of Demand Sustainability became the core research question for FA's dissertation work. He now needed empirical grounding. He could of course go back to the field and gather fresh data. That would have meant essentially throwing away all the empirical work he had done already. A more reasonable way was to go back to these papers and "mine" them to come up with the required empirical underpinning for the theoretical concept . The problem was that there was no existing method that precisely described how to do it. After searching the research method literature, personal communication with well-known IS scholars, and constant deliberations with SA, a new research method was born. We call it Grounded Analytic Research (GAR)[3].

3   The Search for an Appropriate Method

The search problem could be formulated thus: *find a method to integrate the empirical findings from research conducted by the same researcher (FA) and insights from a number of articles resulting from this research that had their own research approaches and synthesize a theoretical concept called Demand Sustainability where none of the individual papers had sustainability as the central focus.*

The first method we examined was the grounded theory method (GTM), a classical method for theory generation. After studying basic GTM literature [5, 6, 7], literature on

---

[2] The thesis also studied and refined the concept of "Supply Sustainability".

[3] In FA's dissertation, the method was called Analytic Research. On reflection and to avoid confusing it with the existing method called "Analytical Research" we chose to rename it.

use of GTM in IS research [8, 9, 10], and some practically oriented papers [11,12], one central question emerged: *"Is it possible to start the GTM process (coding etc.) from the existing articles, and not from the primary data?"* (see Figure 1).

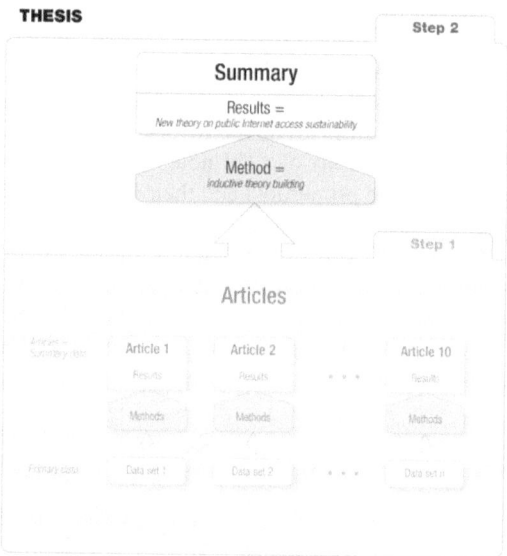

Fig. 1. Thesis structure: The Summary (Kappa) from [18]

The literature provided some cues. Apart from the traditional and explicitly recognised forms of contemporaneous observation and interview, it was unclear what kinds of data are acceptable in GTM [12]. Personal communication with two prominent researchers (Cathy Urquhart and Richard Baskerville), confirmed that GTM is too closely linked to primary data and to certain coding techniques. What we needed was a method to synthesize prior research which in our case comprised of FA's ten articles.

An obvious choice was a "normal" literature review. Several guidelines exist in the literature [e.g. 13]. While these are useful and help in unearthing concepts and ultimately contribute to theory building, and while this method is at first glance appropriate in FA's case, it misses out on one vital aspect: reflection arising not just from the papers, but more importantly, the first-hand and intimate knowledge FA has about the data. Typical literature review papers do not provide any guidelines on how to bring in the primary data that FA had collected but were not part of the findings reported in the published articles. Consequently, an important ingredient of theory building is lost. We needed a method to go beyond simply integrating past findings. We needed an additional process to add the data itself.

The search then led to a closer look at a research strategy known as Analytic Research [14] or Philosophical Research [15]. This methodology defines a purely mental pursuit. The researcher thinks and logically reasons causal relationships. The process is intellectual and the aim is for the flow of logic to be explicit, replicable and testable by others". [15:112]. Analytic research relies on the use of internal logic on the part of the researcher who has the resources required for solving the problem *within* him/herself. No explicit reference to external data sources is necessary: the problem may be solved *logically* or *philosophically*. The emphasis is on cerebration which distinguishes it from the others.

However, GTM was not totally abandoned because of its theory building potential and suggestions that we need to be far more flexible as to what a unit of analysis might be [10:7]. Some of the principles and working methods from GTM were retained. Examples include practical oriented guidelines [10], and the iterative process described as: "The basic idea of the grounded theory approach is to read (and re-read) a textual database (such as a corpus of field notes) and 'discover' or label variables (called categories, concepts and properties) and their interrelationships" [11:2].

The theory building process was also informed by a number of other sources: on getting started and defining the research problem [16], the building blocks of theory development [17], and the process of analytic induction [14]. The overall method for theory building was based on a research methodology framework proposed by Buckley et al. [14] which we describe next (See Figure 2. Our path through the framework is highlighted).

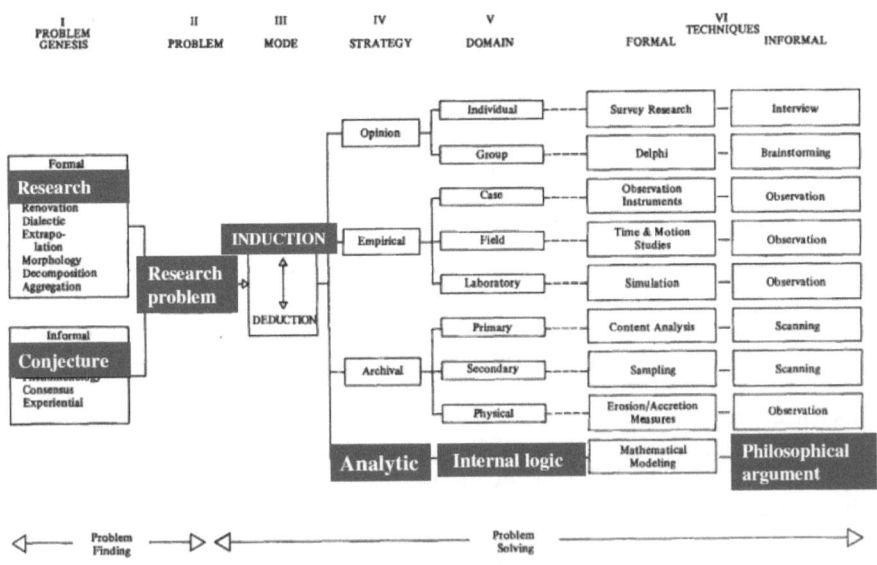

Fig. 2. A Framework for Research Methodology from [14]

4   Placing GAR in a Research Methodology Framework

In our walk through the framework, we illustrate each step by referring to our case. As we have already described the genesis of the problem, we begin with the second step.

4.1   The Research Problem

Problems may be generated formally or informally. The most productive formal approach is reviewing prior research. Our literature review revealed that a broad area of the sustainability issue was not covered This was combined with an informal approach, where the intuitive feeling and experience of FA aroused his interest and curiosity in studying the demand side of sustainability for Internet access in developing countries. Conjecture is frequently used as a useful, informal tool in problem-finding, where the researcher has an intuitive feel regarding a potential problem area, and has a sense that the existing fund of knowledge is insufficient to solve the problem.

In Grounded Theory research, the theory-building process begins as close as possible to the ideal of no theory under consideration. In Analytic Research and general theory building research, however, problem definition up front paves the way for selecting an appropriate research strategy. An initial definition of the research question, in at least broad terms, is considered to be important in building theory from case studies [16]. Analytic induction begins with a rough definition of a research question [5]. A literature review is often preliminary: "on the understanding that it is the generated theory that will determine the relevance of the literature. The literature review is revisited, and extended, once the theory has been generated from data". [10:351]. In our case, the research problem arose from a combination of FA's own experiences and literature reviews conducted by him.

4.2   The Mode: Primarily Inductive

An essential consideration is to decide whether the project is primarily inductive or deductive. We say 'primarily' because both modes are present to some degree in all research. In our case, the mode was primarily inductive.

4.3   The Strategy: Analytic Research

Strategy refers to the essential nature of the data and the process by which it is found and analysed. Of the four suggested avenues [14], we found analytic to be most appropriate for our case. In analytic strategy, problems are solved by breaking it down into its component parts to discover its true nature and the causal relationships among its variables. The solution lies within the interface between the researcher and the problem. This strategy best fits our research problem. The individual articles had been written by FA himself, he knew the research context intimately and had the insights to search for meaningful relationships among the available data through an orderly and disciplined investigation based on logical reasoning.

4.4   The Domain: Internal Logic

The domain, or data source, of analytic research is the researcher's own knowledge and experience. In our case, the theoretical concept was not developed solely by cerebration; the process got support from FA's 'extended memory', namely articles written from his own research. Since this is his own work, it is not in conflict with the intention of Analytic Research "The researcher has the resources required for solving the problem *within* himself" [14:26].

4.5   The Technique: Informal Argument

A variety of formal and informal techniques can be used for data analysis. The most appropriate informal technique in our case was philosophical argument because it relies on inductive reasoning. This technique is in accordance with this observation from the literature [16:532]: "Traditionally, authors have developed theory by combining observations from previous literature, common sense, and experience". For building theory, "the building blocks of theory development" [17:49] was used:

- *What* are the essential variables and parameters of the problem situation?
- *How* are these factors related?
- *Why* does a given condition exist?
- *Who, where, when*. These temporal and contextual factors set the boundaries of generalizability, and as such constitute the range of the theory.

Logical reasoning and an analysis of the findings from the ten articles were used to find factors (What) influencing the public Internet access' sustainability in both a positive and a negative direction, and relations between the factors (How). After that, the relations and the connection to the sustainability issue was explained and reasoned (Why) and the contextual factors were filled in (Who, Where, and When).

To illustrate let us suppose that in Lombok (Where) users (Who) with some IT competence (What) visit Internet cafés more frequently than users without such competence (How) because they get more benefits from the Internet use (Why). If this is true, the users' IT competence is one of the demand side elements playing a role in Internet café sustainability.

5   The Resultant Theory

As we stated earlier, the objective of the research was to conceptualize Demand Sustainability of PIAPs in developing countries. Using GAR, findings and concepts from ten published articles (based on research conducted by FA) were analysed. The resultant conceptualization is depicted in Figure 3. [4] The concepts and their interrelationships came from different papers. For example, "Economic capacity" and its link to "Demand Sustainability" were based on two papers on internet café use in Tanzania and Indonesia respectively.

---

[4] A full description of the theory building process is provided in FA's dissertation work [18].

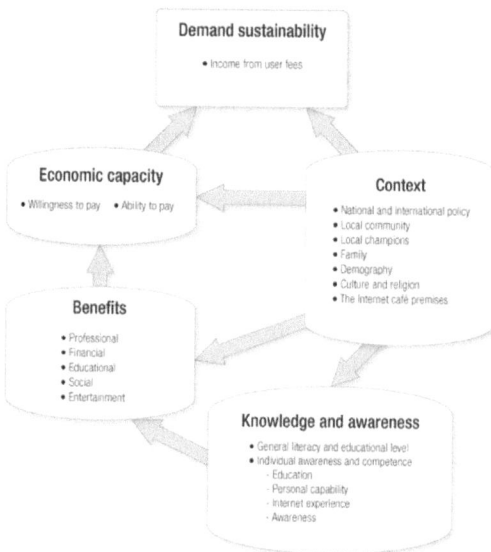

Fig. 3. Demand sustainability from [18]

6   Discussion

Grounded Analytic Research was born when we needed a method to build theory through a two-step process. Step 1 was conducting a number of empirical studies not explicitly related to one another other than being all carried out under the rubric of "bridging the digital divide". Step 2 was going through the resultant published research articles to unearth concepts not explicitly focused on in these articles, but has lain latent in the material. The aim was to develop a theoretical concept called Demand Sustainability. We found Grounded Theory Method to be useful but inadequate for our purpose. Neither of the two conventionally acceptable sources for data in GT studies - first person observations and face-to-face interviews - fit with our data sources which were the articles.

We therefore developed GAR which combines pure reasoning with empirical data. An obvious advantage of GAR is obviation of the need to search for additional data. Instead there is a search for meaningful relationships among the data which are already available. The articles represent the researcher's memory trace – an essential aspect of GAR – and the basis of reasoning. This distinguishes GAR from GTM. While we did use the coding procedure of GTM, it was not from raw or primary data. Rather it was "smaller ideas as a premise for a grander idea" (to quote Baskerville in a personal communication).

It may be argued that GAR's analysis process is not primarily inductive. That is because individual papers employed both inductive and deductive approaches. As such, perhaps abductive is a better description of the process. Yet, we hesitate to categorize GAR as such. The main reason is that reflection and reasoning are vital ingredients of GAR. Deductive approaches in individual papers simply provide the "raw material" for such reflection.

At the same time, GAR also differs from extant Analytic Research or Philosophical Research. The premise for these methods is pure reasoning and reflection. Data is not needed. In GAR the reasoning and reflection is grounded in empirical data. Although the data are seemingly secondary because they come from articles, they were actually gathered by the researcher himself and thus have the characteristics of primary data. His close proximity to the research context gave him the insights that only primary data can give. GAR does not preclude drilling down to the original data, an aspect that distinguishes it from "meta-analysis" of qualitative studies.

Thus, it differs epistemologically from literature reviews that often result in developing concepts or conceptual models by integrating multiple studies [13]. Unlike GAR, such literature reviews build on the findings and the reflections of multiple authors which the reviewer interprets and thus brings in her own thought processes and reflections into theory building. The process is purely based on secondary data. By contrast, GAR has the advantage of being based on a single author's thought processes.

We began the paper by citing the call by Markus and Saunders [3] for submissions to the revamped Theory and Review department of MIS Quarterly. In citing them, we listed a number of methods and formats suggested by them. It is appropriate at this point to check how well GAR has heeded this call.

GAR is a method for comprehensive syntheses (using qualitative, grounded theory, meta-analytic, set-theoretic, or text mining methods) of previously published research with strong theoretical implications. Use of qualitative, grounded theory and meta-analytic methods are commensurate with GAR. It can generate pure theory papers with strong grounding in prior empirical research and/or practice. It also has some of the "highly valued characteristics" listed in their call: GAR can generate theoretical statements enriched by relevant findings from previously published qualitative and quantitative research through syntheses that consider relevant qualitative, as well as quantitative, studies and employs meta-analytic techniques such as analytic reasoning and reflection.

We see that GAR meets several of the listed criteria [3] *simultaneously*. In doing so, our paper contributes towards the search for appropriate and innovative methods for theory building in IS. We demonstrated the usefulness of GAR by building a theoretical concept called Demand Sustainability which is a meaningful contribution to the knowledge on ICT4D. We claim it is meaningful because this theory building was done as the main contribution of the successful doctoral thesis of the first author.

In the methodology landscape, these are exciting times for an IS scholar. Design research [19] is now widely accepted belying the accusation that the IS community is unwilling to accept innovative forms. Variations to established methods such as Action Design Research [20] and Grounded Delphi Method [21] are also being proposed. We offer GAR in this spirit.

Acknowledgments. We thank the anonymous reviewers for helpful comments. In the abstract, we took the liberty of incorporating a sentence from one reviewer's comments because it was perfect! We gratefully acknowledge this "help" and seek the reviewer's indulgence.

References

1. Zmud, B.: Editor's Comments. MIS Quarterly 22(2), xxix–xxxii (1998)
2. Weber, R.: Theoretically Speaking. MIS Quarterly 27(3), iii–xii (2003)
3. Markus, M.L., Saunders, C.: Editor's comments: Looking for a Few Good Concepts...and Theories...for the Information Systems Field. MIS Quarterly 31(1), iii–vi (2007)
4. Te'eni, D.: Review: A Cognitive -Affective Model of Organizational Communication for Designing IT. MIS Quarterly 25(2), 251–312 (2001)
5. Bryman, A.: Social Research Methods. Oxford University Press, UK (2004)
6. Glaser, B.G., Strauss, A.L.: The Discovery of Grounded Theory: Strategies for Qualitative Research. Aldine Publishing Company, Chicago (1967)
7. Strauss, A., Corbin, J.: Basics of Qualitative Research: Grounded Theory Procedures and Techniques. Sage, Newbury Park (1990)
8. Baskerville, R., Pries-Heje, J.: Grounded Action Research: A Method for Understanding IT in Practice. Accounting, Management and Information Technologies 9(1), 1–23 (1999)
9. Sarker, S., Lau, F., Sahay, S.: Using an Adapted Grounded Theory Approach for Inductive Theory Building About Virtual Team Development. The DATA BASE for Advances in Information Systems 32(1), 38–56 (2001)
10. Urquhart, C.: The Evolving Nature of Grounded Theory Method: The Case of the Information Systems Discipline. In: Bryant, A., Charmaz, K. (eds.) The Sage Handbook of Grounded Theory, pp. 339–359. Sage, London (2007)
11. Borgatti, S.P.: Introduction to Grounded Theory. Lecture notes, Boston College (2006), http://www.analytictech.com/mb870/introtoGT.html (consulted June 2008)
12. Warburton, W.I.: What are Grounded Theories Made of? In: 2005 University of Southampton LASS Faculty Post-graduate Research Conference, Southampton, UK, June 6-7. Faculty of Law, Arts and Social Sciences (LASS), pp. 1–10 (2005), http://eprints.soton.ac.uk/16340/ (consulted June 2008)
13. Webster, J., Watson, R.T.: Analyzing the Past to Prepare for the Future: Writing a Literature Review. MIS Quarterly 26(2), xii–xxiii (2002)
14. Buckley, J.W., Buckley, M.H., Chiang, H.-F.: Research Methodology & Business Decisions. National Association of Accountants and The Society of Industrial Accountants of Canada, New York (1976)
15. Jenkins, M.: Research Methodologies and MIS research. In: Mumford, E., Hirschheim, R., Fitzgerald, G., Wood-Harper, T. (eds.) Research Methods in Information Systems, pp. 103–117. North-Holland, Amsterdam (1985)
16. Eisenhardt, K.M.: Building Theories from Case Study Research. Academy of Management Review 14(4), 532–550 (1989)
17. Whetten, D.A.: What Constitutes a Theoretical Contribution? Academy of Management Review 14(4), 490–495 (1989)

18. Furuholt, B.: Bridging the Digital Divide: Sustainable Supply and Demand of Internet Access in Developing Countries. Publication No. 49, Department of Computer Science. Aalborg University, Denmark (2009)
19. Hevner, A.R., March, S., Park, J., Ram, S.: Design Science in Information Systems Research. MIS Quarterly 8(1), 75–105 (2004)
20. Sein, M.K., Henfridsson, O., Purao, S., Rossi, M., Lindgren, R.: Action Design Research. MIS Quarterly 35(1), 37–56 (2011)
21. Paivarintaa, T., Pekkola, S., Moe, C.E.: Grounding Theory from Delphi Studies. In: ICIS 2011 Proceedings, Paper 4 (2011)

Using Photo-Diary Interviews to Study Cyborgian Identity Performance in Virtual Worlds[*]

Ulrike Schultze

Southern Methodist University & Lund University
PO Box 750333, Dallas TX, 75205, U.S.A.
uschultz@smu.edu

Abstract. People's identities (i.e., who they are) are increasingly performed in both physical and digital spaces. Individuals become cyborgs as they extend their presence and bodily senses through digital bodies (e.g., social media profiles, blog posts and avatars). To gain insight into how people make sense of who they are in the face of their digital extensions, a photo-diary method is advanced in this paper. Using a single photo-diary entry and its associated interview, this short paper illustrated empirically the material and discursive practices a user of the virtual world, Second Life, enacted to dynamically draw boundaries to construct her and her avatar's identities.

Keywords: cyborg, photo-diary method, performative identity, material and discursive practices.

1   Introduction

People's identities (i.e., who they are) are increasingly hybrid, simultaneously performed in physical and digital spaces with physical and digital material. Using technological platforms such as Facebook, Twitter, YouTube and virtual worlds, more and more people rely on digital material to present themselves in multiple settings. They are cyborgs, that is, human beings whose presence and senses are extended through technology [1] and whose identities are entangled with it [2, 3].

The type of cyborg that is particularly prevalent in our contemporary computer-mediated world is the individual extended by digital bodies, ranging from traces of online transactions through blog posts and social media profiles to 3D avatars. As cyborgs many users find themselves entangled with these digital bodies and operating in a space where distinctions between the on- and the off-line and between the "real" and the virtual are increasingly blurred [4].

---

[*] Funding from the National Science Foundation, Grant IIS-0848692, made this research possible. Any opinions, findings, and conclusions or recommendations expressed in this material are those of the authors and do not necessarily reflect the views of the National Science Foundation. I am also deeply indebted to the research participants for fully embracing this study and sharing their experiences and insights openly.

A. Bhattacherjee and B. Fitzgerald (Eds.): Future of ICT Research, IFIP AICT 389, pp. 79–88, 2012.

The purpose of this research is to gain insight into how people make sense of who they are in the face of their digital extensions. To this end, a study of users of the virtual world, Second Life (SL), was conducted using a photo-diary interview method. The purpose of this short paper is to illustrate the photo-diary method and its application in the study of cyborgian identity performance.

2   Cyborgian Identity

Even though identity is typically seen as the answer to such questions as "who am I?" and "what am I like?" [5], there are different theoretical perspectives on what identity is. Broadly speaking, identity is either conceptualized in *representational* or *performative* terms [6]: the former regards identity as a more or less stable object (i.e., a self) that is carefully performed for others in an act of impression management [7], whereas the latter regards identity as an ongoing process of identification in which an individual is performed by (and subjected to) the material and discursive conditions that are operating it a given social space [8].

In the context of computer-mediated communication, much prior research has adopted a representational lens, separating on-line from off-line identity [9, 10]. Virtual bodies are conceptualized as passive, disembodied signifiers that refer to – and are separated from – the 'real' thing, namely, the user's physically embodied self [11]. This suggests a unidirectional relationship in which the user controls his/her virtual re-presentation.

In contrast, the cyborgian notion of identity implies a performative orientation in that it regards the physically and digitally embodied user as entangled. This means that the two interacting bodies – one flesh and blood, the other digital – that constitute the cyborgian user, form a single system, or assemblage [12]. However, the bodies in this entanglement "are not objects with inherent boundaries and properties; they are material-discursive phenomena" [12: 823]. In other words, the boundaries between them are always in the making and the result of material-discursive practices.

To illustrate the boundary-drawing practices through which cyborgian identities are performed, Nyberg [3] presents an example from a call center. To a customer, the components that comprise the service delivery (i.e., the telephone system, the computer systems, the customer service representative, etc.) are experienced as an entangled whole until customer service representatives distance themselves from the (failing) technology with such utterances as "the computer has a mind of its own" or "it is not happy." By means of such performative utterances, identities, properties and agency are materialized.

3   Photo-Diary Interview Method

Diaries that are solicited for research purposes are not so much intimate journals as contemporaneous, personal records kept by individual research participants themselves [13]. Diarists essentially take on an adjunct-ethnographer role, observing and recording their own performances and well as those of the people around them at or close to the time that events unfold [14]. As such, diary methods are particularly useful in situations where first-hand observations are not possible [15], e.g., in computer-mediated environments where participants are simultaneously physically sitting in front of the computer and present in a virtual space.

Diary methods address some of the shortcomings of interview research. Retrospective interviews are subject to the vagaries of memory and thus frequently generate abstracted biographical narratives, idealized accounts and general opinions [13]. Because diaries are kept contemporaneously, diary-based research is better able to capture the specificity of decisions made and actions taken by individuals. They tend to make visible experiences that are often hidden, thus producing more complete and honest accounts than other methods [16]. Thus, like ethnographic methods, diaries are conducive for studying practices.

By recording everyday incidents in their diaries, participants' consciousness is raised about the things that happen, their surroundings and their interactions with others. Making sense of these events frequently entails the kind of self-reflexive identity work Giddens [17] describes, as diarists narrativize what they did and why in an effort to construct an authentic, coherent self [18]. As such, diaries can be seen not only as a contemporaneous record of events, but also a situated, storied construction of the diarist and the social reality around him/her [13]. They provide insights into the linguistic, cultural and material resources on which diarists draw in their narrativization, thus making diaries conducive for studying identity performatively.

The "photo-diary: diary interview" method [19] — referred to here simply as the photo-diary interview method — combines visual representations (photos), diaries (written text), and interviews (verbal interactions), in an effort to elicit as complete an account possible of diarists' experiences. In particular, images can make different parts of human consciousness, such as tacit knowledge, accessible to both the researcher and the interviewee because they address the limitations of language [20].

Furthermore, by incorporating snapshots of the space in which events took place, the material conditions of incidents (e.g., the configuration of the space, how people were positioned vis-à-vis objects and others, their gestures and what they were wearing), which are frequently left out of textual diary descriptions, become part of the record. In this way, the role of material resources and practices in the performance of identities can be investigated more readily.

4   Studying Cyborgian Identity Performance in Second Life

In order to illustrate the photo-diary method, this paper relies on data from a single photo-diary entry drawn from a study of the avatar-self relationship in Second Life (SL), for which 35 participants were interviewed between July 2008 and March 2010.

Each participant lived in the southwestern United States and spent at least 10 hours a week in-world. The data collection method was intended to gain maximal insight into the participants' own understanding of their identity performance in-world. It proceeded in two phases:

- Initial 2-hour, face-to-face interview: This interview was held in a wi-fi equipped bookstore so that the interviewee could log into SL. A key objective of the face-to-face meeting was to acknowledge the role of physical embodiment in cyborgian identity. Furthermore, this in-person encounter was intended to build rapport and trust between the researcher and each participant.
- Weekly photo-diaries (for 3 weeks), which provided the basis for interviews: Photo-diary interviews [19] were conducted by phone and took about 1 hour each. Participants were asked to proceed with their SL activities as they normally would, but to take at least five snapshots a week of incidents that were in some way meaningful, significant or important to them. These snapshots were then pasted into a researcher-supplied photo-diary template, which outlined the annotation questions, i.e., the when, what, why, who, and how for each incident. The incidents documented in the photo-diary were then used as the basis for intensive interviewing.

Participants were recruited via SL groups that had some association with the targeted geographic area. Participants were paid $150 after completion of the interviews. With the participants' permission, all interviews were tape-recorded.

4.1   Data Analysis: Dialogic Narrative Analysis

Viewing the interview as a dialog in which narratives that construct and reconstruct the teller's cyborgian identity are co-created by the investigator and the participant, a *dialogic narrative analysis* approach was adopted. Dialogic narrative analysis focuses not purely on the content and structure of the text (i.e., "what" was said and "how"), but also on "to whom" it was said and "why" [18]. Furthermore, it regards the interview as a local accomplishment within a given interview scene in which situated and morally adequate accounts of the interviewee are produced [21].

5   Empirical Illustration: Abigail as Independent Agent

As Abigail[1] and Ozman, their avatars, Terry and Daniel had met, fallen in love and married in SL. They then married in real life (RL) also. They both worked in

---

[1] To protect the participants' identities, all names are pseudonyms and the photo-diary image was converted to a line drawing using an image editor.

IT-related jobs in RL and ran businesses in SL. Abigail had a photography studio, specializing in profile images and promotional material. She was forty and had been in SL for 22 months at the time of the interview.

The photo-diary entry (Figure 1) was part of her second photo-dairy. The entry focuses on Terry's experience of her avatar, Abigail, as an independent being. This incident was prompted by the material conditions of the technology: Abigail appeared on the screen as a virtual body independent of Terry's control at the keyboard. Thanks to the animations embedded in SL objects, Abigail looked alive as she was sitting on the swing, playing with her necklace and gazing in different directions.

Looking at this image in Figure 1, it is not surprising that Terry attributed a cognitive and emotional life world to her avatar. Indeed, she sensed that her avatar was deep in thought and, drawing an analogy between this serendipitous encounter with Abigail and a RL "sweet moment" in which one observes another without being noticed, she wanted to "cherish" the moment rather than disturb her. Terry experienced a deep sense of love for and emotional connection with her avatar. She believed that she could read Abigail's mind and sense her emotional state.

Discursively Terry made a clear distinction between herself and Abigail by referring to herself in the first person ("I"), while referring to Abigail by name and in the third person. Additionally, she referred to the Abigail's life-world as "SLife," thus materializing a cut between "real" and "second" life.

She also relied on the third person ("you" as a surrogate for "one") to universalize the experience of 'capturing someone in a sweet moment.' In this way, she turned this very personal encounter with her avatar and her feelings of love for and connectedness with her digital body into an experience potentially shared by everyone. This discursive strategy normalizes what might otherwise be a contestable claim, making this assertion more credible to both Terry and others.

The photo-diary interview revealed additional insights into how Terry made sense of her cyborgian identity. The first part of the interview related to Figure 1is presented in its totality below, albeit in sections for ease of interpretation. In line with the tenets of dialogic narrative analysis, the interviewer's utterances, identified by initials, are included in the transcripts.

When:

- **Date:** July 19, 2008
- **Start and end time:** 6:20PM

Where: My Photography Studio

Why: I found it interesting

Who: just me ☺

What: – [my husband] Daniel and I stepped away in RL to have some dinner, and spend some time together…when I came back, my screen was exactly what you see in the photo. Abigail was just sitting there at her favorite tree, playing with her necklace, patiently waiting for me to return. It just seemed "sweet" to me. Abigail looked as if she was just contemplating "SLife" – the new studio, Ozman [Abigail's husband], the happiness she feels, etc.

How: I felt like I was sneaking up on Abigail – you know, as you do in real life when you capture someone in a sweet moment…you don't want to disturb them, but you look at them and feel emotionally connected – loving – cherishing a moment with a loved one.

Fig. 1. "Sneaking up on Abigail" Photo-Diary Entry

U.S.:   So, your first picture really, really stunned me. ... Tell me about it.

Terry: Well, I thought it was interesting because, you know, Daniel and I were in Second Life. I was doing something. I was just sitting on the tree. I think I was actually talking with someone before then and I just left Abigail sitting on the pose ball, and I had zoomed in on that, just in that general area, and then walked away. We walked away, had some dinner, spent some time together. I said, "Okay, well I think I'm gonna go back to my computer now." It just seemed like she was just sitting there, just patiently waiting, just looking in different directions, playing with her necklace. And it really did seem like I was kinda sneaking up on her. I didn't want to disturb her (laughing).

U.S.:   (laughing) So, was that the first time you sort of really saw her as this, I mean, it seems like an independent person? ... or, is that not how you felt in this picture?

Terry: Yes. As a matter of fact, Abigail is -- well I guess. I mean, it just seemed like at that moment, Abigail was Abigail, in her self. And I had, you know, I really had nothing to do with controlling her avatar at that point or you know, controlling the shot, or anything like that. It just seemed like she was just sitting there, patiently waiting for me to come back (laughing).

Fig. 2. Photo-Diary Interview Excerpt 1

Notable about Terry's narration of the events that led up to the photo-diary entry (Figure 2), is that the boundaries between RL and SL, as well as between herself and Abigail were ambiguous. Initially, she used "I" to refer to herself acting through Abigail in SL ("I was sitting on a tree"). However, she quickly moved to describing her interaction with her avatar in more technical terms. She referred to "sitting" Abigail "on a pose ball" and "zooming" the camera into "that general area" where Abigail was seated. This suggests that the extent to which such material practices as clicking "sit" options on pose balls and training the camera on a certain scene are salient to the user, they enact boundaries between users and their avatars. In these material practices, the avatar is a technological artifact.

However, the separation between her and Abigail deepened when Terry saw the avatar acting ("looking in different directions, playing with her necklace") without Terry "controlling" either the virtual body or "the shot" (i.e., camera). At this point, Terry acknowledged "Abigail was Abigail, in herself." In addition to bestowing a self to the avatar, she suggested that as an independent, living being, Abigail had a digital body through which she manifested herself (i.e., "I really had nothing to do with controlling her avatar"). In other words, Abigail was accorded a mind, body and identity distinct from Terry's.

> U.S.:   (laughing) And how did that make you feel?
>
> Terry: Oh! I just thought it was sweet. It's endearing to me. Because I have, you
>   know, obviously, I have connected with the avatar, Abigail. And you
>   know, it's almost as if she's my child or something. And when I walked up
>   and saw Abigail just sitting there, I really didn't want to disturb her. I just
>   felt like, "Oh!" you know, "how sweet!" (laughing) So, I really just kinda
>   felt full at the moment. I felt, you know, full of pride. It just kind of helped
>   me to think about all of those things that are going on in Second Life and
>   just started thinking about, you know, "Wow! We've really come a long
>   way on the studio" and Abigail is just so happily married to Ozman. And,
>   it just broadened my thinking a little bit, I think.

Fig. 3. Photo-Diary Interview Excerpt 2

In the next section of the interview (Figure 3), Terry tried to make sense of her connection to an avatar that she has just described as an independent being. She drew on the mother-child relationship ("sweet" and "full of pride") to describe the emotional connection with her avatar. However, instead of being proud of her child Abigail's accomplishments, she was proud of their joint accomplishments in SL (i.e., "we've really come a long way"). In other words, the mother metaphor allowed her to own some of Abigail's accomplishments – and the pride that went with it -- for herself.

> U.S.:   You're thinking on what, specifically? I mean, just her life in general or ...?
>
> Terry: Yes, it was just a reflective thought, I think. Just reflecting on the time that
>   I've spent in SL. The time that has gone into building this new island and
>   the new studio and everything. And you know, there comes a pride with
>   something that you create and you get so close to being finished, and you
>   just have to stand back and look at it and say, "Wow! This really turned out
>   nice." I think that in that moment for me, it was "Okay, we're about to open
>   the studio and I think I've done the right thing, and Abigail thinks so too."
>   (laughing)

Fig. 4. Photo-Diary Interview Excerpt

As the interview continued (Figure 4), Terry shifted attention away from Abigail onto herself for a while. She acknowledged that she, Terry, was contemplating her life in SL and that she felt proud of growing her business by building a new photographic studio, which was about to open. However, she again relied on the discursive strategy of the third person "you" to universalize the experience of 'feeling pride for something you created.' Thus, through the course of the interview she was working her way towards legitimating the pride she felt of her own accomplishments, by first attributing this pride to her child Abigail and then universalizing it.

At the end of this excerpt, Terry re-introduced Abigail as an independent agent. Albeit laughingly, she indicated that the avatar approved of Terry's business decisions (i.e., "I think I've done the right thing, and Abigail thinks so too"). This might be seen as an attempt to return to the identity narrative of Abigail as a living, thinking and feeling being.

U.S.:	So is it almost like you're feeling that you as Terry, are in some ways the owner of all that you have created in Second Life, and Abigail just sort of being an onlooker in this sense?
Terry:	Yes, it could be. I think that I sometimes feel like I'm the onlooker (laughing) and Abigail is the one doing all the creation. But yes, I mean, I guess for the real part of me is just -- I'm a creative person anyway and to be able to have an outlet for creativity in this way, it allows me to think more in terms of just, you know, not a 2D image. I can't draw for anything but I have all of these thoughts in my head and to be able to actually create something in 3D and say, "This is what I wanted it to look like." It just really brings a lot of really good thoughts and good moments for me to sit back and say, "Wow! That's pretty cool!" (laughing)

Fig. 5. Photo-Diary Interview Excerpt 4

In this final section of the interview (Figure 5), the interviewer pressed Terry on agency, especially to whom she attributed ownership of the creative content in SL. After initially wavering ("I sometimes feel like I'm the onlooker … and Abigail is the one doing all the creation"), Terry later conceded that she was "a creative person" with "all of these thoughts in my head." SL served as her outlet because she "can't draw for anything." Being able to see her creativity materialize in 3D then allowed her to acknowledge that her ideas are "pretty cool." Again, Abigail disappeared during this narrative as Terry's identity as the creative power behind her SL business emerges.

6   Conclusion

The objective of this short methodology paper was to illustrate the utility of the photo-diary interview method for studying cyborgian identity performance. Adopting a performative rather than a representational conceptualization of identity performance, this paper focused on identifying the material and discursive practices through which situated and dynamic distinctions are made between the user's physical and virtual embodiments, between reality and virtuality and between human an non-human agency. The empirical illustration demonstrates users' ongoing negotiation of these boundaries as they try of make sense of who they are in light of their increasing entanglement with virtual bodies. The photo-diary interview method is conducive for identifying both the digital materiality and their meanings that users relied on to enact an identity in Second Life, as well as the material and discursive practices through which identities were performed.

References

1. Borer, M.I.: The Cyborgian Self: Toward a Critical Social Theory of Cyberspace. Reconstruction: Studies in Contemporary Culture, vol. 2 (2002)
2. Introna, L.D.: Towards a Post-Human Intra-Actional Account of Socio-Technical Agency (and Morality). Moral Agency and Technical Artefacts. NIAS, Hague (2007)
3. Nyberg, D.: Computers, Customer Service Operatives and Cyborgs: Intra-actions in Call Centres. Organization Studies 30, 1181–1199 (2009)
4. Hardey, M.: Life Beyond the Screen: Embodiment and Identity through the Internet. The Sociological Review 50, 570–585 (2002)
5. Chatman, C.M., Eccles, J.S., Malanchuk, O.: Identity Negotiation in Everyday Settings. In: Downey, G., Eccles, J.S., Chatman, C.M. (eds.) Navigating the Future: Social Identity, Coping and Life Tasks, pp. 116–139. Russell Sage Foundation, New York (2005)
6. Gregson, N., Rose, G.: Taking Butler Elsewhere: Performativities, Spatialities and Subjectivities. Environment and Planning D: Society and Space 18, 433–452 (2000)
7. Goffman, E.: Behavior in Public Places: Notes on the Social Organization of Gatherings. Free Press, New York (1963)
8. Butler, J.: Gender Trouble: Feminism and the Subversion of Identity. Routledge, New York (1990)
9. Turkle, S.: Life on the Screen: Identity in the Life of the Internet. Simon & Shuster, New York (1995)
10. Bessiere, K., Seay, A.F., Kiesler, S.: The Ideal Elf: Identity Exploration in World of Warcraft. Cyber Psychology & Behavior 10, 530–535 (2007)
11. Bardzell, J., Bardzell, S.: Intimate Interactions: Online Representation and Software of the Self. Interactions, 11–15 (2008)
12. Barad, K.: Posthumanist Performativity: Toward an Understanding of How Matter comes to Matter. Signs: Journal of Women in Culture 28, 801–831 (2003)
13. Alaszewski, A.: Using Diaries for Social Research. Sage, Thousand Oaks (2006)
14. Zimmerman, D.H., Wieder, D.L.: The Diary: Diary-Interview Method. Urban Life 5, 479–498 (1977)
15. Czarniawska, B.: Shadowing and Other Techniques for Doing Fieldwork in Modern Society. Liber, Copenhagen (2007)
16. Kenten, C.: Narrating Oneself: Reflections on the Use of Solicited Diaries with Diary Interviews. Forum: Qualitative Social Research 11, Article 16 (2010)
17. Giddens, A.: Modernity and self-identity: Self and society in the late modern age. Polity Press, Cambridge (1991)
18. Riessman, C.K.: Narrative Methods for the Human Sciences. Sage, Thousand Oaks (2008)
19. Latham, A.: Research, Performance and Doing Human Geography: Some Reflections on the Diary-Photograph, Diary-Interview Method. Environment and Planning A 35, 1993–2017 (2003)
20. Bagnoli, A.: Beyond the Standard Interview: The Use of Graphic Elicitation and Arts-Based Methods. Qualitative Research 9, 547–570 (2009)
21. Alvesson, M.: Beyond Neopositivists, Romantics, and Localists: A Reflexive Approach to Interviews in Organizational Research. Academy of Management Review 28, 13 (2003)

Track III

Emerging Themes
in Interpretive Case Study Research

Living in a Sociomaterial World

Eric Monteiro[1,*], Petter Almklov[2], and Vidar Hepsø[3]

[1] NTNU, Dept. of Computer and Information Science (IDI), 7491 Trondheim, Norway
ericm@idi.ntnu.no
[2] Studio Apertura, NTNU Social Research, Dragvoll, 7491 Trondheim, Norway
pettera@svt.ntnu.no
[3] NTNU, Dept. of Applied Geosciences, 7491 Trondheim, Norway
vidar.hepso@ntnu.no

Abstract. The Internet of Things (IoT) – the proliferation of networked sensors, gadgets, artefacts and measurement devices – increase the presence, scope and potential importance of mediated information in collaborative work practices. This underscores the material aspects of sociomaterial practices. We study an extreme case where work practices rely heavily, almost entirely, on representations. In line with the research programme on sociomateriality, we acknowledge the performative role of representations. Representations are thus actively embedded in practice rather than passive re-presentation of data. Extending the programme of sociomateriality, we contribute by identifying and discussing three strategies detailing how sociomaterial practices get performed: *extrapolate* (filling in gaps), *harmonise* (ironing out inaccuracies) and *abduct* (coping with anomalies). We draw empirically on a longitudinal (2004-2011) case study of the subsurface community of NorthOil. This community of geologists, geophysicists, reservoir engineers, production engineers and well engineers rely on sensor-based (acoustic, electromagnetic, radioactive, pressure, temperature) data when exploring and producing oil and gas resources several thousand meters below the seabed where direct access to data is difficult and/ or limited.

Keywords: Sociomateriality, performativity, representation.

1 Introduction

Sociomateriality is a label for a research agenda into the conceptualisation of the interplay between (material) technology and (human) use [1]. Rather than an independent theory or set of concepts, sociomateriality summaries and highlights salient aspects and insights gained in information systems research over the last couple of decades, emphasising the inherent contingency involved with enacting technology [2, 3], the considerable discretion for users [4, 5] and the modular/ interconnected/ networked nature of ICT [6].

A defining feature of sociomateriality, stemming from its commitment to the 'entanglement' of human and material practices [1], is to dismiss a representational

---

* Corresponding author.

A. Bhattacherjee and B. Fitzgerald (Eds.): Future of ICT Research, IFIP AICT 389, pp. 91–107, 2012.
© IFIP International Federation for Information Processing 2012

view of technology in favour of a *performative* one. Here the meaning (hence use) of representations is neither fixed nor stable but emerge through practice (as they are 'performed'). Representations, then, are not passive re-presentations but active, *constitutive* features of (sociomaterial) practice.

Building on, but ultimately extending, the research programme of sociomateriality, the purpose of our paper is to identify and discuss how practice get entangled with technologically mediated representations i.e. we study the strategies at play. Sociomateriality states *that* use/ technology is entangled; we analyse *how* these entanglement play out. We empirically identify three strategies of entanglement: extrapolate (fill in the gaps), harmonise (sorting out errors and inaccuracies) and abduct (coping with anomalies). We have consciously selected an extreme case where work practices are saturated by ICT based visual and textual representations of the data, a consequence of access to the 'reality' (i.e. referent, in a representational vocabulary) being either unattainable or very limited. Moreover, the work practices we study matter: their implications pose significant risks to economic value, the environment and human safety as made painfully clear by Obama's commission following the Deepwater Horizon blowout [7]. Empirically we draw on a longitudinal (2004-2011) case study of work practices within the so-called subsurface community in NorthOil (a pseudonym), a community crucial to efficient, innovative and safe oil and gas exploration and production.

2   Conceptualising Technology: Sociomateriality in Context

The discourse on how to conceptualise technology runs long in information systems research. As a counter-reaction to overly deterministic accounts, the significant discretion for users to appropriate information systems was established decades ago from both empirical studies [2, 5, 8] and theoretical concepts (e.g. the 'situated' nature of action proposed by Suchman [4]), the presence of 'workarounds' by Gasser [5] and Giddens' structuration theory as proposed by [9]). In their historical recapitulation, Orlikowski and Scott [1] describe three, broad categories of approaches: (i) discrete entities (with uni-directional causal effects of technology), (ii) mutually dependent ensembles (with bi-directional relationship) before outlining (iii) sociomaterial assemblages. The decisive distinction between the former two and the latter, Orlikowski and Scott (ibid., p. 455) point out is that the latter see "tools...as constitutive of both activities and identities".

Sociomateriality is a 'banner' or 'signal' (opus cit., pp. 455 and 456) for this agenda rather than an independent theory in itself. In our perspective, the thrust of insights of sociomateriality is essentially drawn from science and technology science (STS), especially actor-network theory. The constitutive use/ technology entanglement defining sociomateriality, corresponds exactly to the 'strong principle of symmetry' found in actor-network theory [10, 11]. Illustrating actor-network theory based work in information systems research prior to [1], Quattrone and Hopper [12, p. 216] explain how "agency and an object's identity reside neither in an individual nor a technology but in a chain of relations between actors (and actants)". Similarly echoing the principle of symmetry between the social and the technical, [13] discusses the 'inscription' of behaviour (i.e. agency) into a variety of materials including technical standards, habits and training programmes.

The constitutive entanglement [14] of use/ technology embedded in the notion of performativity is a "central idea entailed in" [1, p. 460]. We argue this insight was arrived at prior to its formulation within sociomateriality. *That* use/ technology is entangled is a shared insight with e.g. STS. The true, remaining challenge is how to push further, how to explore entanglement in more detail.

An interesting avenue of the pursuit of performativity is the emphasis on extreme cases i.e. cases where representations (constitutively entangled with practice) saturate or dominate the empirical settings. In STS, this has for some time prompted a strong interest in work settings relying heavily, at times almost entirely, on representations. The work-settings thus take on an almost semiotic character. Knorr-Cetina's [15] study of high-energy physicists illustrates this well.   Studying the behaviour of (sub)particles that are inaccessible by direct means, the empirical material of high-energy physicists is exclusively drawn from visual and numerical representations extracted from the apparatus surrounding particle accelerators. The heavy reliance on sensor and measurement devices – inherently error-prone - is challenging [16]. Sensors decay, contain bugs or need calibration. This dilemma is central also to our case from the oil and gas sector. Another setting attracting STS attention is electronic markets [17]. The work practices of traders lean heavily on the real-time representations (readings, computational analysis, visualization) of selected events in the electronic market. In a widely cited study of the option market, MacKenzie and Millo [18, p. 107], cited in [1, p. 461]) explicitly set out to demonstrate the performativity of a formula (the so-called Black-Scholes model) by that it "succeeded empirically not because it discovered pre-existing price patterns but because markets changed in ways that made its assumptions more accurate and because the theory was used in arbitrage".

What the STS studies compellingly demonstrate is the constitutive entanglement of use/ technology. This provides strong empirical evidence for sociomateriality. What remains elusive, however, and the aim of our paper, is to spell out the structure and content of entanglement. We analyse the sociomaterial practices of a subsurface community focusing on how they develop, maintain and revise so-called reservoir models. Operating in an almost semiotic world, the subsurface community have to live with the imperfections, glitches and shortcomings of the reservoir model stemming from its input from incomplete, error-prone and uncertain sensor-based data.

3   Method and Case

3.1   Approach and Access

We employ an interpretative approach that is geared towards an understanding of the context of the information system and the process over time of mutual influence between the system and its context.   A deep-seated conviction we held was that a longitudinal case study was crucial for providing the level of detail that we sought regarding the process of organisational dynamics [19]. In line with [20, p. 537]'s advice for facilitating generalisations from case studies of single organisations, we relied on a theoretical sampling of the case site. We were actively seeking a work setting where the performativity of representations would stand out due to the particularly heavy reliance on representations: we selected a case where 'direct' access to the data referred to was cumbersome at best.

The selection of the organisation for the case study was also influenced by pragmatic concerns of access; we know NorthOil well. The first author is an experienced IS researcher with a prolonged research project portfolio within NorthOil e.g. a study of standardization of well maintenance. The second author has an MSc in geological engineering, and based his PhD in social anthropology on a yearlong ethnographic fieldwork in the subsurface departments of one of NorthOil's field organisations. He has since worked on several (applied) research projects within the Norwegian petroleum industry. The third author has been an employee of NorthOil for 20 years. He has been involved in a variety of projects in and around the subsurface community. He was involved in intervention-oriented research projects as part of his fieldwork for a PhD within NorthOil.

3.2   Data Collection

Pollock and Williams [21] point out the importance of broad, longitudinal research designs to allow for what they call the *biography* of a technology (artefact) to supplement what dominates interpretative IS research viz. the single site case study of an implementation. Given the all too real constraints on research projects – they have confined time spans, they are targeted at given issues, involved PhDs have time constraints for delivery – Pollock and Williams (ibid.) propose a 'synthetic' form of longitudinal case study where formally independent research projects by the research group is chained together to make a bigger picture. Continuity is achieved by maintaining continuity in research approach, overall themes and transparency in documentation. Our study follows Pollock and William's (ibid.) proposed form of a longitudinal case (2004 – 2011). We rely on three types of data collection that ran in parallel: participative observations, semi-structured interviews and document studies (details in Table 1).

Participative observation was of different types. Predominately conducted by two of the authors, we have participatory observations from subsurface operation centres, departments and on offshore rigs. One author has participated in asset workshops where future production plans are discussed. Participatory observations provided insight into everyday practices as we followed people around, informal chatting over coffee, attending meetings and work at their desks.

Interviews were semi-structured and lasting 45 minutes – 1,5 hours. Some have been interleaved with participatory observation, as a way to clarify and expand on observations. Seven selected interviews particularly discussing the use of the reservoir model in operational settings have been fully transcribed. 260 pages of field notes were written during observations and the interviews closely linked to the observations.

Document study of both paper based but more importantly electronic documents have been conducted. Electronic documents include electronic archives, database readings, PowerPoint presentations, well plans, email discussions and policy- and operational regulations.

Table 1. Overview of the three modes of data collection: participatory observations, interviews and document study

Participatory observations	<ul><li>Participatory observation of production optimization 18 days during 3 months in 2005</li><li>Participatory observation of product optimization of another asset for 14 days during 4 months in 2006</li><li>Participant observations 3 months in 2004 every day of one of the assets</li><li>Two field trips to offshore installations, 5 days in 2007</li><li>Participatory observation of subsurface departments, 4 days during 2008-2010</li><li>Participatory observations from 4 asset workshops</li><li>Participation in numerous small, informal meetings and discussions with subsurface and management (2004 – 2011)</li></ul>
Semi-structured interviews	<ul><li>IS/ IT management: 13 interviews 2005 – 2010</li><li>Subsurface members: 55 interviews 2004-2011</li></ul>
Documents	<ul><li>Electronic archives (presentations, memo, documents)</li><li>Database readings (from subsurface tools)</li><li>Email discussions</li><li>Intranet: policy- and operational regulation</li><li>Extranet: newletters and corporate presentations</li></ul>

3.3   Data Analysis

We alternated between data collection and analysis. Following van Maanen's [22] suggestion, we made extensive use of field notes, making sure to separate 'raw' data from own comments, reflections, and questions. Given that all authors, albeit unequally, were involved in both data collection and analysis, we were able to conduct numerous sessions comparing, contrasting and challenging each other's (preliminary) interpretation, thus enjoying the benefits noted by [20, p. 538]. The three authors of this paper have over a period of more than a decade worked together in various configurations of research collaboration. Though collaboration has been in bursts rather than continuous, we are fairly close research partners. By using temporal bracketing and graphical process maps, which are two strategies for data analysis that were proposed by [23], we generated visual illustrations of how the chronological development, including technology implementation projects, within the subsurface community resonated with broader themes and trends within NorthOil.

Beyond internal discussions, our data analysis relies on a series of workshops, meetings, and informal discussions with NorthOil managers, subsurface members, IT department, in which we presented our findings and preliminary data analysis. This contributed importantly to an external validation and criticism of our analysis. For example, when presenting empirical findings on how one reservoir model is used operationally, professionals will often contrast our findings with how things are done differently at other fields. Thus we are painfully aware that our account, complicated as it may be for outsiders, of how the reservoir model is used operationally is simplified and stereotypical.

In our data analysis, we strived to adhere to Klein and Myers' [24] principle of multiple interpretations. This hinges crucially on an ability to discern distinct, potentially diverging, voices among the actors. An example of the results of our efforts in this direction is that the differences between the subsurface community and management when it comes to reservoir estimates, a highly political assessment. Also within the subsurface community clear differences in perspectives were manifest. An example of this is the difference in perspectives between drilling engineers, who wants a clear-cut drilling target in order to build an operationally robust drilling project, and the geologists and reservoir engineers, who often want to keep options open for eventualities and opportunities that may appear during operations.

We utilized the added flexibility in data collection that results from overlapping data collection with analysis [20]. Our data analysis moved between inductively generating aggregated categories from codes (manually: using colour, post-it notes, annotations) and drawing deductively on prior theoretical ideas, notably actor-network theory. We were thus anything but clean slates [25]. The first construct in our theoretical template underpinning our analysis (see Table 2: extrapolate) drew inductively on aggregated categories on practices of navigating in extensive but ill-structured historical data, and resonated with notions of workarounds and improvisation known from practice-based research. The second construct (harmonise) drew inductively on aggregated categories about heuristics for producing trustworthy information that resonates with performativity found in actor-network theory. The third construct (abduct) is drew inductively on break-down situations where 'small' observations challenge overall understanding. This ties in with the way subsurface members in general and geologist in particular collectively arrive at interpretations [26].

Table 2. Our interpretative template with the 3 constructs underpinning our analysis

Construct	Illustration
Extrapolate	In the absence of complete data sets, e.g. when you have but a few wells in designated locations but nothing in-between, "you interpolate between these wells"
Harmonise	Smaller inconsistencies or outright errors are not worth spending a lot of time and resources to iron out e.g. "Local changes based on single observations in new wells are, at least on fields with fairly complex models, often too resource demanding to integrate into the [reservoir] model".
Abduct	When "data doesn't make sense" there is sometimes a need for a more fundamental new understanding of the reservoir e.g. "this fault [line] has been misinterpreted. It's shifted downwards, not upwards. The faults we see here are the results of a landslide pattern".

3.4   Case Context: The Reservoir Model

NorthOil (a pseudonym) is a company in northern Europe with some 30.000 employees operating in about 40 countries worldwide. The focus in this paper is on the work within the subsurface community in NorthOil. The subsurface community is involved intimately with the core value generating activities of any O & G company as they are principally responsible for locating commercially interesting fields, planning, development and optimizing daily production. Subsurface departments consist of numerous specialized disciplines: geophysicists, geologists (with different sub-specialties), reservoir engineers, production engineers, drilling engineers and well completion engineers to name the most common. The subsurface professionals partly work in interdisciplinary teams co-located around the different O & G field organizations and partly in disciplinary defined networks cutting across geographically separated field sites.

The empirical focus of our paper is on the *reservoir model*. It consists of grid cells ascribed with a set of properties based mainly on interpretation of geological data. The model in Figure 1 consists of roughly 45.000 active cells. Information about the reservoir is fragmented and incomplete. The reservoir model is a concerted effort of creating one model representing the whole reservoir. The grid cells of a model are, depending on geology and available data, "about the size of this office building".

NorthOil's fields are predominantly deep-sea hydrocarbon reservoirs most commonly located 1500-3000 meters below the seabed. The hydrocarbons are contained in Jurassic sandstone buried over millions of years by layer upon layer of new sediments. Wells are drilled from concrete platforms, floating rigs or ships. With current drilling technology it is possible to hit a defined target with a precision in the magnitude of meters. To make use of the accuracy in drilling, the reservoir model also

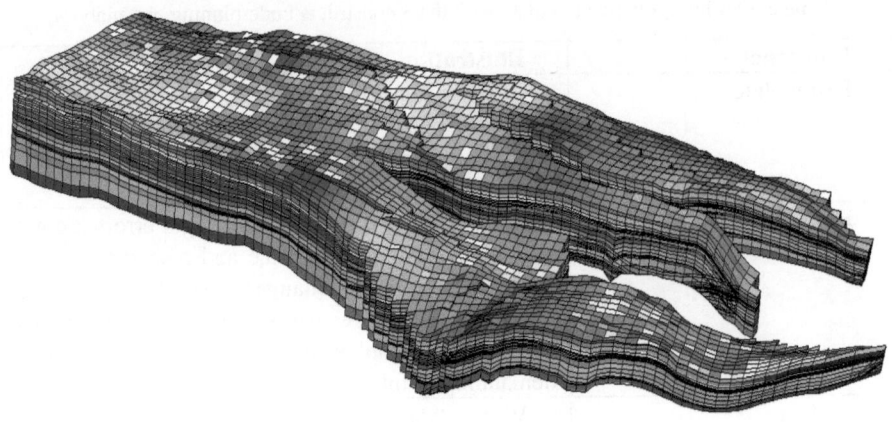

Fig. 1. Visual representation of a reservoir model

need to be fine-grained hence enormous efforts are invested into new technologies and methods in reservoir description. The pace of innovation is high, especially in the ongoing "digitalization" of the industry. Three main types of sensor-based data are essential to the subsurface community.

Seismic data are digital recordings of the reflections of acoustic waves sent down to the reservoir in seismic surveys. It is a very advanced echogram, able to "see through" at least thousands of meters of overlying rock. By specific arrangements of sound sources and microphones and extensive computer processing, geophysicists are able to outline layers and other structures in the rock based on contrasting acoustic properties (see Figure 2, left picture). Most importantly, such contrasts reveal density differences between porous and non-porous rock, the former being more likely to contain hydrocarbons. The data sets from modern seismic surveys are normally three-dimensional and they cover the whole volume of a reservoir. The main weakness of seismics is the low resolution, at best around 30 meters.

Well logs are collections of sensor-based measurements from logging assemblies lowered into the wells, normally in connection with drilling or well operations. The sensors measure physical properties associated with geological properties, e.g., gamma radiation is higher in shale than in sand stone and electrical resistivity is higher in oil than in water. The log plots different measurements and observations along the well (see Figure 2, middle picture) along a downward axis representing length of the well.

Production data are real-time measurements of the oil and gas, volumes transported out of (and in the case of injection for pressure support, pumped into) the reservoir. These can be plotted in various ways, for example as in Figure 2 (right). The pressure development in the reservoir also is monitored. These data give the subsurface group clues about how much oil there might be left in the reservoir, and aid them in day-to-day optimizing existing wells and planning production.

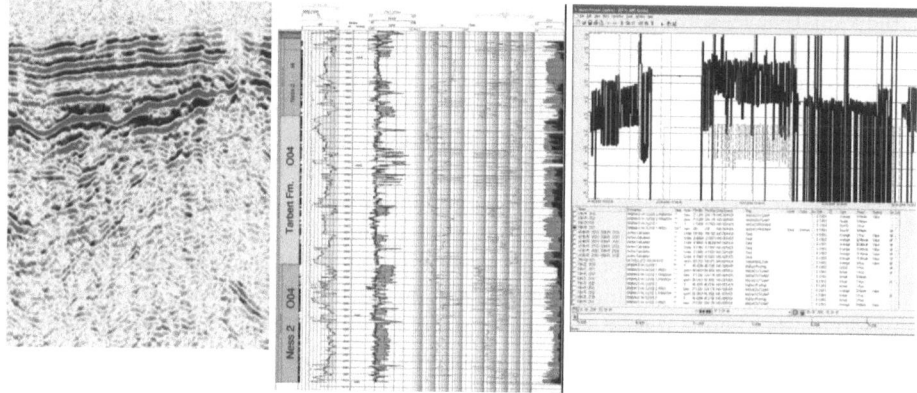

Fig. 2. Typical visual representations of the 3 principal types of data: seismic data (left), well logs (middle) and production data (right)

Building a reservoir model is an extensive project lasting months to years. The model (Figure 1) is used throughout the lifetime of the field to simulate fluid movement in the reservoir, and it is updated by history matching towards recorded production data. Our informants willingly admit to the shortcomings of the reservoir model: "The only thing we know for sure is that the [reservoir] model is wrong". Our concern with the reservoir model is how this imperfect representation gets entangled with, and is constitutive of, everyday work practices.

4   Results

4.1   Extrapolate: Filling in the Gaps

Modelling the reservoir is a creative endeavour where the reservoir is conjured into existence by active interrogation of the available data. We analyse how detailed observations with coarse remote sources are combined in creative extrapolations into the unreachable volumes, between and beyond well observations and beneath the resolution of remote sources.

Wells are just thin lines of high quality data points in kilometre-wide reservoirs. These are interpreted in combination with the vague patterns seen on the seismics. A geologist explains how he proceeds to build an understanding of a new reservoir that has only three wells:

> "Obviously, if you have three wells they're going to tell you a lot about the vertical [well paths]. So you have at least the understanding of the vertical sense of the layers and you can build your sedimentological understanding…You have three wells and … you try to interpolate between those wells with your information and then you try to extrapolate away from those wells into areas that are further away. And then with the help of the seismic, you try to calibrate and use the seismic to help you, and then come up with some sort of feeling about whether, you know, how much reservoir you've actually captured with the data you have?"

Individual have some value of their own in specific situations, but it is in the combinations of data that conceptions of the reservoir as an entity are constructed. This is concretely manifested in the log as a visual representation: The individual measurements of radioactive and electrical parameters plotted on the log do not primarily speak directly of the geology themselves; rather it is certain patterns in the combinations of the different measurements that reveal the reservoir behind them. The log, as a visual presentation also promotes specific combinations. Maybe the most striking example of this is shown in Figure 3. The measurements of two independent physical properties are superimposed on the plots with their scales adjusted so that the one is higher in sand and the other in shale. Thus, when the curves cross, it represents a transition between shale and sand, and the space between them will be green (representing shale) when one is higher and yellow (representing sandstone) when the other is higher. Like in the tale of seven blind Indians and an elephant, each sensor picks up only fragments of the reservoir, but when combined based on theory and experience their referent appears.

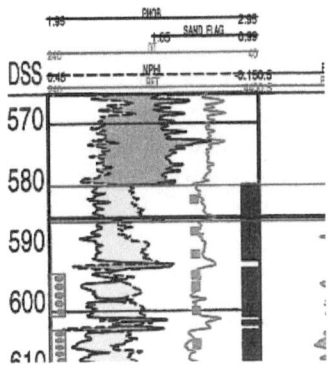

Fig. 3. A section of a well log superimposing two independent measurements, gamma radiation and neutron density. The axes of these measurements are adjusted to make the lines intersect, and the area between them change colour, when there is a transition from shale to sandstone. Thus, only a glimpse on the readings will indicate sandstone (yellow) or shale (green).

New, detailed information from the well path gives a lot of information about the surroundings beyond its actual range, if one is able to interpret it in combination with the seismic of the general structures in the area. We have on several occasions observed collective interpretation where boundaries are drawn in the reservoir based on such combinations. A typical example is when a well log displays a transition from tight shale to sandstone at a certain depth. If the depth corresponds with a reflection on the seismic chart, the well observation "confirms" the seismic and one may assume that the reflection *represents* this transition. Consequently, one can assume that the areal distribution of the seismic reflection represents the boundary between two layers, and one can, more speculatively guess that the properties of these volumes, for example the porosity of the sand stone, are represented by the properties registered in the log.

4.2   Harmonise: Resolving Inaccuracies and (Smaller) Inconsistencies

The subsurface professionals cope with imperfect representations of the reservoir every day. One way of coping is by making informal adjustments or selectively dismissing inconsistent data. We discuss practices by which smaller inaccuracies, errors and inconsistencies are handled, not primarily to represent the reservoir better, but rather to respond to the organizational need to get on with work.

As information arrives from new wells and from production data, the reservoir model should ideally be updated to fit this information. However, local changes based on single observations from new wells are normally too resource demanding to fit into the model. Local changes may have ripple effects to connected areas of the reservoir:

> "[Then] we have to figure out, how the heck are we going to update this monster? Because, if you start fiddling with two wells, then you do something with the rest as well."

The most common way of updating reservoir models, and a method that is subject to much current research, is history matching. History matching is basically a mathematical method where the static properties of the reservoir model are adjusted to best fit the actual historical (dynamic) production development. This operation is very demanding in terms of computer processing resources. It is also demanding in terms of manual labour with programming and constraining of the mathematical problem, so that the resultant history matched model makes sense geologically:

> "Without history matching the model is just an academic exercise with little practical predictive value. When we get production data [..] we actually find out if things match or if the model fits reality."

However, the resultant model will not be perfect and "[i]n the end it is almost always the case that the history matched models violate some important geological constraints". History matching is a calibration of the model towards measured production and will, if it is successful, improve the accuracy of the model. Still, one of our informants stresses that the updated model is not something that passively represents the reservoir:

> "[I]f we can do history matching that is the best. Because then you learn something about the flooding processes in the reservoir, in the process. But that doesn't mean that you should use the model afterwards [laughs]. It is the understanding, the understanding of the reservoir, which is important to gain from it. And if you have that, then a good engineer will be able to work intuitively with the model he has in his head and be able to do much of his work"

The understanding of the reservoir is relatively robust in the sense of being able to absorb both contradictory and missing data. Given the truly extensive network of sensors and measurement devices and the considerable physical stress they are subject to, equipment is anything but fault-proof. One informant explained how they resolved errors generated from erroneous equipment:

> "We've given up fixing that choke. It's too costly to replace. I tell [the production engineer] that he simply has to shut his eyes and disregard the readings from it."

4.3   Abduct: Challenged by Anomalies

In this section we discuss what happens when new information radically challenges the existing knowledge of the reservoir. We observe that whereas local ad hoc interpretations of new data can be creative and open ended, the reservoir model has a certain inertia upheld by workarounds and other modifying practices.

The model of the reservoir may be challenged in many ways. We illustrate contradictions stemming from information from well logs from new wells. Drilling a new well is the moment of truth for subsurface specialists. They may have planned wells for years. In the course of a few days when the drill bit with its logging sensors penetrates the reservoir, their interpretations and predictions are tested. The results will hardly ever fit their expectations, and they always imply adjustments of their ideas of the reservoir:

> "But when we begin to drill, the only thing we know from all our
> experiences is that when we drill we find out things are not the way we
> think they are. "

One of the authors did his fieldwork at a subsurface department when several wells were drilled Though the field is one of the most studied on the continental shelf, with logs and production data from over 100 wells, each well contributed with new information. Most of the time, new well data meant that they had to make smaller adjustments but on a few occasions the well log, as it ticked in meter by meter, left the whole group in utter confusion. At the time of the fieldwork, most wells were drilled on the fringes of the reservoir. The geological theory of the area is that when the reservoir was a mountain on dry land, some large blocks on its fringes have loosened and slid downwards. Though located on one of these fault blocks, the well was expected to penetrate the common stack of known sedimentary layers in the reservoir. As drilling progressed, however, the observed geology "did not make sense". Expected sandstone-layers were "missing" and they lost track of "where they were" in the stratigraphic layers. Unexpected data during drilling was commonplace (cf. previous sections), but this was one of the rare occasions where it seemed impossible to make sense of it. The communal workroom of the geologists turned into a hothouse as experts and the curious seeped in from the entire department, conducting discussions along several paths. Some were discussing technical issues, like whether the positioning equipment in the drill string could be damaged. A geologist commented that the log looked upside-down and suggested that the fault block may have been rotated. Some tried to look at details in the log for a positive identification of the zones they had penetrated. Some discussed (more or less) similar situations with other well projects and the outcomes of those. Taken-for-granted assumptions were critically revisited. The project manager for the new well rather briskly tried to keep the crowd away as he studied the seismics intensely, shifted perspectives and visualization modes on his screen to study a vague vertical shape. He pointed at the screen and concluded, "this fault has been misinterpreted. It's shifted downwards, not upwards". This error did not in itself explain the data directly, but it supported a hypothesis, that the geologist explained later on. The fault was indicative of a certain landslide pattern that he had seen on a field trip to another geological site. According to this understanding there could be several smaller faults beneath seismic resolution (thus invisible) associated with the fault he could see. One of these smaller faults could have shifted the rock structures in a way that could explain the strange data. He drew on a piece of paper and told a geological story of how a major landslide had resulted in a pattern of smaller faults in the block. Gradually new data strengthened his hypothesis. When confronted by anomalies that challenge not only details of their understanding, but also whether they understand anything at all, all resources are drawn upon including field visits to geological fields on dry land in England.

5   Discussion

Proclaiming the performativity of sociomateriality is in itself not very bold. Our analysis is intended as a necessary detailing of sociomaterial practices. How, then, to characterise the emerging performativity?

Representations simplify. The subsurface community are painfully aware of the many details, nuances and variations lost when captured in the representations. Latour [27, p. 71] makes a relevant observation when discussing trade-offs, i.e. what you gain and what you loose, related to his notion of a circulating reference. Reporting from a team of researchers' efforts to analyse certain developments in the Amazon rainforest (whether a designated area of the forest was expanding or retreating), the scientists employ a number of different representations for the 'same' section of the forest: embodied observations from the area, dividing the forest into a grid pattern to select designated cells of forest, a sample of earth from one cell and a set of measurement/ tests from that sample. The richness of the former representations gets successively traded for increased mobility and ease of communication in the latter. Geologists are systematically trained, to use Latour's notion, to move up and down the steps of a circulating reference i.e. moving back and forth between rich representations to abstracted models/ representations. The touch and feel of the reservoir, its structures and tactile qualities, and its scale and complexity are not presented to their bodies and perception, and must be conjured out of the data. Figure 4 shows a picture from a field trip where geologists travel to 'analogous' sites to the O & G fields they are primarily interested in.

Fig. 4. Tactile experience of the porosity and permeability of the rocks from geologists' field trip to an analogue field accompanied by one of the authors

The reservoir model is largely taken for granted in the sense that there is no anxiety over the fact that it is not 'real'. The subsurface community are of course acutely aware of the many shortcomings, inaccuracies, inconsistencies and debatable assumptions embedded in the representation, but the strategies dubbed extrapolate and harmonise in the previous section demonstrate vividly how far they are willing to press the reservoir model. The construction of the reservoir model needs to be understood in light of its purpose. Given the very significant resources involved in revising it ("we do it perhaps every tenth year"), the reservoir model functions like a kuhnian paradigm insofar as being robust despite conflicting data. Rather than spending valuable resources keeping the reservoir model up to date with the latest data, the performativity is strikingly pragmatic: you happily sacrifice perfection and completion of the representation for something good enough for the purpose at hand. The representations are expected to answer the pragmatic question par excellence, what to do next? Are the predicted volumes big enough to justify the cost of a new well? Should they drill or not?

Relying on representations presuppose *trustworthy* representations. Why should anyone trust representations positively known to neither accurate nor complete? Trustworthiness, as pointed out by scholars [28, 29], is not an attribute of the data but an acquired quality (a performed achievement, if you want). The underlying performances in NorthOil's subsurface community include: *triangulating* between different representations and data sources (e.g. during history matching when the reservoir model is calibrated with real-time production data), maintaining multiple *versions* (including historicised ones) of the data (e.g. when some engineers make and rely on a stock of private and local data and analysis) and, arguably the ultimate safety net, numerous formal and informal arenas to collectively discuss, assess and converge on interpretations of the representations (e.g. the weekly meetings between reservoir and production engineers on production optimization or during asset management workshops).

Radical, discontinuous changes in the in the interpretations of representations rely on an ability, systematically harnessed, to zoom in and out of representations i.e. to move from detailed accounts to the larger picture. This ability is manifest on different levels. At an analogous site, one geologist explained why sketches were often more useful than photographs:

> "Photography makes things simpler but might lead to situations where
> you do not see the big picture and significant issues. One has to develop
> clear mental pictures of the structure up front."

The drawings are not mere low-resolution images, but have representational qualities of their own, emphasizing the 'big picture' and 'significant issues'.

6　Conclusion

The proclaimed performativity of sociomateriality is in itself valuable but inadequately specific for compelling theoretical, methodological and practical implications. Our detailing into three strategies is intended as a necessary step towards a more fine-grained grasp of the 'entanglement'.

As in STS, also IS research demonstrates an increased attention to settings saturated by representations. Supplementing what has traditionally been a cornerstone of IS research – workplace oriented studies and the role of technology – more media-oriented studies are emerging. For instance, [30] reports from an ethnography of the practices and presentation of identities of game-playing users of the online game World of Warcraft (WoW) and [31] explore the embodied character of avatars in virtual space. An important motivation for our paper is the relative paucity of work-oriented studies of the performativity of sociomateriality. This underscores Barley and Kunda's [32] point of "bringing work back in". We focus on the strategies of performativity in work-practices saturated by representations. Hence the purpose of our study is to analyse how performativity – in a work setting with cross-pressure from managerial obligations for efficiency, safety issues and professional identity [33] – is shaped.

Practical implications that follow from our work are related to perspectives on safety as known from the notion of high-reliability organisations (HRO). Though not explicitly addressing safety in this paper, our observations of the work of the subsurface professionals display clear HRO characteristics. The reservoir models, so central to everyday practices and operational decisions, are never really taken-for-granted. They are constantly, to use HRO vocabulary, willing and able to suspend simplifying assumptions. Left to themselves, studying the reservoir, workers display a "reluctance to simplify interpretations" and a "preoccupation with failure", important aspects of the "collective mindfulness" making up the cornerstone of HRO [34].

References

1. Orlikowski, W., Scott, S.: Sociomateriality: Challenging the separation of technology, work and organization. Academy of Management Annals 2, 433–474 (2008)
2. Kling, R.: The control of information systems after implementation. Comm. of the ACM 27, 1218–1226 (1986)
3. Orlikowski, W.: A Practice Perspective on Technology-Mediated Network Relations: The Use of Internet-Based Self-Serve Technologies. Information Systems Research 15, 87–106 (2004)
4. Suchman, L.: Plans and situated action. University Press, Cambridge (1987)
5. Gasser, L.: The integration of computing and routine work. ACM Trans. on Information Systems 4, 205–225 (1986)
6. Pentland, B., Feldman, M.: Narrative Networks: Patterns of Technology and Organization. Organization Science 18, 781–795 (2007)
7. National commission. BP Deepwater Horizon oil spill and offshore drilling, Report to the President by the National commission (2011),
   http://www.oilspillcommission.gov/final-report
8. Barley, S.: Technology as an Occasion for Structuring: Evidence from Observations of CT Scanners and the Social Order of Radiology Departments. Administrative Science Quarterly 31, 78–108 (1986)

9. Orlikowski, W., Robey, D.: Information Technology and the Structuring of Organizations. Information Systems Research 2, 143–169 (1991)
10. Scott, S., Wagner, E.: Networks, negotiations, and new times: the implementation of enterprise resource planning into an academic administration. Information and Organization 13, 285–313 (2003)
11. Walsham, G.: Actor-network theory and IS research: current status and future prospects. In: Lee, A.S., Liebenau, J., DeGross, J.I. (eds.) Information Systems and Qualitative Research, pp. 469–483. Champan & Hall (1997)
12. Quattrone, P., Hopper, T.: What is IT?: SAP, accounting, and visibility in a multinational organisation. Information and Organization 16, 212–250 (2006)
13. Hanseth, O., Monteiro, E., Hatling, M.: Developing information infrastructure: The tension between standardization and flexibility. Science, Technology & Human Values 21, 407–426 (1996)
14. Barad, K.: Posthumanist performativity: toward an understanding of how matter comes to matter. Signs 28, 801–832 (2003)
15. Knorr Cetina, K.: Epistemic cultures: How the sciences make knowledge. Harvard University Press (1999)
16. Shapin, S., Schaffer, S.: Leviathan and the air-pump: Hobbes, Boyle and the experimental life. Princeton University Press (1985)
17. Knorr Cetina, K., Preda, A. (eds.): The sociociology of financial markets. Oxford University Press (2005)
18. MacKenzie, D., Millo, Y.: Constructing a market, performing theory: The historical sociology of a financial derivates exchange. American Journal of Sociology 109, 107–145 (2003)
19. Pettigrew, A.: Longitudinal field research on change: theory and practice. Organization Science 1, 267–292 (1990)
20. Eisenhardt, K.: Building Theories from Case Study Research. Academy of Management Review 14, 532–551 (1989)
21. Pollock, N., Williams, R.: Moving Beyond the Single Site Implementation Study: How (and Why) We Should Study the Biography of Packaged Enterprise Solutions. Information Systems Research 23, 1–22 (2011)
22. Van Maanen, J.: Qualitative studies of organizations. Sage publications (1998)
23. Langley, A.: Strategies for theorizing from process data. Academy of Management Review 24, 691–710 (1999)
24. Klein, H., Myers, M.: A Set of Principles for Conducting and Evaluating Interpretive Field Studies in Information Systems. MIS Quarterly 23, 67–93 (1999)
25. Suddaby, R.: What grounded theory is not. Academic of Management Journal 49, 633–643 (2006)
26. Frodeman, R.: Geological reasoning: Geology as an interpretive and historical science. Geological Society of America Bulletin 107, 960–968 (1995)
27. Latour, B.: Pandora's hope. Harvard University Press (1999)
28. Porter, T.: Trust in numbers: the pursuit of objectivity in science and public life. Princeton University Press (1996)
29. Ellingsen, G., Monteiro, E.: Mechanisms for producing working knowledge: enacting, orchesterating and organizing. Information and Organization 13, 203–229 (2003)
30. Nardi, B.: My Life as a Night Elf Priest: An Anthropological Account of World of Warcraft. Univ. of Michigan Press (2010)

31. Schultze, U., Leahy, M.M.: The Avatar-Self Relationship: Enacting Presence in Second Life. In: Proc. ICIS (2009)
32. Barley, S., Kunda, G.: Bringing work back in. Organization Science 12, 76–95 (2001)
33. Perin, C.: Shouldering risks: the culture of control in the nuclear power industry. Princeton University Press (2005)
34. Weick, K., Sutcliffe, K.: Managing the unexpected: assuring high performance in an age of complexity. Jossey Bass (2001)

Co-materialization: Digital Innovation Dynamics in the Offshore Petroleum Industry

Thomas Østerlie

NTNU Social Research,
Trondheim, Norway
thomas.osterlie@samfunn.ntnu.no

Abstract. This paper empirically explores the concept of co-materialization to explain the digital innovation dynamics in offshore petroleum production. The central insight developed is that the very nature of subsurface processes and phenomena that may be monitored and controlled is transformed as offshore petroleum production is digitalized. The paper shows how digital technologies are intrinsic to this transformation as material reality and abstract concepts take on meaning together through digital technologies. The central dynamic driving this transformation is the process wherein digital technologies, physical phenomena, and work processes for monitoring and controlling these phenomena evolve together in continuous interplay.

Keywords: digital innovation, industrial transformation, materiality, performativity.

1 Introduction

Digitalization[1] remained low within offshore petroleum production in the North Sea region well into the 1990s. Once available only by boat or helicopter, offshore installations in these inhospitable waters are today electronically available from the mainland. Massive developments of subsurface data communication cables have increased data transfer speed and capacity between offshore and onshore facilities [2]. Advances in data communication technology during the late 1990s enabled real-time communication between down-hole sensors and topside facilities, sparking a proliferation of remote sensor technologies connected in large sensor networks [3]. These sensor networks stretch across the seabed and deep into individual wells for entire oil fields. By connecting on- and offshore facilities through subsurface cables, these remote sensor networks have become constituent parts of a larger digital infrastructure [1] that the offshore petroleum industry has built up over the past decade or so.

---

[1] This paper draws upon Tilson et al.'s [1] distinction between digitizing, understood as "the process of converting analog signals into a digital form", and digitalization, described as "a socio-technical process of applying digital techniques to broader social and institutional contexts that render digital technologies infrastructural" (p.750).

A. Bhattacherjee and B. Fitzgerald (Eds.): Future of ICT Research, IFIP AICT 389, pp. 108–122, 2012.

Significant re-organizations of petroleum production in the North Sea have taken place during the same period, and personnel previously located at offshore installations have been moved to onshore operations centers [4]. Onshore personnel that used to focus on developing plans and recommendations that were handed over to offshore personnel to implement are today an integral part of daily offshore activities. With the availability of real-time sensor data and new engineering applications for visualizing and manipulating this data, onshore engineers can actively participate in monitoring, diagnosing, and controlling offshore processes. Since this new organization of offshore petroleum production is geographically distributed, communication technologies such as video conferencing, e-mail and instant messaging have become integral to the collaboration between offshore and onshore personnel [5].

The digitalization of offshore petroleum production is creating wakes of digital innovations [6] within the distributed network of petroleum companies, technology vendors, service companies and research institutions [7], and these wakes have spawned both actual and anticipated changes in the organizing logic [8] of the offshore petroleum industry. With a basis in the ongoing digitalization of the offshore petroleum industry, both the actual and anticipated changes have collectively functioned as an organizing vision [9] for the future organization of petroleum production. Heralded under different labels, such as e-Fields, Smart Fields, i-Fields, Digital Energy, and Integrated Operations, the core vision is fully digital oil fields in which mass volumes of sensor data are used for computer-assisted, or even completely automated decision-making.

This dominant view of the ongoing transformation of offshore petroleum production focuses on the innovation outcome, namely that of increased digitalization, though it says little about the dynamics driving the innovation processes related to digitalization. Yet, understanding these processes is important in order to achieve a better understanding of the relationship between digitalization and the ongoing transformations in the offshore petroleum industry. In a first step towards unpacking this relationship, this paper asks: *What are the dynamics driving digital innovation in the offshore petroleum industry?*

Through an analysis of empirical data from studies within the offshore petroleum industry, this paper explores a possible answer to the question. Building and elaborating upon the insight that digital technologies play an integral part in creating the materiality of the physical world [10], this paper contends that the impact of digital innovation in offshore petroleum production lies in a transformation of the fundamental relationship between work and the physical phenomena to be monitored and regulated. The central dynamic driving this transformation is the process wherein digital technologies, physical phenomena, and work processes for monitoring and controlling these phenomena evolve together in continuous interplay. *Co-materialization* is forwarded as a concept describing this process.

Co-materialization is offered as the main contribution of this paper. The paper contributes towards current developments of a performative agenda within IS research [11]. This agenda is a response to continued calls to better account for the constitutive role played by computing technologies in studies of work and organizing [12-14].

Much of the existing work towards a performative agenda has, therefore, been to conceptualize the relationship between technology, work, and organizing through concepts such as sociomateriality [11] and imbrication [15]. This paper contributes towards the performative agenda by showing the necessity of expanding upon the notion of materiality to encompass the materiality of the physical world when studying the role of digital sensor technologies in transformations of work and organizing. This insight should be of general interest to researchers for the continued development of a performative agenda within both IS and IS-related fields.

The remainder of the paper is organized as follows: First, a section outlining a performative approach to studying digital innovation dynamics in offshore petroleum production is presented. The attention is then turned towards the methods and materials that the paper is based on. A case story is presented, before the concept of co-materialization is empirically elaborated based on the case story. The paper concludes by drawing some implications of the concept.

2   Digital Innovation and Materialization

While innovation is a much studied topic within the IS literature over the past decades, Lyytinen and Rose [16] observe that this literature is predominantly concerned with IS adoption and diffusion patterns. With basis in the observed lag between first availability of novel computing technologies and their adoption within organizations, the IS innovation literature has focused on how information systems come to be applied in novel ways to transform organizations' administrative, IS, or core business functions [17]. Focusing predominantly on the social processes related to adoption and diffusion dynamics, the IS innovation literature do not account for the constitutive role played by computing technologies as a driver in IS innovation.

The broader innovation literature has been concerned with what Dosi [18] refers to as the "'prime mover' of inventive activity" (p.148), i.e. innovation dynamic. These theories follow two broad categories: demand-pull and technology-push. Demand-pull theories see the marketplace and the identification of needs as the central dynamic driving technological innovation. These theories have been criticized for treating technology as a black box, failing to account for just how technology contributes to innovation. Technology-push theories, on the other hand, see innovation driven by technological development. Somewhat crudely put, this group of theories typically conceptualizes innovation as a linear process of science-technology-product. While technology development is the prime mover in technology-push theories, these theories tend to ignore the environmental feedback that shapes technologies as they are taken into use, which has been a central concern within the IS literature.

As such, neither the IS innovation literature, with its focus on adoption and diffusion patterns rather than innovation dynamics, nor the broader demand-pull/technology-push theories on innovation dynamics, offer much traction for studying the dynamics driving digital innovation in offshore petroleum production. More recently, Tilson et al. [1] forward content digitizing coupled with functional convergence of computing and media platforms as the driving dynamic in transforming communication and media industries. Digitizing is also central to the transformation of offshore petroleum production. Drawing upon the works of Barad [19-21], Østerlie et al. [10] show how digital sensor technologies used in petroleum production play an integral part in creating the materiality of the physical world when digitizing physical phenomena. As such, digitizing the physical world is significantly different from content digitizing, which Tilson et al. [1] defines as "converting analog signals into a digital form" (p. 750).

Building upon the insight developed by Østerlie et al. [10], this paper further mines Barad's work to further develop a performative approach for analyzing the dynamics driving digital innovation in offshore petroleum production. Specifically, this section will, with some help from Rouse [22], elaborate on Barad's use of the concept of *materialization*. Barad uses materialization to describe the processes through which the world takes on meaning. Central here is that meaning is not inherent in the world, but rather, Barad assumes the position that meaning, which she refers to as "local intelligibility," is performed within phenomena in the world. Three elements in this position are of particular relevance here: the primacy of phenomena, material (re)configurations and discursive-materiality.

First and foremost, phenomena are the basic ontological unit in Barad's work: "phenomena are constitutive of reality" ([21], p. 205). The world exists independent of humans and our understanding of it; however, this does not mean that it is made up of pre-existing entities with more or less clearly delineated boundaries and properties that are to be grasped and represented. On the contrary: Rouse [22] contents that Barad's position is that "the world is articulated by overlapping, intra-acting phenomena, but most of these fail to disclose any pattern of local intelligibility" (p. 149).

If the world is not made up of delineated phenomena with fixed properties, what is it that we can have knowledge of? This is the point where Barad pushes performativity to encompass material reality. Instead of representations that mirror preexisting phenomena, phenomena take on meaning through processes of diffraction. While the world appears as phenomena with more or less clearly delineated boundaries and properties, these are not basic properties of the world. Instead, they are enacted through material (re)configurations in the world. When the world does disclose patterns of local intelligibility, i.e. when the world takes on meaning, it does so through particular material (re)configurations. Throughout her works, Barad uses various experimental scientific setups as pedagogic examples to illustrate such material (re)configurations:

> [C]onsider an experiment in which light is scattered from a particle. The scattered light may be directed towards a photographic plate rigidly fixed in the laboratory and therefore used to record the position, or the light may be directed towards a piece of equipment with movable parts used to record the momentum of the scattered light. The first case essentially describes the process of taking a picture of the particle with a flash camera. In that case, the light is part of the measuring apparatus. In the latter case, the light's momentum is being measured and hence it is part of the object in question. ([19], p. 171)

In this example, position is not a property of light as a preexisting entity with properties, but rather is enacted through the scientific instrument setup. Yet, the boundary between light as a phenomenon with properties such as position or momentum to be measured, and the instrumental setup, is not fixed either. When measuring momentum, light is part of the instrumental setup, and to this end, Barad argues that scientific instruments are not external to the reality being grasped, but are always part of the material (re)configuration that makes reality intelligible. But, if "the belief in the power of words to mirror preexisting phenomena" ([20], p. 802) is misguided because phenomena are enacted through material (re)configurations, what then is the function of concepts such as position and momentum?

This leads to the third element of Barad's concept of materialization: discursive-materiality. Instead of refuting the dualism between discursivity (in this example understood as abstract concepts such as position and momentum) and materiality, Barad posits that phenomena are discursive-material. In so doing, Rouse [22] observes that Barad includes concepts as part of the material (re)configuration that makes reality intelligible: "the natural world only acquires definite boundaries and concepts only acquire definite content, together" (p. 146). Barad offers an interpretation of Bohr's quantum physics philosophy to illustrate this point. For Bohr, position is not a property of a particle, nor is it an abstract concept. Instead, the concept of position only has meaning through an experimental setup or a material (re)configuration in Barad's vocabulary, with fixed rulers and a particle.

To summarize, with a basis in an ontology of phenomena, reality takes on meaning through discursive-material (re)configurations in the world, a process Barad refers to as materialization. Nyberg [23] juxtaposes Barad's work with actor network theory [24]. He observes that whereas ANT seeks to explain how phenomena become stable, Barad retains the poststructuralist sensitivity towards reality as becoming rather than being. As such, her work emphasizes the fluidity and constant unfolding character of phenomena.

A central premise for studying digital innovation in offshore petroleum production is that the physical phenomena that petroleum professionals monitor and control are physically inaccessible to human inspection. It is therefore meaningless to distinguish between material reality, understood as the stuff the world is made up of [25], and the digital technologies for knowing about it. Thus, the attraction of materialization for studying digital innovation in offshore petroleum production lies in Barad's formulation of a performative ontology that creates no such separation between phenomena and the physical arrangements for knowing about them.

3   Methods and Materials

This paper draws upon data collected through two consecutive studies within the Norwegian petroleum industry. The first of these studies did not focus on digital innovation, but rather on ICT use for safe and reliable petroleum production. This study was conducted as an independent part of a larger joint industry research and development project (JIP) within the Norwegian petroleum industry [26]. The JIP is a form of generic project organization used within the petroleum industry to facilitate cooperation between petroleum companies, the vendor industry and research institutions to build competency and develop technologies regarded as particularly critical to the industry as a whole. The particular JIP reported from here gathered participants with long and extensive experience from the ongoing digitalization of the North Sea in order to study the feasibility of expanding petroleum production into the polar region. I participated in workshops and meetings organized regularly within the JIP. Seeing the JIP as a rich site for learning more about the ongoing digitalization of offshore petroleum production, I approached project workshops and meetings as fieldwork using breaks and after hour activities to learn more about other project participants' experiences from the ongoing digitalization of offshore petroleum production.

In parallel with attending project activities, I conducted 10 months of ethnographic fieldwork [27] in the onshore operations center of an international petroleum company operating in the Norwegian sector of the North Sea. This operations center houses the onshore personnel of several offshore petroleum fields. Onshore and offshore personnel work closely with each other, communicating through different media such as instant messaging, e-mail, phone, and video conferencing. At the time of conducting the fieldwork, the petroleum company was in the final stages of implementing a new engineering application for the real-time monitoring of wells for use in the onshore operations center. I had, therefore, collected quite a lot of data on the relationship between digitalization and work transformation when asked to do the second study this paper builds upon. I had even developed the outlines of a model on digital innovation dynamics as part of the analysis for the first study.

Digital innovation in offshore petroleum production was the topic of the second study. Financed as an independent study, I was asked by the same petroleum company where I had previously conducted ethnographic fieldwork to come up with policy advice to improve the organization's ability to implement research-based software in their operational units. Deciding to base this study on the model of digital innovation dynamics I had previously outlined, I conducted a total of 24 interviews with people who had been involved in developing new digital technologies used within the petroleum company: 13 researchers and 4 software engineers working in the corporation's R&D division, 3 engineers from different operational units who had been the customer for new digital technologies, 1 engineer working in the corporation's central IT division, as well as 3 software engineers working in vendor companies who develop new digital technologies put to use within the petroleum company under study. The interviews focused on the respondents' experiences from research-based software development projects. Instead of focusing on single projects, I inquired about general experience. Nevertheless, throughout the period of the interviews, I acquired insight into a number of specific projects and digital technologies.

This paper, therefore, draws upon a diversity of materials. I made daily field notes [28] throughout the ethnographic fieldwork in the onshore operations center. Jotting down notes in a pad throughout the day, I would transcribe the field notes during periods of calm or latest the same day upon returning from the fieldwork. Similarly, I made field notes during JIP project workshops and meetings, which I transcribed later the same day. Conducting the first study as a grounded theory study [29], I coded the field notes shortly after writing them up, writing theoretical memos to record conceptual insights emerging during coding. In addition to the field notes taken during the first study, the theoretical memos related to innovation were used as materials for the analysis presented in this paper. From the second study I have transcribed each of the interviews conducted. I also conducted a document search of OnePetro (http://www.onepetro.org) to collect supplemental data on the projects and technologies mentioned during the interviews. OnePetro archives all papers published through the Society of Petroleum Engineers' conferences and journals, making it a key source for reports on the experience and development of new technologies from the global petroleum industry.

The concept of co-materialization emerged from the analysis a large number of projects and technologies developed over the past 20 years. For the ease of presentation, I choose to empirically ground the elaboration of co-materialization in a single case story. This particular case has been chosen because it intensely manifests central properties and dimensions of co-materialization.

4   Case Story: Predictive Maintenance of Topside Chokes

Petroleum is produced from hydrocarbon molecules contained within fluids trapped in subsurface reservoirs. On the Norwegian Continental Shelf (NCS), a subsea plateau that forms the Norwegian sector of the North Sea, these reservoirs are located thousands of meters beneath the seabed. Wells have been drilled to drain the fluids containing hydrocarbon molecules out of the reservoirs. Reservoir pressure pushes the fluids, referred to by petroleum professionals as the well flow, out through the wells and through kilometers of pipelines leading topside towards an offshore production platform. Onboard the platform, a petrochemical processing plant separates crude oil and gas from the hydrocarbon molecules contained within the well flow. The gas is exported by pipeline to onshore refineries, while supertankers feed refineries across the globe with crude oil from the NCS.

This section outlines the major steps towards one of the more recent innovations in offshore petroleum production: predictive maintenance of offshore chokes. It starts with an outline of sand influx, the basic problem addressed by predictive maintenance. It then outlines the major developments towards predictive maintenance of offshore chokes. The purpose is to outline the case story that forms the backdrop for the discussion of co-materialization as a concept describing and explaining key dynamics driving digital innovation in offshore petroleum production.

4.1   Sand Influx and Sand Control

NCS reservoirs are typically found within geological sand stone layers. The porous sand stone structures function as sponges, trapping fluids containing hydrocarbon molecules. Over time, as increasing amounts of fluids are drained out of a reservoir, changes in the fluid balance may cause these sand stone structures to loose integrity. As the sand stone looses integrity, large areas of the reservoir start crumbling and may even collapse. Sand particles from the crumbling reservoir is then swept along with the fluids that are drained out of the reservoir, into wells and through the pipelines towards the topside platform.

Sand swept along with the well flow end up as sand deposits in the petrochemical processing equipment on the topside platform. Sand deposits stand the danger of contaminating the crude oil and thereby degrading its quality. In addition, sand clogs up the processing equipment. Parts of the processing plant have to be taken offline to clean the processing equipment of sand deposits. This reduces the plant's processing capacity for the duration of the cleanup procedure. More critically, though, sand particles create a sand blasting effect on chokes (the valves used to control fluid flow rates within the piping) and in pipeline bends as they are swept along with the fluids streaming at high speeds through the piping. Sand can, in extreme cases, erode through piping and choke casing and thereby puncturing the equipment. A punctured pipeline subsea may cause immense environmental damage as oil gushes into the ocean. On the topside platform, a punctured pipe or choke casing will send high-speed fluids jetting onto the deck. This is a significant safety risk as the high-speed fluids may cause human injury or even death. The well flow also contains gas. Punctured equipment topside will, therefore, also cause a gas leak. Leaking gas is considered among the most dangerous situations on a petroleum installation as it may ignite and explode.

Sand problems are not particular to the NCS. Referred to as sand influx, sand-related problems are reported in the American petroleum literature as early as the late 1940s. Sand influx as a concept describes the physical processes in the subsurface reservoir that cause sand to be swept into the well. To this end, well screening technologies for preventing sand from entering wells have been developed. It comes with a set of technologies and work practices aimed at preventing sand from entering wells. These technologies and work practices are collectively referred to as sand control. Sand control routines builds on the premise that wells can only produce at rates where there is no sand influx. As such, these routines focus on establishing the maximum fluid flow rate where sand is not swept from the reservoir into the well. While this may significantly reduce the production rates of a single well, this is usually not a significant problem as long as only a few wells produce with such restrictions.

4.2   Sand Content and Sand Monitoring

Sand deposits started appearing in the topside petrochemical processing equipment of offshore platforms on the NCS in the late 1980s early 1990s. By then, the fluid balance within reservoirs on fields developed in the early 1970s and 80s was causing sand stone formations to collapse. Production restrictions related to producing at maximum sand free rate on a single well has limited impact on a field's overall production volumes. However, when a large number of wells experience sand influx it significantly reduces the field's overall production capacity. This was the situation, or at least the prospective situation, for an increasing number of fields on the NCS at the beginning of the 1990s.

Sand monitoring emerges in the mid 1990s as a response to this problem. Sand monitoring builds on the premise that limited amounts of sand in the well flow constitutes no significant risk to safety or operations. Instead of establishing the maximum sand free rate on a well, sand monitoring seeks to ensure that wells produce within what is called maximum safe sand rate. However, producing with maximum safe sand rate requires real-time monitoring of the amount of sand in the well flow.

Sand monitoring as an alternative strategy for dealing with the effects of sand is proposed in a period where early digital sensor technologies are being put in use on offshore platforms. In parallel with developing safe operational constraints for producing with sand in the well flow, different digital sensor technologies for quantifying sand content were being experimentally developed. Several vendors sought to offer this technology, but in the end acoustic sand sensors are chosen. Acoustic sand sensors detect the ultrasonic sounds of sand particles hitting the inside piping in bends. Based on an algorithm that combines well flow velocity with the frequency of ultrasonic sound signals, the sand sensor quantifies the number of sand grains passing across it per second.

Sand monitoring requires significant changes in the operating conditions for the platform. Producing with sand in the well flow increases wear and tear on pipes and chokes. Sand monitoring is therefore coupled with more frequent and extensive inspections and maintenance of pipes and chokes. Sand monitoring required pipe and choke vendors to develop new inspection and maintenance frequencies, and changes in the maintenance regimes of the subcontractors in charge of plant maintenance.

4.3   Erosion Potential and Predictive Choke Maintenance

Chokes are used to control fluid rates within the pipelines. The valve opening and thereby accuracy degrades as the choke wears out. This gives offshore operators less control over fluid rates, making it increasingly difficult to regulate the production process in such a way that it optimizes the plant's processing capacity. Chokes on fields with the sand monitoring therefore tended to be replaced well before they were worn out. This is expensive and causes unnecessary downtime.

By the turn of the millennium petroleum companies operating on the NCS had started building up onshore operations centers.   Data communication capacity between on- and offshore installations was steadily increasing, and operators were exploring the possibilities of involving onshore personnel more closely with daily offshore activities. A key task for the onshore personnel was to optimize daily production. Production optimization seeks to prioritize between wells in such a way that the offshore petrochemical plant's processing capacity is used most efficiently within the restrictions incurred through the gas and crude oil export capacity.

As part of these efforts, one operator along with a software vendor and an engineering company joined forces to develop predictive choke maintenance to give onshore engineers better control with the accuracy of the offshore chokes used to optimize production. This was developed for a field already running with sand monitoring strategy. To this end, the engineering company developed a set of models describing and prescribing the degree of wear and tear on individual wells over time depending on the amount of sand having passed through the choke. This, they called erosion potential. The software vendor developed a tool that used these models together with sand sensor and other data sources to predict the current state of offshore chokes.

While the basic models for erosion potential remained unchanged, the software tool underwent a number of revisions. The greatest challenge was related to poor data quality of the input data. A number of visualizations and work processes were developed to allow onshore engineers to determine accuracy of the choke erosion models.

5   Discussion: Digital Innovation and Co-materialization

With basis in the case story above, I will now explore a possible answer to the question 'what are the dynamics driving digital innovation in offshore petroleum production?'. The difference between innovation, on the one hand, and technology adoption and organizational change in general, on the other, is that some form of novelty accompanies innovation [16]. To answer the research question, we, therefore, first have to establish what constitutes novelty in the case story. Having established this, we can then turn our attention to the dynamics driving digital innovation in offshore petroleum production.

With the organizing vision of fully digital oil fields in which mass volumes of sensor data are used for computer-assisted, or even completely automated decision-making, most of the petroleum industry literature forwards novel digital technologies as 'prime-mover' [18] of the ongoing transformation of offshore petroleum production. In the case story above, however, neither the acoustic sand sensor that measures sand in the well flow nor the software developed to monitor erosion on individual offshore chokes is based on novel digital technologies. The acoustic sand sensor is based on a technology for detecting ultrasonic sounds. While never previously used to measure sand content in fluids, the technology itself was, at the time, by no means a novel technology. Rather, it had been developed for other uses and used for a number of applications prior to developing digital sensors for detecting and quantifying sand. Similarly, the software developed to predict choke erosion was crafted around a series of familiar visualization techniques such as plotting data in graphs for comparison between data sources and breaking down the physical infrastructure in a tree hierarchy to ease navigation.

Instead, novelty in the case story lies in a transformation of the very nature of subsurface processes and phenomena that may be monitored and controlled. The case story above traces two such transformations: the transformation of sand and of erosion from approximated to quantified phenomena. We can use the transformation of sand from an approximated, delayed action phenomenon to sand as a real-time, quantifiable characteristic of the well flow to exemplify this. Prior to the introduction of digital sand sensors, sand in the well flow materialized as accumulated deposits in the processing equipment. It would take hours from measures to limit sand influx had been taken before sufficient deposits had accumulated in the processing equipment so that offshore personnel could determine the effect of their actions; sand was a delayed action phenomenon. Offshore personnel would, furthermore, refer to sand deposits in approximate and relative terms such as significant or small amounts of sand observable when cleaning up the processing equipment.

Digital technologies are intrinsic to transforming sand from an approximated, delayed-action phenomenon to a real-time, quantified characteristic of the well flow. Physical phenomena materialize through complex discursive-material performances that involve undifferentiated matter, physical artifacts and digital technologies. Sand content emerges through the material setup of an acoustic sand sensor, along with a pipeline bend, and the undifferentiated matter of the well flow rushing from the well towards the topside platform. The acoustic sand sensor is mounted on the outside of this bend. The well flow creates a sound as it hits the outer bend of the piping, where the sand sensor is mounted, at high speeds. The acoustic sand sensor is designed to isolate the sound of solid particles hitting the piping, and transforms this sound into a digital signal. Through laboratory experiments, the sensor vendor had developed an algorithm that combines well flow velocity with frequency of ultrasonic sound signals to calculate sand content, measured as grains of sand passing across the sand sensor per second. The acoustic sand sensor's controller software implements this algorithm to transform the digital signals generated by the acoustic sand sensor into a measurement of sand content. Sampling the digital signals each second, the material setup of acoustic sand sensor, controller software, piping, and well flow performs sand as a real-time, quantified characteristic of the well flow.

In this analysis, sand content as a quantifiable characteristic of the well flow is not a property of the physical world simply waiting to be represented. Instead, it is performed through the material setup where digital technologies – both acoustic sand sensor hardware and controller software – play a constitutive role in creating the materiality of the physical world [10]. As such, sand content is not merely an abstract concept (i.e. discursive). Rather, material reality and abstract concepts take on meaning together through digital technologies; they co-materialize.

This is not to be interpreted as a form of radical constructivism claiming that sand in the well flow as a figment of social construction. Such a position would reduce physical phenomena to being purely discursive. The argument pursued is, on the contrary, a refutation of reducing physical reality to constructs and representations, and instead to offer a realist analysis of how the world takes on meaning through the use of digital technologies. There were undeniably solid particles in the well flow before introducing the acoustic sand sensor, with accumulated sand in the processing equipment being a testament to this. Yet, it is through the discursive-material reconfigurations outlined above that sand content, as a quantitative characteristic of the well flow, comes to be performed as a pattern of local intelligibility, to use Barad's terminology.

Having established what constitutes novelty in the case story, we can turn our attention towards the dynamic driving digital innovation in offshore petroleum production. Sand had been a well-known operational problem within the global petroleum industry for almost half a century when platforms on the NCS started experiencing sand influx in the late 1980s. While measures for handling sand in the well flow along with research on reservoir geology to better understand the causes of sand influx had been in continuous development since the 1970s, it is with the advent of digital technologies in the 1990s that sand content emerges as a real-time, quantified characteristic of the well flow. This does not mean that some sort of technological imperative drives the emergence of sand content. An engineer working with a vendor company offering a sand sensor technology competing with the acoustic sand sensor in the case story, explained that their sand sensors built on a technology that the vendor had developed for significantly different purposes. They had never thought of using the technology to detect and quantify sand. Yet, when petroleum companies operating on the NCS started developing sand content as a concept, the vendor saw the possibility of adopting their technology to implement the sand content concept.

As such, digital technologies emerge as part of an evolving understanding of how to regulate subsurface processes and phenomena. Subsurface processes play an important role in shaping this understanding. Digital sensor technologies for quantifying sand in the well flow emerges at a point in time when a growing number of oil fields on the NCS were beginning to experience significant reduction in production capacity due to sand influx. Petroleum companies came to identify sand control as a significant production limitation to be addressed. Sand monitoring, as a concept emerges from the convergence of aging oil fields on the NCS and the technological possibilities of technological developments at the time. The senior research engineer commonly attributed as the key originator of the sand monitoring concept participated in the industry R&D project that this paper draws from. He described the sand monitoring strategy as an egg of Columbus: once formulated, everybody was wondering why nobody had come up with the idea before. Clearly proud to be attributed as the originator of sand monitoring, he carefully pointed out that formulating the concept was "a matter of timing". The timing was right in that increasing computerization of offshore installations opened up for the possibility of instrumenting the production process with digital sensors, which made the production restrictions caused by sand control to be a solvable problem.

The evolving understanding of how to regulate subsurface processes and phenomena emerges from recognized needs and relevant technologies for responding to these needs. Sand content co-materializes with technologies for measuring sand content and sand monitoring in a space of possibilities where changes in fluid distribution in maturing reservoirs lead to increased sand influx in wells, where existing sand control strategies significantly reduce production volumes on fields with much sand influx, and where measuring sand content is technologically feasible. It is, therefore, possible to say that recognized needs and relevant technologies for responding to these needs co-materializes out of the same space of possibilities.

6   Conclusion

This paper has empirically explored the concept of co-materialization to explain the digital innovation dynamics in offshore petroleum production. The central insight developed is that the very nature of subsurface processes and phenomena that may be monitored and controlled has been transformed as part of digitalizing offshore petroleum production. The paper has shown how digital technologies are intrinsic to this transformation through a process where material reality and abstract concepts take on meaning through digital technologies. The central dynamic driving this transformation is the process wherein digital technologies, physical phenomena, and work processes for monitoring and controlling these phenomena evolve together in continuous interplay.

As such, this paper offers an interpretation of the ongoing digitalization focusing on change processes. This supplements the focus on innovation outcome predominant in the organizing vision of fully digital oil fields (see Section 1). While this organizing vision has been central to securing top-level commitment to the massive investments required for developing the digital infrastructure and making the organizational changes required to transform offshore petroleum production. Now that the infrastructure is more or less in place, the industry is entering a new phase: that of capitalizing on the digitalization. Co-materialization offers a perspective that may contribute towards this second phase. By emphasizing the creation of new phenomena forms the thrust of digital innovation, co-materialization suggests that focus for this second phased of digitalization should lie on finding new ways of using existing data sources to create phenomena that may be regulated in order to improve and optimize production.

Through the concept of co-materialization, this paper suggests that digital innovation not only changes the nature of work but the very phenomena to be regulated through technology and work. Common to both sand monitoring (Section 4.2) and predictive maintenance (Section 4.3) is that they constitute a fundamental shift in the industry's relationship to the materiality of offshore petroleum production. Both sand monitoring and condition monitoring constitute a shift away from static towards a more dynamic relationship with the materiality to be monitored and controlled. Such a shift is a common denominator to digital innovation in offshore petroleum production. This may suggest that the ongoing digitalization of offshore petroleum production constitutes a shift towards an increasingly dynamic relationship that transforms the offshore petroleum industry as it redistributes competency within petroleum companies, as well as between petroleum companies and other actors within the offshore petroleum industry on the one hand, while transforming the nature of work, technology and organizing within the offshore petroleum industry on the other. This, however, will have to be explored further in later publications.

References

1. Tilson, D., Lyytinen, K., Sørensen, C.: Digital Infrastructure: The Missing IS Research Agenda. Information Systems Research 21, 748–759 (2010)
2. Henderson, J., Hepsø, V., Mydland, Ø.: What is a capability platform approach to Integrated Operations? An introduction to key concepts. In: Rosendahl, T., Hepsø, V. (eds.) Integrated Operations in the Oil and Gas Industry: Sustainability and Capability Development, pp. 1–19. IGI Global, Hershey (2012)

3. Watson, R.T., Boudreau, M.-C., Chen, A.J.: Information Systems and Environmentally Sustainable Development: Energy Informatics and New Directions for the IS Community. MIS Quarterly 34, 23–38 (2010)
4. Gulbrandsøy, K., Hepsø, V., Skavhaug, A.: Virtual collaboration in oil and gas organizations. ACM SIGGROUP Bulletin 23, 42–47 (2002)
5. Bayerl, P.S., Lauche, K.: Technology Effects in Distributed Team Coordination: High-Interdependency Tasks in Offshore Oil Production. Computer Supported Cooperative Work (CSCW) 19, 139–173 (2010)
6. Boland, R.J., Lyytinen, K., Yoo, Y.: Wakes of Innovation in Project Networks: The Case of Digital 3-D Representations in Architecture, Engineering, and Construction. Organization Science 18, 631–647 (2007)
7. Acha, V., Cusmano, L.: Governance and Co-ordination of Distributed Innovation Processes: Patterns of R&D Co-operation in the Upstream Petroleum Industry. Economics of Innovation and New Technology 14, 1–21 (2005)
8. Sambamurthy, V., Zmud, R.W.: Research Commentary: The Organizing Logic for an Enterprise's IT Activities in the Digital Era–A Prognosis of Practice and a Call for Research. Information Systems Research 11, 105–114 (2000)
9. Swanson, E.B., Ramiller, N.C.: The Organizing Vision in Information Systems Innovation. Organization Science 8, 458–474 (1997)
10. Østerlie, T., Almklov, P., Hepsø, V.: Dual Materiality and Knowing in Petroleum Production. Information and Organization 22, 85–105 (2012)
11. Orlikowski, W.J., Scott, S.V.: Sociomateriality: Challenging the separation of technology, work, and organization. Academy of Management Annals 2, 433–474 (2008)
12. Leonardi, P.M., Barley, S.R.: Materiality and change: Challenges to building better theory about technology and organizing. Information and Organization 18, 159–176 (2008)
13. Monteiro, E., Hanseth, O.: Social Shaping of Information Infrastructure: On Being Specific about the Technology. In: Orlikowski, W.J., Walsham, G., Jones, M., DeGross, J.I. (eds.) Information Technology and Changes in Organizational Work, pp. 325–343. Chapman & Hall, London (1996)
14. Orlikowski, W.J., Iacono, C.S.: Research Commentary: Desperately Seeking the 'IT' in IT Research-A Call to Theorizing the IT Artifact. Information Systems Research 12, 121–134 (2001)
15. Leonardi, P.M.: When Flexible Routines Meet Flexible Technlogies: Affordance, Constraint, and the Imbrication of Human and Material Agencies. MIS Quarterly 35, 147–167 (2011)
16. Lyytinen, K., Rose, G.M.: Disruptive information systems innovation: the case of internet computing. Information Systems Journal 13, 301–330 (2003)
17. Swanson, E.B.: Information Systems Innovation among Organizations. Management Science 40, 1069–1092 (1994)
18. Dosi, G.: Technological paradigms and technological trajectories: A suggested interpretation of the determinants and directions of technical change. Research Policy 11, 147–162 (1982)
19. Barad, K.: Getting real: Technoscientific practices and the materiality of reality. Differences 10, 87–128 (1996)
20. Barad, K.: Posthumanist Performativity: Toward and Understanding of How Matter Comes to Matter. Signs 28, 801–831 (2003)
21. Barad, K.: Meeting the universe halfway: Quantum physics and the entanglement of matter and meaning. Duke University Press, Durham (2007)
22. Rouse, J.: Barad's Feminist Naturalism. Hypatia 19, 142–161 (2004)

23. Nyberg, D.: Computers, Customer Service Operatives and Cyborgs: Intra-actions in Call Centres. Organization Studies 30, 1181–1199 (2009)
24. Law, J., Singleton, V.: Object Lessons. Organization 12, 331–355 (2005)
25. Iedema, R.: On the Multi-modality, Materiality and Contingency of Organizational Discourse. Organization Studies 28, 931–946 (2007)
26. Verhelst, F., Myren, F., Rydlandsholm, P., Svenson, I., Waaler, A., Skramstad, T., Ornæs, J.I., Tvedt, B.H., Høydal, H.: Digital Platform for the Next Generation IO: A Prerequisite for the High North. In: SPE Intelligent Energy Conference and Exhibition, pp. 1–11. Society of Petroleum Engineers (2010)
27. Fetterman, D.M.: Ethnography: Step by Step. SAGE Publications, Thousand Oaks (1998)
28. Emerson, R.M., Fretz, R.I., Shaw, L.L.: Writing Ethnographic Fieldnotes. The University of Chicago Press, Chicago (1995)
29. Charmaz, K.: Constructing Grounded Theory: A Practical Guide Through Qualitative Analysis. SAGE Publications, Thousand Oaks (2006)

Mutability and *Becoming*: Materializ*ing* of Public Sector Adoption of Open Source Software

Maha Shaikh

Warwick Business School, University of Warwick, Coventry CV4 7AL, UK
Maha.shaikh@wbs.ac.uk

Abstract. Juxtaposing two local council cases of open source software adoption in the UK we highlight their differences and similarities in open source adoption and implementation. Our narratives indicate that for both cases there was strong goodwill towards open source yet the trajectories of implementation differed widely. We draw on Deleuze and Guattari's ideas of becoming, tracing versus mapping and multiplicity to explain how *becoming* occurs at different speeds. Our data shows that the *becoming* of adoption can be both constrained and precipitated by various forms of materiality (of the assemblage of the open source ecosystem). The interesting point of departure of our study is how open source software – a much touted transparent and open phenomenon – is by its nuanced and layered mutability able to make the process and practices surrounding it *less visible*.

Keywords: open source, public sector procurement, becoming, mutability, materiality.

1 Introduction

Why is it that when two different local councils adopt open source software that one proves to become more adept at it, while the other finds itself implicated in different machinations? This paper approaches this question with a focus on the *becoming* (performative understanding [1, 2]) of the primary adoption process. Our contribution lies in unpacking the adoption and procurement of open source software (OSS) by two different local councils in the UK sensitized by ideas of becoming, mutability and materiality. We recognize and show how the becoming (complicated, uncertain, never stable or complete) of OSS adoption indicates that the process of *becoming* occurs at different speeds [3]. The speed of becoming is managed and controlled and can be purposively directed. Our cases show how management in the local councils reined in (or otherwise) the process of becoming via material instantiations of OS. The nature of materiality was manipulated in both cases to different ends, and results.

We draw on Deleuze and Guattari's [4] ideas of becoming, tracing versus mapping and multiplicity alongside the shared ontology of Actor Network Theory (with [4] – ie a relational ontology where information technology and users are not defined outside their relationship but *in* their relational networks [5]. This consideration moves the focus of the analysis from the actor, either human or non-human, towards a more

A. Bhattacherjee and B. Fitzgerald (Eds.): Future of ICT Research, IFIP AICT 389, pp. 123–140, 2012.

complex and less defined phenomenon, which is the interaction [6-8]. It has a "relational materiality" [9]. This reflects an aversion to accept *a priori* the pre-existence of social structures and differences as somehow intrinsically given in the order of things, or what Barad terms "agential realism" [10, p810]. This ontological predisposition sensitizes us to the idea that more than one reality is possible. Indeed successful software adoption is never a certainty but drawing on ideas of becoming takes our analysis further by laying bare both successful and unsuccessful possibilities that are attempted, but perhaps never quite become. The relevance of such an approach lies in its ability to unpack various criteria, actors, relations and material considerations that a simple adoption study would do little justice to as 'performativity leaves open the possibility of events that might refute, or even happen independently of, what humans believe or think' [11, p323].

These ideas and our theoretical underpinnings are explained further in section 3. Section 2 provides background literature to this study and contextualizes our work, and section 4 and 5 explain the methodology and two cases respectively. Section 6 is the analysis and discussion and the paper concludes with section 7.

2   Open Source Adoption and Procurement in the Public Sector

Adoption of software and IT often does not follow a well-laid out plan and every context is different. Context, as argued by Robey and Sahay [12] plays a very important role as technologies are adopted and used in situ and need to be studied as such. A certain amount of drift is usual [13] and perhaps even necessary as this *performs* acceptance at the individual and collective level. Other IT adoption studies usually focus on workarounds as a manner of performative adoption [14-17]. However, such work has always kept users as central. This paper is not an adoption study in the conventional sense of user adoption. The aim of this paper is to understand higher level procurement decisions where decisions are made by strategists, top IT managers and policy writers so users, unlike for Boudreau and Robey [18], are not the real focus for us. Instead, we look to literature on procurement of open source and primary adoption of open source software (by IT staff and developers, and not secondary adoption by users [19]).

Open source software implies openness of the source code thus making it possible to change, and improve the code. In effect open source encompasses certain freedoms[1] that are embedded in the license of the code[2]. Procurement [20] and acquisition decisions by many governments are currently under question, and greater scrutiny has led to governments in the European Union, UK, Australia [21] and the USA [22] to amend their habits. Research to date in the area of open source use and adoption in the public sector, though growing, is still quite patchy. A UK based study [23] focused on eight different local councils and agencies. This work outlined a number of concerns and key areas that need improving in the public sector before successful adoption can emerge. This was however, a high level study where details

---

[1] http://www.opensource.org/docs/osd
[2] http://www.opensource.org/licenses/index.html

of each case the various struggles were not the focus. Likewise in the US, studies have shown open source use adoption needs top level support and encouragement for success [24]. Brazil is a very interesting case where the success of open source adoption has been explained and emphasized as a product of insurgent experts [25].

The European Commission has an explicit directive to promote software alternatives [26], especially open source software. And very recently, the British Government's Cabinet Office [27-29][3] met with the large and influential system integrators to declare a greater need to have open source choice offered to the government. The argument put forward by the Cabinet Office was that the government was unable to choose open source as an alternative if this was not offered as an option by the integrators. Open source software, along with open data and open standards is fast becoming part of the language that governments all over the world are eager to adopt [30]. It is, for example, one of the basic building blocks of the US government in relation to its encouragement of its open government initiative [31].

Open source software is part of the easing of recession and costs of IT in the public sector in the UK. However, as the UK government is aware, open source software is still a rather unknown phenomenon. The true and complete costs involved with switching to another software, be it open source or not, are not easy to evaluate [32]. Open source software further complicates matters with close to zero license costs, but this does not necessarily translate to lower costs in other aspects [33].

Private companies [34] tend to adopt open source software for a mix of reasons which clearly include the promise of reduced costs of adoption, but there is often a strategic aspect, as well as a strong desire to innovate [35, 36]. The public sector would like to enjoy these benefits as well but till very recently the desire to innovate was not foremost for most governmental agencies. Public sector organizations are not profit orientated yet there is much to learn from private companies and their manner of dealing with open source. The larger idea here is the level of experience and comfort that private companies bring to open source adoption which is sorely lacking in the public sector. There are some exemplary cases of open source adoption by the public sector like the Extremadura case in Spain [37, 38] but there are far more 'success' stories of open source adoption by commercial companies [39-42]. What we found missing in the literature was attention to the role played by politics within and external to public sector organizations attempting to adopt OSS.

Our research was thus motivated by a desire to make sense of OS adoption while deliberating on politics and other heretofore ignored actors. More specifically we were driven by a need to understand how open source software adoption was being managed by public sector organizations and why, when the circumstances and reasons

---

[3] http://webarchive.nationalarchives.gov.uk/+/
http://www.cabinetoffice.gov.uk/resource-library/
procurement-policy-note-ppn-use-open-standards-when-specifying-
ict-requirements

for adopting open source for both councils were so similar the results were so very different. Thus, our main research question is: *How can, and is the becoming of open source software adoption managed and controlled?*

3   Ontological Positioning

Becoming is not a specific state but rather a focus on movement from the then to now, not a move from one state to another. It reflects a passing of time and a process, 'becoming thus sees the idea of an organization's existence not as an ontologically stable, but rather as something that exists only in its duration' [43]. It is in this becoming that organizing materializes with a focus 'on movement rather than that which is moved' [43, p159]. The previous tradition of studies of change have been criticized for focusing on stability in order to understand change [15, 16, 44]. This suggests the need to reverse 'ontological priorities' [2] and for keener perceptions of the ongoing nature of change or 'changing' [45]. This reversal is helpful not least if it allows a better understanding of the micro-processes of change, treats change as dynamic and unfolding rather than as a fait accompli, and makes it ontologically possible to 'see' change by directly looking for changing, rather than as a byproduct of some comparative stabilities [2]. Thus in developing the concept of becoming Clegg et al. [43] emphasize the focus on movement, not on what has moved or where it arrives (at best mere snap shots, moments in time); becoming is about travel and mutation rather than what has mutated. Stability is then at best fleeting but more likely to be illusionary; change is reality.

Drawing on various interpretations of organizational change [15, 16, 45] Tsoukas and Chia [2] argue that improvisation within a context is somewhat narrow in recognizing the prevalence of change, changing routines focus solely on human agents and agency, and any and all collectives and organizations never quite become, and indeed are in a constant form of changing (becoming). And becoming is performative [2, 15] where performative [46, 47] implies that something becomes into existence and has effect and materiality through action and performance – action through words, movement or some more abstract change is needed.

Becoming implies an ontological understanding where the world (reality) has a middle but there is no beginning or end. Reality is not seen as hierarchical but rather as a rhizome of multiplicities that can and do fracture, rupture, and entangle. Such an ontological position creates an imposition on the researcher to make a methodological cut into reality where Law [9] has argued that attention to differences and interactions can become that cut. Drawing on this idea we 'map' rather than trace the unfolding performance of OSS in two local councils. The idea of a map builds on the importance of change and seeing the world as constantly new in its emergence. Tracing implies almost a replication of the old that is stifling (and unrealistic?). A map is thus performative, a becoming – we do not know and will find it difficult to predict assemblages or rhizomes (various possible futures). A tracing, on the other hand, is a static understanding of the world.

The desire to understand the status quo does not mean we must have a static view of the world [48]. The trapeze artist walks across the tightrope appearing to be not doing very much and keeping straight, however this keeping upright requires many muscles and nerves are in a constant flux else the artist would fall. In an organizational setting this form of changing occurs all the time but is difficult to perceive. Thus an ontological understanding that becoming brings with it nudges the researcher to focus on ruptures as an epistemological tool to cut into the data and allow the changing to emerge for us.

4   Methodology

We carried out in-depth, semi-structured interviews with core personnel in each organization. We chose two local councils within the UK, Camden and Bristol City. Our choice was dictated by their deep and long interest in open source software where they had experienced rather different results to date.

4.1   Data Collection

We conducted 32 in-depth interviews over the course of late 2010 to early 2012. The personnel interviewed ranged from the open source policy writer, IT and developer team, floor-walking members, users, and strategy level staff, but also those involved in making procurement decisions and strategy of open source use in the organization. Each of our interviews lasted for an hour or more. Our short interview guide covered questions relating to basic information about the length of open source adoption, and the role of the interviewee in the process to more detailed examination of obstacles, opportunities, and challenges involved.The main ideas the respondents focused on included the lack of maturity level of open source software, there is no policy in most councils for open source adoption, license confusions and lack of knowledge about the implications of various open source licenses (see Table 4).

4.2   Data Analysis

The material from the interviews was analyzed [49] systematically (using Atlas.ti software) for the main lessons, decisions, challenges, strengths, advice, best practices, consequences and other interesting elements that emerged from the interviews. Our code book consisted of phrases consistent with ideas of becoming, change, rhizomes and mutability, but we also allowed the data to give rise to new codes.

We focused on open and axial coding of the data. For nearly half of the interviews we open coded very finely by studying phrases. As we progressed through the coding process we noticed that few new codes or ideas were emerging so we began to code *paragraph by paragraph*. Our coding process thus remained rigorous and we stayed faithful to our data and the ideas emerging from it. Table 1 shows some sample data and the manner of coding we employed.

Table 1. Sample of Data and Coding

Open codes	Sections of Data	Axial codes
Code TCO Requirements	There is a procurement template we have had to develop... it will have the magic box of hidden costs. If we invite a number of suppliers, they are all asked the same questions.....there are some essential criteria that must be met.	**Embedding materiality**
Ownership Responsibility Sustaining community	We need laboratories set up to force them to work through such ideas and we are struggling for techniques of how to do that..... need to make it part of people's job description and they are monitored on it ....otherwise I am left buffering between developers and businesses which is a compromise.	**Transparency via materiality**
Conversion issues License differences User resistance	But there were users that were doing somewhat complex things with spreadsheets ... their material would not convert so easily and such users were more difficult to bring around to open source use.	**Recalcitrant materiality**
Certification Documentation Reliability Persuasive standards Interoperability	An issue did arise. We are part of a government connect called Extranet. It is a part of a government secure intranet. There is a code of connection to connect up to this service which we are required to do. That code of connection is built upon the advice of the CESG. CESG certified Blackberry as the only IL3 secured email product. Blackberry only support Exchange, Notes....then how could we choose an open source email platform? It was not an issue of security, it was an issue of whether it (open source product) was certified.	**Material control(ling)**
Content mutability Resistance Open source breakdown	We had an issue with document fidelity – documents would not display as they were intended to in the open source application. We tried hard to convert with fidelity- but it wasn't easing their work, these were genuine problems.	**Mutating materiality**

5   Two Cases of Open Source Software Adoption

Juxtaposing two local council cases of open source software adoption in the UK we highlight their differences and similarities in open source application and implementation. One can now be distinguished by its 'success' (Camden Council) whereas the other (Bristol City Council) has undergone a very mixed engagement with open source. Our narratives indicate that for both cases there was strong goodwill towards open source right from the start and yet the trajectories of implementation are widely different.

Camden Council guided the open source process internally with a strong manager as leader. He built up a team of IT staff over the last ten years that progressed from a simple interest in open source to what is now considered to be an evangelist team of highly skilled developers. Camden co-created on an open source project and is now able to offer its expertise to other local councils that share an interest in moving to open source software and platforms.

Bristol City Council was in the media spotlight from the moment it announced its open source intentions. There was a grand move to open source desktop software use. However, this euphoric open source sentiment did not last for more than a year, after which stories of open source failure began to leak. Open source software was then discarded and Bristol was forced to return to proprietary software. More recently Bristol has shown a renewed interest in open source but this time there is a more cautious approach to such change.

There are many similarities across both cases in the UK and we found it intriguing to make sense of where in this process of open source adoption did open source play a role, and what provoked the failure in one case and the relative success of the other.

Table 2. Chronological Tracing of Open Source Software for CC

Year	Tracing IT/IS Events at Camden Council
2001	Took part in the Pathfinders project by submitting a proposal for an open source content management system which would be reused by other local councils.
2002	CC won some funding for the CMS. A partnership of five local councils began work on the CMS in collaboration with Philip Greenspan of the MIT.
2003-04	Won second round of funding to build an expanded version that had more functionality, be easier to install and would work on an open source database as opposed to Oracle. The CMS was taken up by 30 UK local authorities and then also Australia, Malaysia and China. CC faced growing complexity of working closely with an external open source community with different motivations, deadlines and agenda.
2004	Began to build an ecosystem around their open source projects by enrolling SME help and enthusiasm (and also the funding they had left).
2005	The ecosystem proved harder to maintain as there were not enough tenders to keep the companies afloat. The number of support vendors began to disappear from the market forcing CC to find other forms of support. CC found another academic institution that was willing to work on the CMS.
2006	CC created a validation process for incoming contributions from external sources. CC hired the services of Red Hat to objectively validate the contributions thus creating a meritocratic process of acceptance. CC toyed with the idea of setting up a subscription payment for the CMS but dismissed it considering that this would not be open source friendly.
2005-2011	CC now works in conjunction with the academic institution that took up the development of the CMS. The academics nurture the community and manage it. The development is done partly by university students, CC IT staff and some contributions are from external developers and opens source communities.
2011-12	CC has a strong team of IT developers and staff that are busy building up open source projects, and expertise. The growing concern is however, that this team and its energy are being nudged towards more maintenance work rather than challenging new open source projects.

5.1   Camden Council (CC)

Camden council and its move towards open source has been lead by a strong IT leader who has a reputation for doing things differently. The clear objective is to have a content management system which can manage the load of thousands of constituents and where many dissimilar functions are possible. The decision to go open source was not dictated by any form of ideology but rather it was a practical decision based on a need to work with other local councils and cut back on a waste of resources and expertise. Table 2 traces the chronological history of open source adoption by Camden Council.

Camden Council faced numerous challenges with its decision to adopt and co-create open source software in the form of community management, limited funding, a dying ecosystem of SME vendor support, and lack of uptake of the CMS by as many councils as expected yet it has persisted in its endeavor with some good degree of success.

5.2   Bristol City Council (BCC)

Approximately 15 years ago (1997-1998) the IT staff of BCC were using open source software to support the council's first experiments with websites (see Table 3). There was no philosophy or political backing for open source at this point. It was simply a practical need to create a website that led the BCC IT staff to use open source software options. The interviewees added that there were always 'overtones of being open' but no clear direction or strategy was apparent in the first five years.

Evaluating various open source options has not been cheap – indeed this part of the selection process was lengthy and consuming in terms of time and various resources. This expense would be more acceptable if it had led to a viable set of OSS options. The issue was that BCC was recommended a package where numerous products were 'sewn together' to provide a solution that did not meet all the functional requirements. While Microsoft offered BCC the usual standard government option – no extra expenses or strings attached – and still emerged cheaper than the OS option.

BCC has a roadmap for changes required over the next few years. This will no doubt entail exit costs but BCC believes that with the many companies offering support in migration from proprietary to open source software nowadays there is a clearer idea (and value attached) to exit costs, which makes migration less problematic and fuzzy.

Table 3. Chronological Tracing of Open Source Software for BCC

Year	Tracing IT/IS Events at Bristol City Council
1997-98	Open source used to create and host the first BCC website
2001-2004	BCC evaluated and selected StarOffice rather than Microsoft products because the former was cheaper. Initial research with local government system vendors indicated that integration with StarOffice would be technically possible, and several key vendors expressed a willingness to do the work necessary.
2005-06	StarOffice rolled out across the council to over 5000 users, supported by 8 person team of floorwalkers and technical specialists, providing document conversion, training and coaching to staff. BCC shared experience and learning from evaluating and selecting StarOffice by publishing guidance documentation via "Open Source Academy", a UK National e-Innovations Project.
2007-08	BCC continued to invest in StarOffice, rolling out version 8 and working with Sun and key third party integration system vendors (ISVs) in the local government market, seeking to establish integrations with a variety of business systems. Vendors began to step back from willingness to do integration work without Bristol contributing significant extra funds, citing lack of market take-up of StarOffice and open document format (ODF). BCC staff shared challenges and options for addressing them with Sun, IBM, and other EU governments interested in the issues in a series of conferences and seminars.
2008-09	Continued use of StarOffice became problematic, as fidelity of file conversion was still not as effective as necessary for problem free "round-tripping" of documents, and lack of system integration meant that a high number of MS Office licenses had to be retained.
2009	BCC adopted a new Information Systems & Technology Strategy and restructured the ICT Service, introducing Enterprise Architecture and establishing a new approach to evaluating and selecting applications and technology to ensure fitness for purpose. Open Standards were made a formal and central part of the strategy at this point. EA team recommended that due to experiences between 2005 and 2009, it was no longer viable to continue using StarOffice, and that MS Office should be adopted. Project created to develop business case and plan.
2010	BCC Cabinet approve business case for adopting Windows 7 and MS Office 2010 on all council PCs, with other elements of "desktop and collaboration" software stack to be selected through a rigorous "level playing field" approach of comparing OSS and proprietary options to business requirements. OSS would be selected wherever it met requirements and provided best value for money. Computacenter and Sirius (OSS SME subcontractor) were taken on as System Integrators to design and deliver the project.
2011	Breakdown of relations between Computacenter (SI) and SiriusIT SME support led to delays in selection and design stages. LinuxIT eventually selected as replacement by Computacenter. Some OSS options were selected, e.g. Big Blue Button for web-conferencing and video conferencing, and Alfresco for team collaboration. MS software selected for other elements, e.g. email, IM and presence management, directory services. EA team led separate series of evaluations and selections for an integration platform, business process management system (BPMS), website, and electronic document and records management system (EDRMS). Open standards based products from Tibco chosen for integration and BPMS. OSS products Drupal and Alfresco chosen for website and EDRMS.

6   Analysis

Our study finds that becoming occurs at different speeds [3, 50]. Considering the uncertain nature of becoming this is not so surprising, but what is more interesting is the question of the nature of becoming – how and what can impede or accelerate the process? Our data shows that the becoming of adoption can be both constrained and precipitated by various forms of *materiality* (of the assemblage of the open source ecosystem) [51]. Open source and its transparent process, character, code and license do not necessarily lead to more transparency. The interview material lead to this interesting conclusion forcing us to reconsider and unpack open source software based on our data (and literature) – see Table 4.

6.1   Mutability of Open Source

Open source software and its development process have a number of key elements (see Table 4) such as license [52], community [53], the code [54], coordinating mechanisms [55], and documentation [56]. This is a fairly familiar characterization of OSS but we want to highlight how all these characteristics are not fixed – even within the same project. They are changing, indeed in a state of constant becoming. Scant attention, if any has been paid to the idea of how OSS mutates within a project or over time. The two cases, in their own manner, emphasize how malleable and yielding OSS was, and is. The license of an open source product can range from a variety of accepted (OSI approved) types, however, each license offers some form of viral control mechanism. Some licenses like the General Public License (GPL) are more viral than others. This in turn affects the ability of code to mutate and restricts the variation in becomings possible. The materializing of each element matures the becoming and expedites it in a manner that makes further (variations in) becomings less likely (see Table 5). Thus open source use and adoption can be controlled and managed. In the case of BCC their choice of enterprise open source software was based on an open core model rather than a more 'pure' open source license. Such a model implied that the enterprise edition of the software being procured by BCC was actually not strictly open source as the code was not necessary viewable. Open core models are a form of dual licensing where there is an open source version whose functionality is often limited by comparison to the enterprise open core version, thus giving rise to the term crippleware to describe the reduced functionality OS version. Such choices are becoming more common yet as were told by the developer team, such a model often undermines community contributions eventually killing the project itself.

Community in turn, is a multifaceted phenomenon where variations are visible in the level of skills and expertise of the members and contributors. The size of the community in both cases not only varied but there was a constant flux of developers experienced. Another form of mutability was introduced into the BCC case because it relied on commercial vendor support. Such projects can see diverse forms of sponsorship and resource injection which give rise to changing loyalties, and focus. On the other hand, when questioned about the community support side of their OS project, CC replied that, "I suppose there was and there wasn't. Because there is a community of local government. There are…potentially 399… members of that community. There wasn't at that time any kind of community of webmasters. So there were these relatively new posts being created in local authorities but there wasn't any communication or anything set up to communicate. So that's one of the first things we did as part of the project, we set up five webmasters from the five partners. But then we got them to try and go out and invite people …we did a couple of workshop meetings where we just invited people. So that was the basis of the community.

Table 4. Implications of Open Source Mutability

Mutability of Open Source		
	Areas and Level of Mutability	**Implication**
License	• Choice of license • Version of license • Level of reciprocity involved • Level of transparency	The varied viral nature of some licenses makes them more (or less) amenable to change. Dual licenses are yet another form of mutability.
Community	• Skill level of members • Core team size • Turnover rate • Number of company backed employees	A community with a strong core team of developers backed by company resources and high skill level has greater potential to adapt and change.
Code	• Level of stack • Reusability • Language • Modularity	Code, depending on which language is used, the level of application or product being built and its reusability can affect the sort of mutability possible.
Coordinating Mechanisms	• Public or private discussion groups • Face-to-face meet-ups • Levels and types of mailing lists • Access level of version control software	Coordinating mechanisms in open source are key. Some mechanisms are open to the public, whereas others need to be for developer only access. Such variations in access can blur the level of transparency offered.
Documentation and Metadata	• The type of (detail) documentation provided • Level of updating documentation • Access to metadata • Search-ability of documentation and metadata	Documentation in open source can be patchy and incomplete thus eroding transparency and changing the mutable nature of open source.

Source code, depending on which language is used, the level of application or product being built and its reusability can affect the kinds of mutability possible. As can the variety of coordinating mechanisms at the disposal of a developer community. Much of the discussion about development is carried out over public forums but this is not always true. There is also a growing trend for face-to-face meetings in open source development where traceability of ideas is less transparent and archivable. The various OS projects in both cases used tools such as version control to manage the code, contributions and metadata as explained by an IT manager at CC, "the software does have full version control and there is you know, a nightly build that kind of rolls up all of the code contributions and produces the head build as opposed to like a version" but as he clarified that not all members of the community had equal access to all levels of the tool and code. This again built in varying degrees of transparency and mutability.

6.2   Materializing of Open Source – Speed and Time Control

In table 4 we illustrated how each element of open source software like the license, community, code and so on, encapsulates the potential for more or less mutability. Our two cases of open source adoption by the public sector in the UK narrate this story, and help us to explain the difference in adoption ability and 'success' of both in terms of mutability of open source software, and how this mutability was constrained or encouraged by the material inscriptions adopted for manoeuvre. As much of Science and Technology Studies literature explains materiality is more than tangible 'things', it includes ideas, feelings, and silent action.

It may well be considered that when anything becomes more materialized that it would be less vague and opaque, however, we found that this was not necessarily true. In fact, there was little ability to trace all the possible trajectories of becoming when the situation was as complex as a politically infused public sector organization. There were more than one possibilities for mapping but experienced bureaucrats in both councils were able to manage the possible rupturing of the adoption process. Instead of building transparency into the system with a greater reliance on materiality, the local council IT staff and policy writers were able to contain the opaqueness in a strategic manner to their advantage.

In both councils we saw that license of the software was a key concern. For BCC the open core model created complications and a strong possibility for lock-in. however, it was in its practicing (of the license) that the license materialized. Each license of open source may be slightly different but they are all alike in behaving as the Constitution of the project. As Constitution it dictates what can be done with the code, who owns it and how this ownership can change in processes of redistribution and even multiple licenses. Camden Council adopted a single (as opposed to dual license) and it was the BSD. With the BSD it is possible for anyone to take the source code and change the license of their particular strand. So though the practicing of the license makes open source more material it does little to solidify its mutability thus leaving the possibility of managing the speed of open source adoption. Another manner of understanding such becoming made visible was to make sense of in terms of time [57]. More than license and thus different code branches make visible multiple becomings or *multiple parallel times*.

The community leaves traces in its process of collaboration, turnover, expertise sharing and so on. Its materializing is manifested in this very change and flux where members join while others leave. Other forms of materializing involve sponsoring employees to become a part of the community, and the training (through the community or on the job) of members. This is part of the process of making open source software prepare for *future present time*. The possible future is being pulled back in the present becomings to force a certain tracing (not mapping) of the adoption process. This is because the future is unknown so the way the councils made sense of future software and requirement needs was by using the present as indication. However, this becoming was constrained as and constraining as new emergent changes were inevitable – yet by attempting to trace the future both councils were restricting new possibilities.

Table 5. Becoming Manifested as Materializing

Becoming and **Materializing**		
Areas and Level of Mutability	**Materializing**	**Time**

• Choice of license
• Version of license
• Level of reciprocity involved
• Level of transparency
	License is the Constitution – written and in practice.
	   • Changing license
	   • Practicing the license
	   • Implementing the license
		Multiple parallel times

• Skill level of members
• Core team size
• Turnover rate
• Number of company backed employees
	Community traces, voices, decisions, sense of belonging (expressed through T-shirts, brand, etc).
	   • Community in flux
	   • Sponsoring employees
	   • Training of developers
		Future present time

• Level of stack
• Reusability
• Language
• Modularity
	Code, requirements, functionality and use
	   • Changing requirements
	   • Greater encapsulating
	   • Reusing code
		Hiding time Revisiting time

• Public or private discussion groups
• Face-to-face meet-ups
• Levels and types of mailing lists
• Access level of version control software
	Coordinating Mechanisms
	   • Making discussions transparent
	   • Increasing security level of access
	   • Varying governance structure to cope (change) access levels
		Traceable time

• The type of (detail) documentation provided
• Level of updating documentation
• Access to metadata
• Search-ability of documentation and metadata
	Documentation and Metadata
	   • Making the search algorithms visible (or not)
	   • Maintaining documentation
	   • Detailed documenting and instructions
		'Moment' of time (capturing)

Speed of becoming is managed through the code by controlling the changing nature of requirements, varied forms of encapsulation and even encouraging reuse of code. These are material forms of the code where traces are left and can be followed. Code and its materializing thus make it possible to *hide time*, yet at the same *revisit time*. Camden Council was hopeful of reusing its code and system across other councils and did manage this for a while, "and so we built our proposal to the funding around that basis that we were going to produce an open source content management system that would be reused by other local authorities... And so that release got taken up by more than 30 UK local authorities and then started being taken up in Australia and Malaysia and China and all kinds of places in the world. However, a shrinking ecosystem of vendor support over time made a change in code less possible This in turn led to impaired materializing of the code, and the objectives of Camden Council.

Traceability and materializing in relation to open source coordination are (theoretically) built into the open development process. Discussions between developers are made visible, and traceable, access to discussion forums and version control software are managed by security levels, and we also found in our data that the governance structure changes in relation to security access and expertise of the developer. The materiality of code makes time *traceable* and retraceable (though each retracing will no doubt be a variation of other becomings and not quite a tracing).

Finally, time, or moments of it can be *captured*. This reinforces the idea of materializing of open source because good documentation of code makes algorithms visible, and future documentation easier and more possible. However, as the example of BCC shows poor documentation, and impaired interoperability can force a breakdown of software use. The fact that other councils that BCC needed to work with did not use open source made it difficult for BCC to share documents without trouble. Often the documents created by BCC using open source were not rendered in the expected manner by other councils or were completely illegible, "we had an issue with document fidelity – documents would not display as they were intended to in the open source application".

7   Conclusion

Considering each element of open source individually is useful to understand mutability, materializing and transparency (or lack of) but as one interviewee explained open source is complex and has 'vectors of lock-in'. It is an entanglement of all these elements in proportions that are beyond complete control that build in uncertainty make the becoming of open source software so challenging. The data revealed a richness in its material element (as the codes show). Literature on open source procurement and adoption in the public sector has not only ignored this idea but we find that it is in general (though not true for all) often atheoretical. We have attempted to redress this issue by sensitizing our data collection and analysis with ideas of becoming. Such an ontology allowed us to move beyond a focus on only the human [15], or practices, or likening change to merely improvising [16]. There has been more recent work in IS that shows concern for a relational ontology where the social and material are understood to be entangled [58] and imbricated [59] but there has been little use of such ideas to understand OSS in the public sector, and how this implicates the process of becoming.

In this paper we understand better how the becoming of open source software adoption by two different local councils in the UK indicate that the process of becoming occurs at different speeds because of the nature of their materiality. Our data shows that the becoming of adoption can be both constrained and precipitated by various forms of materiality (of the assemblage of the open source ecosystem) [51]. The interesting point of departure of our study is how open source software – a much touted transparent and open phenomenon – is by its nuanced and layered mutability [60, 61] able to make the process and practices surrounding it *less visible*.

Acknowledgement. This research was funded by the UK Cabinet Office, OpenForum Europe and a few other organizations.

References

1. Law, J., Singleton, V.: Performing Technology's Stories: On Social Constructivism, Performance, and Performativity. Technology and Culture 41, 765–775 (2000)
2. Tsoukas, H., Chia, R.: On Organizational Becoming: Rethinking Organizational Change. Organization Science 13, 567–582 (2002)
3. Colville, I., et al.: Simplexity: Sensemaking, organizing and storytelling for our time. Human Relations 65, 5–15 (2012)
4. Deleuze, G., Guattari, F.: A Thousand Plateaus. Capitalism and Schizophrenia. University of Minnesota Press, Minneapolis (1987)
5. Latour, B.: Give Me a Laboratory and I Will Raise the World. In: Biagioli, M. (ed.) The Science Studies Reader, pp. 258–275. Routledge, New York (1999)
6. Latour, B., Johnson, J.: Mixing humans and nonhumans together: The sociology of door-closer. In: Star, S.L. (ed.) Ecologies of Knowledge: Work and Politics in Science and Technology, pp. 257–277. SUNY Press (1995)
7. Callon, M.: Some Elements of a Sociology of Translation: Domestication of the Scallops and Fishermen of St. Brieuc Bay. In: Law, J. (ed.) Power, Action and Belief: A New Sociology of Knowledge?, 32nd edn., pp. 196–233. Routledge & Kegan Paul, London (1986)
8. Callon, M.: The Sociology of an Actor-Network. In: Callon, M., et al. (eds.) Mapping the Dynamics of Science and Technology. Macmillan, London (1986)
9. Law, J.: After ANT: Topology, Naming and Complexity. In: Law, J., Hassard, J. (eds.) Actor Network Theory and After, Blackwell and the Sociological Review, Oxford and Keele (1999)
10. Barad, K.: Posthumanist Performativity: Toward an Understanding of How Matter Comes to Matter. Signs: Journal of Women in Culture and Society 28, 801–831 (2003)
11. Callon, M.: What Does it Mean to Say that Economics is Performative? In: MacKenzie, D., et al. (eds.) Do Economists Make Markets?: On the Performativity of Economics, pp. 311–357. Princeton University Press, New Jersey (2007)
12. Robey, D., Sahay, S.: Transforming Work Through Information Technology: A Comparative Case Study of Geographic Information Systems in County Government. Information Systems Research 7, 93–110 (1996)
13. Ciborra, C.U. (ed.): From Control to Drift. Oxford University Press, Oxford (2000)

14. Gasser, L.: The Integration of Computing and Routine Work. ACM Transactions on Office Information Systems 4, 205–225 (1986)
15. Feldman, M.: Organizational routines as a source of continuous change. Organization Science 11, 611–629 (2000)
16. Orlikowski, W.J.: Improvising organizational transformation over time: A situated change perspective. Information Systems Research 7, 63–92 (1996)
17. Monteiro, E., et al.: The family resemblance of technologically mediated work practices. Information and Organization 22, 169–187 (2012)
18. Boudreau, M.-C., Robey, D.: Enacting Integrated Information Technology: A Human Agency Perspective. Organization Science 16, 3–18 (2005)
19. Fitzgerald, B., et al.: Adopting Open Source Software: A Practical Guide. MIT Press (2011)
20. Phipps, S.: Open Source Procurement: Subscriptions. ComputerWorldUK [blog post] (March 3, 2011), http://blogs.computerworlduk.com/simon-says/2011/03/open-source-procurement-subscriptions/index.html
21. Archer, G.: Open Source Software Policy: Australian Government Information Management Office (AGIMO) Circular, Australian Government: Department of Finance and Deregulation (2010), http://fwd4.me/wY6
22. Kundra, V., et al.: Technology Neutrality: Memorandum for Chief Information Officers and Senior Procurement Executives. Washington DC Executive Office of the President: Office of Management and Budget (2011), http://fwd4.me/wY5
23. Waring, T., Maddocks, P.: Open Source Software implementation in the UK public sector: Evidence from the field and implications for the future. International Journal of Information Management 25, 411–428 (2005)
24. Oram, A.: Promoting Open Source Software in Government: The Challenges of Motivation and Follow-Through. Journal of Information Technology & Politics 8, 240–252 (2011)
25. Shaw, A.: Insurgent Expertise: The Politics of Free/Livre and Open Source Software in Brazil. Journal of Information Technology & Politics 8, 253–272 (2011)
26. Ghosh, R.A., et al.: Guideline on public procurement of Open Source Software, Brussels, Belgium. UN University/MERIT and Unisys Belgium (2010), http://fwd4.me/wXx
27. Ballard, M.: Government IT suppliers claim procurement system excludes open source (February 25, 2011), http://ComputerWeekly.com, http://www.computerweekly.com/Articles/2011/02/25/245598/Government-IT-suppliers-claim-procurement-system-excludes-open.htm
28. Saran, C.: Government plans procurement overhaul to slash IT spend (September 22, 2010), http://ComputerWeekly.com, http://www.computerweekly.com/Articles/2010/09/24/242958/Government-plans-procurement-overhaul-to-slash-IT-spend.htm
29. Hall, K.: Government tells major IT suppliers - we want more open source software (February 23, 2011), http://ComputerWeekly.com, http://www.computerweekly.com/Articles/2011/02/23/245555/Government-tells-major-IT-suppliers-we-want-more-open-source.htm
30. Burkhardt, R.: Seven Predictions for Open Source in 2009 (2008), http://drdobbs.com/open-source/212700284
31. Noveck, B.S.: Defining Open Government (2011), http://cairns.typepad.com/blog/2011/04/whats-in-a-name-open-gov-we-gov-gov-20-collaborative-government.html

32. Russo, B., Succi, G.: A Cost Model of Open Source Software Adoption. IJOSSP, 60–82 (2009)
33. [33] Gallopino, R.: Open Source TCO: Total Cost of Ownership and the Fermat's Theorem (2009), http://robertogaloppini.net/2009/01/08/open-source-tco-total-cost-of-ownership-and-the-fermats-theorem/
34. Agerfalk, P., Fitzgerald, B.: Outsourcing to an Unknown Workforce: Exploring Opensourcing as a Global Sourcing Strategy. MIS Quarterly 32, 385–400 (2008)
35. Sutor, R.: Managing open source adoption in your IT organization (2009), http://www.sutor.com/newsite/blog-open/?p=3260
36. Shaikh, M., Cornford, T.: Understanding Commercial Open Source as Product and Service Innovation. In: 2011 Academy of Management Annual Meeting, San Antonio, Texas, USA (2011)
37. Zuliani, P., Succi, G.: Migrating public administrations to open source software. In: E-society 2004 IADIS International Conference, Avila, Spain, pp. 829–832 (2004)
38. Zuliani, P., Succi, G.: An Experience of Transition to Open Source Software in Local Authorities. In: E-challenges on Software Engineering, Vienna, Austria (2004)
39. Dinkelacker, J., et al.: Progressive Open Source. In: Proceedings of the 2002 ACM International Conference on Software Engineering (ICSE 2002), pp. 177–184 (2002)
40. Dahlander, L.: Penguin in a newsuit: a tale of how de novo entrants emerged to harness free and open source software communities. Industrial and Corporate Change 16, 913–943 (2007)
41. Fitzgerald, B.: The Transformation of Open Source Software. MIS Quarterly 30, 587–598 (2006)
42. O'Mahony, S., et al.: IBM and Eclipse (A). Harvard Business Review Case Study, December 16 (2005)
43. Clegg, S., et al.: Learning/Becoming/Organizing. Organization 12, 147–167 (2005)
44. Weick, K.E.: Improvisation as a mindset for organizational analysis. Organization Science 9, 543–555 (1998)
45. Weick, K.E., Quinn, R.E.: Organizational change and development. Annual Review of Psychology 50, 361–386 (1999)
46. Austin, J.: How to do Things with Words. Oxford, Clarendon (1962)
47. Butler, J.: Excitable Speech: A Politics of the Performative. Routledge, London (1997)
48. Bateson, G.: Steps to an ecology of mind. Chandler, New York (1972)
49. Strauss, A., Corbin, J.: Basics of Qualitative Research: Techniques and Procedures for Developing Grounded Theory. Sage Publications (1999)
50. Weick, K.E.: Organized sensemaking: A commentary on processes of interpretive work. Human Relations 65, 141–153 (2012)
51. Rose, J., Jones, M.: The Double Dance of Agency: a socio-theoretic account of how machines and humans interact. In: ALOIS 2004 - Action in Language, Organisations and Information Systems, Linköping - Sweden (2004)
52. Benkler, Y.: Coase's Penguin, or, Linux and the Nature of the Firm. Yale Law Journal 112, 369–446 (2002)
53. O'Mahony, S., Ferraro, F.: The emergence of governance in an open source community. Academy of Management Journal 50, 1079–1106 (2007)
54. Fitzgerald, B., Feller, J.: A further investigation of open source software: community, co-ordination, code quality and security issues. Information Systems Journal 12, 3–6 (2002)
55. Crowston, K., Kammerer, E.E.: Coordination and collective mind in software requirements development. IBM Systems Journal 37, 227–245 (1998)

56. von Krogh, G., et al.: Collective Action and Communal Resources in Open Source Software Development: The Case of Freenet (2003), `http://opensource.mit.edu/papers/vonkroghhaefligerspaeth.pdf`
57. Kavanagh, D., Araujo, L.: Chronigami: Folding And Unfolding Time. Accounting, Management and Information Technology 5, 103–121 (1995)
58. Orlikowski, W.J., Scott, S.V.: Sociomateriality: Challenging the Separation of Technology, Work and Organization. The Academy of Management Annals 2, 433–474 (2008)
59. Leonardi, P.M., Barley, S.R.: What's Under Construction Here? Social Action, Materiality, and Power in Constructivist Studies of Technology and Organizing. The Academy of Management Annals 4, 1–51 (2010)
60. Mol, A., Law, J.: Regions, Networks and Fluids: Amaemia and Social Topology. Social Studies of Science 24, 641–671 (1994)
61. Moser, I., Law, J.: Fluids or flows? Information and qualculation in medical practice. Information Technology & People 19, 55–73 (2006)

Track IV
New Ideas in Positivist Research

Part IV

Moderating Effect of Environmental Factors on eHealth Development and Health Outcomes: A Country-Level Analysis

Supunmali Ahangama and Danny Chiang Choon Poo

Department of Information Systems, School of Computing, National University of Singapore,
13 Computing Drive, Singapore 117417
supunmali@comp.nus.edu.sg, dannypoo@nus.edu.sg

Abstract. This cross-national study examines how the relationship between national eHealth initiatives and health outcomes are contingent on (1) macro-economic stability; (2) GDP per capita; and (3) institutions. Resource Based View's (RBV) resource complementary perspective and literature on Information Technology and health outcomes are used as the guiding theoretical framework. Publicly available archival data from more than 50 countries are gathered to understand the moderating effect. Health outcomes are measured through Infant Survival Rate (ISR). The results indicated that there is no direct effect of eHealth initiatives on health outcomes; however, eHealth initiatives interact with above three contingencies affecting health outcomes. Macro-economic stability moderated the relationship between eHealth development and health outcomes positively. GDP per capita and institutions moderated the relationship of eHealth development and health outcomes in a negative direction. Implications of the findings for theoretical discourse of the resource complimentary perspective and future research are discussed in this paper.

Keywords: eHealth, Infant Survival Rate, resource complementary perspective.

1   Introduction

eHealth can be recognized as an essential tool in ensuring a safer, efficient and sustainable healthcare delivery around the world[1-4]. Use of eHealth will facilitate the provision of a more patient centered care[5] outside the traditional environment which could be a shift of focus from general practitioners office or from hospitals. According to WHO[4], *eHealth is the use of information and communication technologies (ICT) for health.* This could be for treating patients, conducting research, educating the healthcare personnel, tracking diseases and monitoring public health. eHealth is a field that has become prominent within the last decade and can be identified as a rapidly growing area. Though electronic health records (EHR) is not eHealth, EHR is the heart of eHealth. eHealth is broader and a larger group of stakeholders could be reached through this technology. eHealth resources will be managed or used by medical staff, patients, government policy makers, researchers, general public etc., dispersed in

A. Bhattacherjee and B. Fitzgerald (Eds.): Future of ICT Research, IFIP AICT 389, pp. 143–159, 2012.

different geographical locations. Usage of eHealth will be critical in transforming the healthcare sector into a new level. However, most of the Information Technology (IT) applications are developed targeting administrative and financial transactions rather than to support clinical care[3].

Introduction of eHealth tools to healthcare services is enormously challenging due to numerous factors varying from common factors such as limited financial support available to much more serious factors like, lack of a legal framework to protect the privacy of users. Ensuring the privacy of the patients is a major concern in using eHealth in healthcare industry. Lack of adequate measures to ensure the privacy of patients may reduce the acceptability of this new technology, eHealth by many patients. Such a low acceptance by the major stakeholders group (patients) may limit the potential of achieving the expected benefits of eHealth and it may be detrimental. Moreover, IT is likely to cause digital divide where people with IT access will get a better service compared to people who do not have IT access.

While most of the studies that have been carried out at country-level have mainly considered the contribution of IT to economic growth[6], only a very few country-level studies had been carried out to understand the contribution of IT investments on better health outcomes. In reviewing existing literature, we found that findings of prior studies that examined the relationship between IT expenditure and health outcomes have shown mixed results and had merely identified possible negative consequences related to EHR usage[7]. Moreover, these authors have focused on overall IT expenditure of a nation rather than on specific eHealth expenditure or eHealth initiatives. Thus, assessing the relationship between eHealth initiatives and health outcomes can be considered as a key research gap to be answered.

We address this, by using the resource complementary perspective of Teece[8] and propose that the relationship between eHealth development and health outcomes is moderated by national environmental factors, namely, (1) institutional; and (2) economic factors (GDP per capita and macro-economic stability). Though there can be numerous factors affecting eHealth development and health outcomes (quality and safety), we consider that the institutional factors and economic factors are the key factors capable of affecting any development strategy and its outcomes in any country [9]. While GDP and macro-economic stability indicate the availability of financial resources for implementation of eHealth, institutional factors indicate the capability of individuals and legal framework in health care institutions to generate better health outcomes.

Health outcomes will be measured using Infant Survival Rate (ISR), which is a parallel measure to Life Expectancy Rate (LER) more commonly used as the prime indicator of quality of a healthcare system[10]. These complementary assets will be modeled using archival data of 55 countries. These 55 countries were selected based on the fact that data on all the necessary variables for the study were available only for these countries and a number of countries had to be excluded due to non-availability of data for one or more variables.

RQ: *How do a nation's complementary assets (macro-economic stability, GDP per capita and institutions) interact with national eHealth initiatives in predicting its health outcomes?*

This paper is organized as follows. Theoretical framework is briefly explained in section (1.1) and descriptions on hypothesis development and research design are dealt with in sections (2) and (3). Sections (4), (5) and (6) deal with analysis and results, discussion and conclusion respectively.

1.1 Theoretical Framework

The concept of complementary assets introduced by Teece[8], describes that for commercializing a new product profitably, a firm needs access to complementary assets (manufacturing and distribution facilities) in a favorable manner[11]. Complementary assets are resources or capabilities that allow firms to capture the profits associated with a strategy, technology or innovation[12]. Even though, competitors can duplicate and launch the same new product they will not be able to get a competitive advantage if they do not get access to complementary assets possessed by the producer. Based on Resource Based View (RBV)[13], complementary assets can be categorized into two different areas as resource co-presence view and resource channeling view. Resource co-presence view explains that a resource can be considered to be a complementary asset if its presence increases the value or outcome of another resource. This is also known as interaction perspective. Resource channeling view explains that when resources are used in mutually reinforcing manner, complementary assets are formed[14]. Thus, former can be applied into our study to understand why certain countries have better health outcomes compared to some other countries[10]. Complementary assets will be helpful in achieving high health outcomes from IS innovations related to healthcare. Rather than developing and deploying eHealth tools itself, it is important to understand the complementary assets that could provide a better utility. Moderating variables (macro-economic stability, GDP per capita and institutions[6, 15]) used in this study will be complementary assets that will enhance the relationship between eHealth development and health outcomes.

Many studies have been carried out on the impact of IT investment on quality and safety of healthcare system[16-18]. There had been endorsements from World Health Assembly by passing an eHealth resolution (WHA 58.28) in 2005 for eHealth implementation and development as a means for improving healthcare. Stroetmann and others[18] have found economic benefits of implementing eHealth considering 10 sites in Europe. In reviewing publications on the impact of eHealth on the quality and safety of health care between 1997 and 2010, Black et al.[17] have found only limited evidence indicating achievement of expected benefits and have even found some situations where implementation of eHealth leading to detrimental effects. Particularly, the reviewers have not found sufficient evidence showing improvement in patient outcomes associated with these technologies, though large-scaled projects have been funded and deployed to support eHealth implementations.

It is reported in literature[10] that IT investments influence life expectancy. However, these authors have used the overall IT expenditure for a country as an attribute in their study, rather than considering the ICT expenditure specifically related to healthcare and has identified it as a limitation in carrying out their research. They have identified that the three mechanisms–information integration, workflow coordination and collaborative planning via ICT can influence health outcomes.

According to them, adequate investments on these three mechanisms and collective application of them (eHealth) will lead to positive health outcomes.

2   Hypothesis Development

Better outcomes can be obtained by improving the quality of healthcare system by infusing ICT. It is evident from literature that a more efficient and safer medical service could be provided by using health IT. According to Mithas et al.[10] overall life expectancy of a country can be improved based on the IT expenditure of a country. The authors have identified Information integration, Workflow coordination and Collaborative Planning as the three main areas of IT, which could influence the healthcare sector. Information integration is consolidation of diverse information sources (both semi structured and unstructured data) into structured data (and information). Information integration will allow access to information in 24/7 as and when required for intra and inter hospital activity coordination and management. Thus, better judgments can be made through integration of data from different sources. Workflow coordination is automation of the activities in the care value chain. For example, efficient distribution of drugs avoiding scarcities and endangering patients could be achieved through workflow coordination. Collaborative planning allows effective cooperation between different levels in a hospital.

There is a dearth of published literature on the influence of national environmental factors (moderating variables) on eHealth development and standard of health (Infant Survival Rate, ISR) in a country. Health Standards is a part of Human Development Index (HDI) where life expectancy is used as an indicator for health standards[19].

2.1   Moderating Effect of Macro-economic Stability

Macro-economic stability of a country can be maintained through a low inflation rate with declining budget and trade deficits[15]. The stability of the macro-economic environment is important for success in carrying out eHealth initiatives. With stable macro-economic conditions advanced countries in the world are more likely to implement eHealth effectively as they have done with e-government development[20]. Though, macro-economic stability may not directly affect the overall life expectancy, economically unstable countries over burden with debts may not invest in ICT for healthcare. When the macro-economy of a country is unstable, government would not be able to provide services in an efficient manner[15]. High inflation may lead governments to provide the people with only the essential services even in the health sector rather than attempting on providing them with value added services or preventive care.

Healthcare expenditure is escalating in many countries. In the USA, healthcare expenditure was expected to double between 1998 and 2007. Thus, the governments should be in a position to address the escalating costs. Through eHealth, people can access health services via internet to reduce costs[19] and to improve the survival rate or longevity of life. The following hypothesis was established in identifying the major role played by macro-economic stability of a country in developing and in implementing its IS innovations relevant to healthcare.

H1: The relationship between eHealth development in a country and its Infant Survival Rate is moderated by macro-economic stability. The relationship becomes stronger when the stability of macro economy is high and becomes weaker when macro-economic stability is low.

2.2   Moderating Effect of GDP Per Capita

GDP per capita is an indication of a country's wellbeing and is used to measure the economic development of a country. It has been noted that healthcare expenditure as well as health concerns increase with a nation's economic development[10, 21]. The introduction and use of eHealth tools will mainly depend on the financial support available. If it is accessible only to those who can pay, the benefits of eHealth will be low for poorer sections of the population in less developed regions, and will only be a burden to the public health systems. In addition, financial constraints will play a major role in ensuring the privacy of patients too, which is a major concern related to eHealth. For example, additional financial support will be required to train healthcare workforce or to deploy sophisticated health information safety measures.

It has been found that IT has different impacts depending on whether the particular country is a developing or a developed country. Moreover, it has been identified that higher income leads to increased use of eHealth[19, 22]. Thus low-income groups in poorest countries who are inherently more susceptible to preventable diseases are experiencing the lowest contact with eHealth tools. Having access to eHealth will facilitate access to health information and preventive measures. Mothers will use advice on health nutrition and fitness or on vaccinations to prevent many fatalities of children due to preventable causes. Thus, we postulate that better GDP per capita will allow higher improvement in ISR via access to eHealth.

H2: The relationship between eHealth development in a country and its Infant Survival Rate is moderated by GDP per capita. The relationship becomes stronger when GDP per capita is high and becomes weaker when GDP per capita is low.

2.3   Moderating Effect of Institutions

According to the global competitive index, the institutional environment shapes up the framework within which individuals, firms, and governments interact. It also focuses on how societies share the benefits and bear the burden of development strategies. Thus, factors such as intellectual property rights, ethics and corruption, undue influence, government inefficiency and security have been considered in defining the institutional environment[15]. In the usage of ICT in healthcare, it is important to ensure the transparency in handling patient records while maintaining privacy of patients. Thus, it should be possible to maintain good governance and maintain ethical practices followed in healthcare industry relying on eHealth.

Many political and policy amendments will be required to integrate the eHealth tools to daily operations of healthcare industry smoothly. Importantly there should be a legal framework to facilitate secure transfer of information between various stakeholders even across different geographical boundaries. The transfer of information could be varying from communication between the physician and the patient to sharing of research findings. Organization for Economic Co-operation and Development (OECD) has highlighted in its 2010 report, the importance of having a new legal framework for sharing medical information to improve the efficiency in healthcare service.   They have identified this as a challenge even in world's most advanced countries.

We can hypothesize, that when there is better structure of institution, higher benefits of eHealth can be achieved to increase the ISR.

H3: The relationship between eHealth development in a country and its Infant Survival Rate is moderated by institutions. The relationship becomes stronger when the quality of institutions is high and becomes weaker when quality of institutions is low.

2.4   Control Variables

Four control variables (excluding theoretical constructs of concern) that could explain the variance of dependent variable (ISR) are considered. Firstly, we control number of hospital beds per 10,000 of the population as it is an indicator of quality of healthcare infrastructure of a country[10]. According to World Health Statistics by WHO, number of hospital beds are composed of beds available in public, private, general and specialized hospitals. Secondly, as a proxy for healthcare service, we controlled physician density and nurse and midwife personnel density. These values are taken from the World Health Statistics Report 2010 of WHO. It is the amount of health workforce per 10,000 population[10]. In addition, effect of ICT infrastructure is controlled and the index is computed considering number of PCs, Internet users, main telephone lines, mobile phones and broadband users per 100 people. The data are obtained from UN e-Government Survey Report 2008.

3   Research Design

A cross sectional analysis of 55 countries (See Appendix) is used for testing the hypothesis. 2011 is used as the base year (for dependent variable) and values for all the other constructs are captured in previous years[10]. Archived (retrospective) data are used as it is impossible to collect primary data within the available resource constraints and also because archived data will allow reproducibility with ease and are generalizable[23]. In addition common method bias could be avoided as data are gathered from different sources[24]. The main data sources are (1) World Health Statistics 2011[25] and 2010;   (2) UN e-Government Survey report 2008[26]; (3) WEF Global Competitiveness Report 2008-2009[15]; (4) Digital Planet 2008[27]; and

(5) Global e-Health Survey Results 2009 of WHO (and country profiles developed based on 2009 survey results)[4]. These reports are considered to be reliable sources and many authors have used these data in their research. For example, Digital Planet Report is used by Mithas et al. [10] and Bankole et al. [28] to study the impact of IT expenditure on quality of healthcare system of a country (using WHO statistics). In addition, Global Competitiveness Report and e-Government Survey Report are used by many researchers to apply into various areas[20, 29, 30].

These data collecting organizations follow rigorous procedures to maintain the reliability and validity of these data. To ensure quality of these data, for example, (1) data are collected only from CEOs or equivalent high ranked officials; (2) respondents can answer in their preferred language; (3) administration of survey is done in several modes (face-to-face, telephone and online interviews or surveys); and (4) a careful editing of data is performed before aggregating to get country-level data[15].

3.1   Operationalization of Constructs

Many previous studies[10, 31] used LER, to measure the quality of healthcare systems. However, as suggested by Bankole et al. [28], LER will be more useful in considering the impact over a long term. To evaluate the impact of eHealth on LER, it may require a longer period to be considered. However, the impact of eHealth on Infant Mortality Rate (IMR), a parallel measure to LER can be detected in a shorter period of time compared to LER. LER is the average number of years of life remaining at a given age. According to World Population datasheet, LER at birth (most commonly used) is *"the average number of years a newborn is expected to live under current mortality levels"*. IMR is the number of infant deaths per 1000 live births. ISR is computed by subtracting IMR from 1000 (ISR=1000-IMR). IMR values are obtained from the WHO World Health Statistics 2011.

As an index for eHealth is not available in published literature, a new construct is developed using (1) ICT expenditure on healthcare (for computer hardware, software and services) by a country for 2008 (data obtained from Digital Planet 2008); (2) whether eHealth policy is implemented; and (3) whether ICT capability is provided to healthcare personnel and students (related to healthcare). The data for latter two items are obtained from WHO ATLAS country profiles developed based on Global eHealth Survey Results 2009. The new index is used to indicate the level of eHealth development in a country. This measure is developed based on methods used in the development of similar measures like e-Business development (whether of businesses use internet for buying and selling goods)[32].

Macro-economic stability index is taken from WEF Global competitiveness report 2008-2009[15]. This is composed of (1) government surplus/ deficit; (2) national savings rate; (3) inflation; (4) interest rate spread; and (5) government debt. GDP per capita is also adopted from Global competitiveness report 2008-2009. GDP per capita will be used to represent the economic prosperity of a country. Similarly, Institutions index is obtained from the same report mentioned above and it is developed using (1) intellectual property rights; (2) ethics and corruption; (3) undue influence;

(4) government inefficiency; and (5) security. These three indices had been used in past studies to understand the e-government development[20].

4   Analysis and Results

4.1   Descriptive Statistics

It is evident from Table 1, that most correlations among variables are significant at $p < 0.001$. The correlation among independent and moderating variables are less than the threshold value of 0.8[33, 34] except for between institutions and ICT infrastructure ($r=0.82$). Although this indicates a potential for multi-collinearity, our use of a robust method of moderated multiple regression to test the hypotheses generally ease any undue influences[35, 36]. In addition, since these variables measure different parameters and are used as standard measures (used as two distinct pillars in computing the global competitive index) of WEF global competitiveness report[15], the high correlations may not gravely impinge on the results. Nevertheless, we performed the diagnostic statistical collinearity tests to measure variance inflation factor (VIF). VIF is used to evaluate the impact the other independent and moderating variables have on the standard error of a regression coefficient[19, 35]. If VIF is below 10, then it can be considered as an absence of serious multi-collinearity issue. The variable ICT infrastructure is having a VIF of 5.2, thus, it is not removed as it is below the threshold value of 10. All the other variables show VIF values less than 5 indicating non-existence of multi-collinearity.

Table 1. Descriptive statistics and coorelations

Variables	M	SD	1	2	3	4	5	6	7	8	9
1.Physicians density[a]	2.80	1.02	-								
2.Nurses density[a]	3.38	1.33	46	-							
3.Hospital beds[a]	3.35	0.85	73	34	-						
4. ICT Infrastructure	0.38	0.25	69	52	65	-					
5. eHealth	0.76	0.20	66	37	56	61	-				
6. Institutions	4.47	0.96	50	52	41	82	53	-			
7. MSI	5.03	0.82	40	38	28	53	41	52	-		
8. GDP per Capita[a]	12.76	1.52	34	12	25	33	57	21	30	-	
9. ISR[a]	6.89	0.02	70	43	68	66	53	52	41	30	-

N=55; M=mean; SD=Standard deviation; MSI=Macro-economic Stability; All correlations equal or greater than 0.25 are statistically significant at $p < 0.05$; Decimal points omitted for correlations; [a]Log transformed variables

Note: See page 7 for description of variables

4.2   Hypothesis Testing

Moderated multiple regression[37, 38], an established method is used in many studies to test interaction effect. As per Frazier and others[37], continuously measured predictor and moderator variables involved in the regression equations are standardized (Z-scoring). Since independent variables and moderator variables are highly correlated with the interaction term, centering or standardization will reduce the multi-collinearity problem[39, 40]. Moreover, z-scoring makes it easy to compute with available standard packages, to plot significant moderation effects and also to interpret the effect of interaction effects[40]. Hierarchical multiple regression equation is structured in such a way that variables are entered into the model in series of steps as presented in Table 2. Firstly control variables, secondly predictor variables and the moderator variables (coded or standardized variables) and thirdly the product terms are entered into the equation. All the individual variables used to create interaction terms should be included in the model before the interaction terms[37]. Furthermore, it is important that all the interaction terms are entered simultaneously, thus, their effects can be assessed at the presence of other interactions[38, 39].

R^2 value of 0.71 and adjusted R^2 value of 0.635 (F=9.554, p<0.001) indicates that the overall model is useful in explaining the variance in ISR. The change in R^2 value between step 2 and 3 as shown in Table 2, is 0.112 (F=5.525, p<0.01). Thus, it is possible to interpret the outcome in testing the moderation effects. Though, there is no direct effect of eHealth development on ISR, it can be noted that there is significant moderating effect and eHealth development interact with moderator variables to affect ISR. The relationship between eHealth development and ISR is contingent on macro-economic stability (β=0.337, p<0.05) and the direction of interaction pattern for eHealth development and standard of health is consistent with the initial prediction. Thus, H1 is supported. The relationship between eHealth development and ISR is contingent on GDP per capita (β=-0.418, p<0.01). However, the direction of interaction pattern for eHealth development and ISR is contrary to our prediction. Hence, we can conclude that H2 is not supported. Then the relationship between eHealth development and ISR is contingent on institutions (β=-0.386, p<0.01) in the negative direction indicating that H3 is not supported.

We did plot interaction effects (Figure 1-3) to determine whether the interactions (that are significant) confirm to the proposed direction of interactions as we hypothesized. Moreover, a slope analysis is performed to evaluate whether the gradient differs from zero[37, 38, 40]. Figure 1 presents the disordinal (crossover) interaction of macro-economic stability on the relationship between ISR and eHealth development. When a simple slope analysis is performed on the effect of macro-economic stability on the relationship of ISR with eHealth development, it revealed that when the macro-economic stability is high the relationship of ISR and eHealth development was positive and significant (t=13.46, p<0.001). When the macro-economic stability is low, the relationship is negative and significant (t=-19.81, p<0.001).

Table 2. Regression results

Moderated Multiple Regression Steps			
		β^a	
	Step 1	Step 2	Step 3
Controls			
Hospital beds	0.288*	0.326*	0.298*
Physicians density	0.292*	0.293	-0.002
Nurses density	0.067	0.067	0.043
ICT infrastructure	0.242	0.242	0.493*
Main Effect			
eHealth		-0.60	-0.231
Macro-economic Stability		0.066	-0.039
GDP per Capita		0.062	0.152
Institutions		0.098	0.027
Interaction Effect			
eHealth*Macro-economic Stability			0.337*
eHealth*GDP per Capita			-0.418**
eHealth*Institutions			-0.386**
R^2	0.589	0.598	0.710
Adjusted R^2	0.556	0.528	0.635
F	17.922***	8.543***	9.554***
R^2 Change	-	0.009	0.112
F Change	-	0.246	5.525**

[a]The beta values reported are based on standardised coefficients

N=55   *p<0.05   **p<0.01   ***p<0.001 (1-tailed)

Note: See page 7 for description of variables

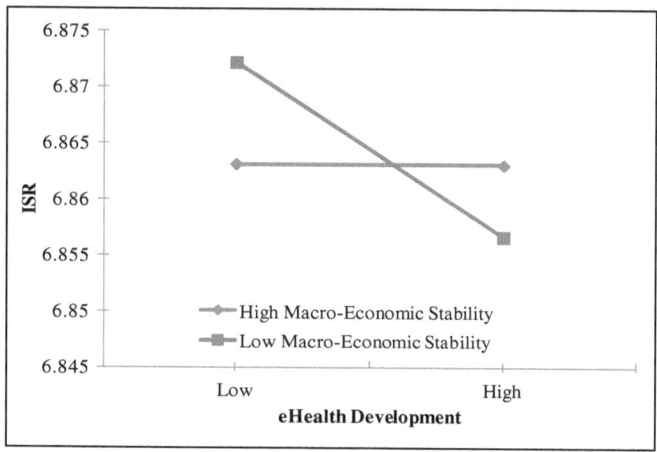

Fig. 1. Moderating influence of macro-economic stability on relationship between eHealth development and ISR (healthcare standard)

Figure 2 shows the disordinal interaction of GDP per capita on the relationship between ISR and eHealth development. When a simple slope analysis is performed on the effect of GDP per capita on the relationship of ISR with eHealth development, it revealed that when the GDP per capita is high the relationship of ISR and eHealth development was negative and significant (t=-3.02, p<0.01). However, when the GDP per capita is low, the relationship was positive and non-significant (t=0.89, n.s.). Interestingly, this indicates that the positive relationship of interaction of GDP per capita and eHealth development on ISR occurs only at low GDP per capita. This finding will be discussed in detail in the next section.

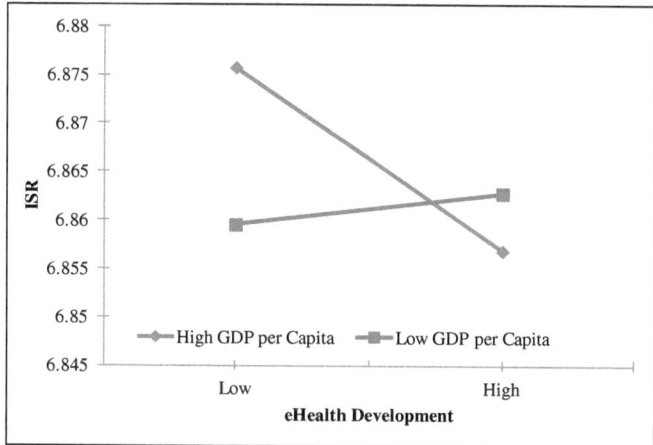

Fig. 2. Moderating influence of GDP per Capita on relationship between eHealth development and ISR (healthcare standard)

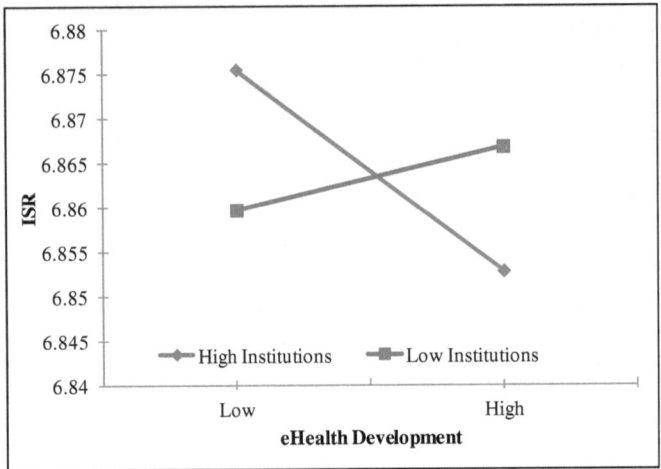

Fig. 3. Moderating influence of institutions on relationship between eHealth development and ISR (healthcare standard)

5   Discussion

Through this research it was expected to understand and assess the environmental factors that affect the relationship between eHealth development and standard of health (ISR). Through the analysis carried out using country-level data, it is identified that macro-economic stability plays a significant role in improving ISR in the presence of eHealth. That is, if the macro-economy is not stable, a country will not be able to achieve high health standards through eHealth development. Thus, the expected benefits from eHealth may not be achieved unless there is macro-economic stability in a country.

However, eHealth development may not affect ISR, at higher levels of institutions (moderated in negative direction). Firstly, having a high level of institutional framework, may burden the deplorers and users and thus, they may not be willing to follow on a cumbersome process and may even reject it. Secondly, this may be possibly due to the maintenance of many eHealth informative websites without any legitimate responsibility to the content provided. Thus, even if there is a high level of institutional framework, a lack of assurance on the validity of content may reduce user confidence in such websites and hence their acceptance. Another fact is that though, many countries have introduced eHealth policies, very few countries (even among advanced nations) such as Singapore and UK[4] have implemented the eHealth policy fully. As such, in most of these countries, the true benefits may not be possible to achieve until a sound legal framework is created. For example, privacy and ethical issues in handling patient data may have not been completely answered, and such partial implementation could be detrimental rather than non-implementation of policies. Further, it has been found that even though there are effective policies, it is important to improve the perception of healthcare workforce if the expected benefits are to be achieved. For example, a medical practitioner may alter the concerns on privacy, depending on where they are working (private or government hospital)[4].

According to this analysis, eHealth development may not affect ISR, at higher levels of GDP per capita. The negatively moderated relationship shown may be due to several probable reasons. Though GDP per capita indicates the economic growth of a country, the benefits of the development may not have reached the common public uniformly. As noted in legal frameworks for eHealth by WHO[4], even though a country is highly developed, still there will be a majority who will not have access to eHealth tools. The tools may not reach the people who really need them and will only be used by a certain class of people in the society (digital divide). The public who do not have access to IT, could suffer from poor healthcare access[10]. Also, it is found that developed countries tend to be less confident in the healthcare system, thus less confidence in eHealth systems. Thus, investing more in ICT for healthcare may not attract public to eHealth, unless the public confidence on the system is simultaneously improved[19] and a uniform accessibility to the public is created.

6   Conclusion

6.1   Limitations

Use of secondary data obtained from various sources can be considered as a limitation in carrying out this research. However, it is not feasible to collect primary data from more than 50 countries considering the budgetary and human resource constraints. Since these data used are collected from some reputable organizations such as WHO, WEF, UN it can be ensured that these data are collected using stringent measures and statistical methods have been used to ensure the validity and reliability of these data. Moreover, several researchers had used similar data for their studies[10, 20].

In this study we considered only ISR as an indicator for standard of health. Thus, to obtain more generalized and robust results, it would be better to take some other health outcomes too for consideration. Also, in the self-developed measure, rather than identifying whether there is an eHealth policy or not it would have been better if the level of implementation was known. However, such data are available only for some countries and even those are indicating only whether partially or fully implemented.

We considered only the countries having data for all the predictors and moderator variables. Thus, we could only consider 55 countries in this cross sectional study. For example, many African countries had to be removed from the consideration due to this reason. In this study, we have used 4 independent variables including the moderators. Therefore, the sample size of 40 is adequate to capture fairly small R^2 values at a significant level of 0.05[35]. Despite these three limitations, the findings are useful in assessing the moderating effect of environment factors on the relationship of eHealth development and health standard.

6.2   Implications and Future Research

As theoretical contribution of this study, we can identify; (1) Contribution made to theoretical discourse of RBV's resource complementary perspective. In previous studies, it is considered that IS innovation and deployment have direct effect on outcomes. However, our study maintains that having a specific resource can improve the outcome rather than having only the predictors (application of IS). (2) Contribution made to the knowledge base of IT-healthcare standard in assessing the influence of environmental factors in national level on the relationship between eHealth development and health outcomes (ISR).

As practical contribution, this study assists practitioners, policy makers and administrators to understand the reasons for various levels of health outcomes and use these findings in development of policy and in management of complementary assets. Getting negative interaction effects indicate that administrators should pay more attention on these complementary resources and should learn from the mistakes made before.

The findings of our research have implications for future research. First, while we show that macro-economic stability, GDP per capita and institutions have interaction effect on eHealth development and ISR, new complementary assets could be introduced to the model. For example, moderation effect of technological readiness and technological innovation can be examined. Second, panel dataset could be used to examine the effect of leads and lags between predictors, moderators and dependent variables. Third, rather than using only ISR to measure the health outcome, new combined measures could be introduced. Specially, since many developed nations are having a high ISR, a new measure could be introduced to indicate national health outcomes. Finally, self-developed eHealth development measure can be further improved by including more items to capture relevant data. However, there should be more complete national eHealth data to achieve that.

In conclusion, this study provides a new perspective to the relationship between eHealth development and national health outcomes by introducing complementary assets, namely, macro-economic stability, GDP per capita and institutions. Through this study, we found the moderating effect of environmental factors on the relationship between eHealth development and national health outcomes. This will be helpful to understand how IS innovations should be managed and to understand the influence of IS innovations in healthcare on health outcomes (ISR) in reference to complementary assets.

References

1. Kohn, L.T., Corrigan, J., Donaldson, M.S.: To err is human: building a safer health system, vol. 6. Natl. Academy Pr. (2000)
2. America, I.o.M.C.o.Q.o.H.C.i.: Crossing the quality chasm: A new health system for the 21st century. National Academies Press (2001)
3. Wu, S., et al.: Systematic review: impact of health information technology on quality, efficiency, and costs of medical care. Annals of Internal Medicine 144(10), 742–752 (2006)
4. World-Health-Organization, Global Observatory for eHealth (GOe) (2006), http://www.who.int/kms/initiatives/ehealth/en
5. Berwick, D.M.: What 'patient-centered' should mean: confessions of an extremist. Health Affairs 28(4), w555–w565 (2009)

6. Kauffman, R.J., Kumar, A.: Impact of information and communication technologies on country development: Accounting for area interrelationships. International Journal of Electronic Commerce 13(1), 11–58 (2008)
7. Lohr, S.: Doctors Raise Doubts on Digital Health Data. New York Times (2009)
8. Teece, D.J.: Profiting from technological innovation: Implications for integration, collaboration, licensing and public policy. Research Policy 15(6), 285–305 (1986)
9. Srivastava, S.C., Thompson, S.: E-Government, E-Business and National Economic Performance (2010)
10. Mithas, S., Khuntia, J., Agarwal, R.: Information Technology and Life Expectancy: A Country-Level Analysis (2009)
11. Teece, D.J.: The Strategic Management of the Oxford Handbook of Strategy, p. 138 (2006)
12. Shaw, B.: Innovation and new product development in the UK medical equipment industry. International Journal of Technology Management 15(3), 433–445 (1998)
13. Barney, J., Wright, M., Ketchen, D.J.: The resource-based view of the firm: Ten years after 1991. Journal of Management 27(6), 625–641 (2001)
14. Ravichandran, T., Lertwongsatien, C.: Effect of information systems resources and capabilities on firm performance: A resource-based perspective. Journal of Management Information Systems 21(4), 237–276 (2005)
15. Porter, M.E., Schwab, K.: The Global Competitiveness Report 2008–2009 (2009)
16. Car, J., et al.: The impact of eHealth on the quality and safety of healthcare. In: A Systemic Overview and Synthesis of the Literature. Imperial College London and The University of Edinburgh, London (2008)
17. Black, A.D., et al.: The impact of eHealth on the quality and safety of health care: a systematic overview. PLoS Medicine 8(1), e1000387 (2011)
18. Stroetmann, K.A., et al., eHealth is Worth it: The economic benefits of implemented eHealth solutions at ten European sites. European Commission (2006)
19. Bagchi, K., Udo, G., Kesh, M.: An Empirical Study Identifying the Factors that Impact eHealth Infastructure and eHealth Use (2005)
20. Srivastava, S.C., Teo, T.S.H.: What facilitates e-government development? A cross-country analysis. An International Journal on Electronic Government 4(4), 365–378 (2007)
21. Groot, W., Van Den Brink, H.M.: The health effects of education. Economics of Education Review 26(2), 186–200 (2007)
22. Diaz, J.A., et al.: Patients' use of the Internet for medical information. Journal of General Internal Medicine 17(3), 180–185 (2002)
23. Kiecolt, K.J., Nathan, L.E.: Secondary analysis of survey data 1985. Sage Publications, Inc. (1985)
24. Woszczynski, A.B., Whitman, M.E.: The problem of common method variance in IS research. The Handbook of Information Systems Research, 66–77 (2004)
25. World Health Organization (WHO), W.H.S., WHO Press, Geneva. and A.o.(2011), http://www.who.int/whosis/whostat/2011/en/index.html
26. United Nations Department of Economic and Social Affairs (2008). United Nations E-Government Survey (2008), http://unpan1.un.org/intradoc/groups/public/documents/un/unpan028607.pdf
27. WITSA, Digital Planet 2008: The Global Information Economy. Arlington: WITSA (2008)
28. Bankole, F.O., Kweku, M.O., Brown, I.: Exploring the Impacts of ICT Investments on Dimensions of Human Development in Different Contexts: A Regression Splines Analysis. In: Proceedings of SIG GlobDev Fourth Annual Workshop (2011)

29. Krishnan, S., Teo, T.: Engaging Citizens in Managing Electronic Government Service Quality: A Country-Level Analysis (2011)
30. Krishnan, S., Teo, T.S.H.: The Effect Of Information Systems Capabilities On Sustainability: A Country-Level Analysis (2011)
31. Ngwenyama, O., et al.: Is There A Relationship Between ICT, Health, Education And Development? An Empirical Analysis of five West African Countries from 1997-2003. The Electronic Journal of Information Systems in Developing Countries 23(0) (2006)
32. Dutta, S., Mia, I.: Global Information Technology Report 2008-2009. World Economic Forum (2010)
33. Gujarati, D.N.: Basic Econometrics, 4th edn. McGraw-Hill, New York (2003)
34. Gujarati, D.N., Porter, C.: Basic Econometrics, Boston. McGraw-Hill International Edition, 5th edn., pp. 260–261, 338 (2009)
35. Hair Jr., J., Black, W.C., Babin, B.J., Anderson, R.E., Tatham, R.L.: Multivariate data analysis (2006)
36. Husted, B.W., Instituto Technologico y de Estudios.: Wealth, culture, and corruption. Journal of International Business Studies, 339–359 (1999)
37. Frazier, P.A., Tix, A.P., Barron, K.E.: Testing moderator and mediator effects in counseling psychology research. Journal of Counseling Psychology 51(1), 115 (2004)
38. Aiken, L.S., West, S.G., Reno, R.R.: Multiple regression: Testing and interpreting interactions1991. Sage Publications, Inc. (1991)
39. West, S.G., Aiken, L.S., Krull, J.L.: Experimental personality designs: Analyzing categorical by continuous variable interactions. Journal of Personality 64(1), 1–48 (1996)
40. Cohen, J., Cohen, P., West, G.S., Aiken, L.S.: Applied multiple regression/correlation analysis for the behavioral sciences (2003)

Appendix: Countries Considered in this Study

Argentina	India	Poland
Australia	Indonesia	Portugal
Austria	Ireland	Romania
Bangladesh	Israel	Senegal
Belgium	Italy	Singapore
Brazil	Japan	Slovakia
Bulgaria	Jordan	Slovenia
Cameroon	Korea (Republic of)	Spain
Canada	Kuwait	Sri Lanka
China	Malaysia	Sweden
Colombia	Mexico	Switzerland
Czech Republic	Morocco	Thailand
Denmark	Netherlands	Turkey
Egypt	New Zealand	United Kingdom
Finland	Norway	United States
France	Pakistan	Viet Nam
Germany	Panama	Zimbabwe
Greece	Peru	
Hungary	Philippines	

Social Networks and Communication Media for Generating Creative Ideas

Yi Wu and Klarissa Chang

13 Computing Drive, Building 'COM2', National University of Singapore,
Singapore, 117417
wuyi@nus.edu.sg, changtt@comp.nus.edu.sg

Abstract. Why some dyadic interactions are more likely than others to trigger hinder the generation of novel and useful ideas? To investigate this question, we examine the attributes of dyadic ties that influence the generation of creative ideas, and how the strength of influence changes contingently on the mix use of communication media. Our study extends previous research by examining the impacts of Simmelian advice tie, Simmelian friendship tie and communication media mix on generating creative ideas. We conducted a survey among students in a knowledge-intensive academic institution. The results show that Simmelian advice tie, Simmelian friendship tie and communication media mix help to trigger the generation of creative ideas. The impact of Simmelian advice tie on creative idea generation is weakened by communication media mix, while the influence of Simmelian friendship tie is strengthened by it. We discuss both theoretical and practical contributions of our research on these findings.

Keywords: generating creative ideas, Simmelian advice tie, Simmelian friendship tie, communication media mix.

1   Introduction

Creativity refers to the generation of ideas that are novel and useful [3]. It is important to study creativity in order to effectively manage the innovation process in organizations. It is even more important to understand how to generate creative ideas because idea generation is the prerequisite for idea evaluation and selection [16]. Generating creative ideas has been studied from different perspectives, including organizational [e.g., 27] and individual [e.g., 31] levels. However, little attention has been devoted to studying creativity at the dyadic level, i.e., generating creative ideas between each pair of individuals. Dyadic exchanges are not only conduits of knowledge but also sources of social support [38]. This paper examines the attributes of dyadic ties that influence the generation of creative ideas; and how the strength of influence changes contingently on mix use of communication media.

A Simmelian tie refers to the extent to which a focal dyad is surrounded by at least one common third party [21]. Two types of ties commonly occur in organizations: tie between coworkers and tie between friends. Advice tie encourages task-oriented

A. Bhattacherjee and B. Fitzgerald (Eds.): Future of ICT Research, IFIP AICT 389, pp. 160–176, 2012.

and norm-supporting interactions to solve challenges that require novel and useful ideas [34]. On the other hand, friendship tie includes personal trust that provides comfortable opportunities to discuss uncertainties and concerns with peers to come out with creative thoughts [34]. However, there is little research looking at the impacts of the presence of third party on generating creative ideas in both advice and friendship networks. Research on absorptive capacity and associative learning has shown that it is easier to absorb diverse knowledge to generate creative ideas when individuals share a common knowledge base of similar third party [32]. Therefore, we initially explore that the existence of common third party around a focal tie substantially changes the nature of generating creative ideas.

Besides the influence of common third party presence in different networks, the mix use of communication media is another factor that would significantly impact on the process of generating creative ideas in dyads. Different media has been widely implied in organizational work, including face-to-face communication, mediated communication. Mediated communication refers to communication that takes place using communication technology (e.g., telephone, computer) [40]. On one hand, communication technology enables diverse groups of people to collaborate and make decisions, regardless of their geographic locations [23]. On the other hand, some research suggests that the potential for process losses exists when using mediated communication [15]. However, process losses that occur because of mediated communication challenges may actually be beneficial when the end result is a creative product.

Due to the knowledge gaps identified above, we address the following research questions in this study:

RQ1: How does Simmelian advice tie impact on generating creative ideas?

RQ2: How does Simmelian friendship tie impact on generating creative ideas?

RQ3: How does communication media mix moderate the impacts of Simmelian advice and friendship ties on generating creative ideas?

This research has significant theoretical contributions. It helps in understanding of how creative ideas are generated between individuals by integration of different theoretical perspective (i.e., Simmelian advice tie, Simmelian friendship tie and communication media mix). Through examining the direct and moderating effects of communication media mix, the research opens a black box to demonstrate how communication media influences the generation of creative ideas. More importantly, it calls for the need to devote significant theoretical attention to dyadic perspective in studies investigating the nuances of social networks in work teams.

The study also provides practical contributions. Organizational managers are often encouraged to form creative teams by structuring Simmelian ties in either advice or friendship network among employees. Organization workers could leverage both face-to-face and mediated communication to assist in generating creative ideas. Additionally, technology system designers can better understand how to integrate multiple technology artifacts (e.g., verbal and non-verbal cues) by considering specific communication tools with corresponding artifacts.

2   Theoretical Background

2.1   Creativity: Generate Creative Ideas

Generating creative ideas is often the result of novel combinations of different perspectives individuals are exposed to via social interactions [2]. Social interactions are defined as the transfer of information between the source which is sending information and the recipient who is receiving information [38]. Social interaction between two individuals includes the following basic stages: the recipient's acquiring of knowledge from the source and processing that knowledge, and then the realization of the potential value of the interaction outcome [32]. Processing knowledge that yields creative ideas has been the subject of studies that adopt a cognitive psychology perspective in studying creativity [37]. Within this context, creative ideas are associated with the occurrence of two distinct sets of cognitive processes: generation of creative ideas and evaluation of the generated ideas to select the ones for further pursuit. This model is consistent with the "blind-variation and selection-retention" model of creative thought by Simonton [37]. As the recipient evaluates the ideas after interacting with the source, that recipient is able to realize the novelty and usefulness of the ideas.

We rely on the recipient to assess the novelty and usefulness of his/her ideas because we focus on the generative aspect of ideas before the ideas are exposed for further evaluation. It is important to recognize that what the recipient considers as potentially creative may not necessarily be considered as creative by others.

2.2   Simmelian Ties for Generating Creative Ideas

In reality, a social tie between two individuals includes different relationships such as advice or friendship tie. Previous research suggests that supportive behavior on the part of others in a work-place (such as coworkers) enhances employees' creativity [29]. On the other hand, friendship tie considers with whom individuals share perceptions and rely for social support [12]. It includes personal trust that provides comfortable opportunities to discuss uncertainties and concerns with peers to come out with creative thoughts [34]. Particularly, Simmelian advice tie indicates whether a connection between two coworkers is Simmelian or not; meanwhile; Simmelian friendship tie describes whether a friendship is Simmelian or not .

Generating creative ideas requires individuals to hold common knowledge and shared understanding to derive personal thinking and solutions from a new perspective. We contend that Simmelian tie can enhance generating creative ideas. Simmel and Wolff [36] argued that network size does not fundamentally change the impact of a network on behavior, rather, the change from a dyad to a triad or a larger network changes an individual's behavior. Simmelian tie facilitates the formation of shared understanding and the pursuit of common goals by mitigating competition and self-interest. This is important, because informational advantages can be quite limited if the parties involved, acting opportunistically, avoid sharing sensitive [41].

A distinction between a Simmelian tie and a non-Simmelian tie may provide novel insights into how individuals leverage common knowledge and shared understanding to generate creative ideas from a new perspective. Simmelian advice tie increases the stability of interaction to achieve the successful integration of different perspectives to generate creative ideas [9]. Meanwhile Simmelian friendship tie enhances the generation of creative ideas by improving open communication to foster a collaborative environment [28].

2.3   Communication Media for Generating Creative Ideas

Compensatory adaptation theory (CAT) is based on the idea that human brains are initially designed for face-to-face communication [20]. Users of mediated communication exerted greater cognitive effort and experienced more communication ambiguity than dyad engaging in face-to-face communication. Regardless of the problems and challenges that have been associated with mediated communication, the ambiguous communications or inaccurate communication fluency that results from it actually leads to increase in creativity [40]. Creative solutions to problems have sometimes developed as the result of accidents or misunderstandings. Moreover, studies in cognitive psychology have shown that when individuals do not have all the information they need to make a conclusion, they "fill in the blanks" based on their individual knowledge base [20].

As recipients of information do not spend significantly more time compensating for the obstacles presented by mediated communication, they have more time to interpret presented information and combine it with existing knowledge which may help in the development of creative ideas. Since too many social and nonverbal cues may provide irrelevant information and interfere with message content, too much face-to-face communication (as a rich medium) may be detrimental to generate creative ideas [44]. Thus, the value of applying CAT to generate creative ideas is that the ambiguity and lack of communication fluency inherent in the move away from continual face-to-face interactions provides individuals with opportunities to perceive information in ways different than that in which it was intended.

A second main theoretical perspective we draw upon to understand the relationship between communication media use and generating creative ideas is dual coding theory. Dual coding theory (DCT) posits that individuals learn and retain information through both verbal and nonverbal systems [11]. In reality, individuals present and receive information in multiple ways; the use of multiple media allows us to process different facets of information in a variety of ways [25]. Thus, receiving information through mediated media and in face-to-face situations not only influences how one receives information but affects how one perceived information and influences the amount of time one engages in communication-related activities [40]. Use of non-face-to-face communication media provides individuals more time to ponder the information contained in a mediated interaction [14]. Thus, DCT would suggest that because generating creative ideas requires that an individual eventually bring divergent ideas together, have a mix of mediated communication and face-to-face interactions is important.

3   Research Model and Hypotheses Development

3.1   Effect of Simmelian Advice Tie

The increased stability promotes the formation of a common knowledge among the coworkers involved at work [41]; common knowledge is critical to overcome interpretive barriers and achieving the successful integration of different perspectives to generate creative ideas [9]. Another element that differentiates Simmelian advice tie from non-Simmelian advice tie is the higher level of cooperation observed within the dyads at work [41], regard of norms of reciprocity that facilitate advice exchanging for solving problem [32].   Cooperation becomes a shared value in densely connected structures, and individuals with common-third coworker(s) are naturally inclined to devote time to knowledge sharing with others. When a dyad shares common-third coworker(s) that strengthens the collaborative environment around them, it improves the conditions to generate creative ideas between the dyads [12, 28]. Therefore, we hypothesize:

H1: The presence of Simmelian advice tie is positively associated with the generation of creative ideas between dyads.

3.2   Effect of Simmelian Friendship Tie

Strong friendship tie influences shared values [18], and such shared value can induce the common knowledge to trigger generating creative ideas between individuals. As well, friendship enhances open communication [19], due to the emotional attachment [6] that is intrinsic to the relation.   These factors are associated with the fostering of a collaborative environment favorable to creativity [28]. As well, the presence of common-third friend(s) can foster trust of the interacting individuals to engage more closely at work, which could form the collaborative conditions needed to generate creative ideas [28]. Therefore, we hypothesize:

H2: The presence of Simmelian friendship tie is positively associated with the generation of creative ideas between dyads.

3.3   Effects of Communication Media Mix

Researchers have found that communication tools can provide an environment conducive for sharing new and novel ideas.   Too many social and nonverbal cues found in face-to-face communication (as a rich medium) may provide irrelevant information, distract from the task at hand, and be detrimental to creativity [44]. In contrast, a mediated communication environment is conducive to creativity because it prevents distraction from face-to-face communication. The intent of communication media mix is to determine how often individuals engage in mediated communications (e.g., email, Google Documents) relative to face-to-face interactions. According to dual coding theory, humans process information differently when it arrives in diverse forms [30]; thus, it is important to use more than one form of communication.   When multiple communication media are used, the total amount of possible communication activity expands, allowing all participants more air time. The increase in possible communication combined with the potential to generate creative ideas to arise from mediated communication ambiguity, suggest that more mediated communication is better for generating creative ideas. Therefore, we hypothesize:

H3: The degree of communication media mix is positively associated with the generation of creative ideas between dyads.

Simmelian advice tie is strong relationship, according to the definition of Simmilian tie [21]. Results from the network studies suggested that strongly connected coworkers prefer to stick on group-wide media; and at onsite teamwork, the most frequency media is face-to-face communication. Communication media choices influence how individuals interact, the type of information conveyed, and the amount of information conveyed in teamwork [25]. Interaction in teamwork in non-face-to-face communication is less likely than those who in face-to-face communication to exchange private and relational information [26]. This decrease in the amount and type of information shared may hinder the ability of individuals to generate creative ideas, as knowledge diversity is useful to generate creative ideas [38]. As CAT proposes, it is important to see visual cues when explaining something novel using language to be better able to share in face-to-face communication. Thus, individuals who are better able to understand and clarify others ideas in teamwork will be more likely to generate creative ideas. This will be more likely to occur in face-to-face communication. Hence, we hypothesize:

H4: The impact of Simmelian advice tie on the generation of creative ideas will be weakened by the degree of communication media mix.

Simmelian friendship tie indicates close friendship [21]. Close friends are less comfortable when expressing views that are different from others. This discomfort may be lessened when communicating in ways that do not highlight differences, such as in a computer-mediated environment where the recipient and source do not see each other [10]. Additionally, friends can rely on multiple communication media to interact with each other, due to the geographic and time issues. DCT suggests that use of different forms of communication media would help individuals develop and express creative ideas [30]. Therefore, we hypothesize:

H5: The impact of Simmelian friendship tie on the generation of creative ideas will be strengthened by the degree of communication media mix.

The theoretical propositions are summarized in figure 1. Next, we present a detailed description of the mechanisms of our design, which will be used to examine our research questions.

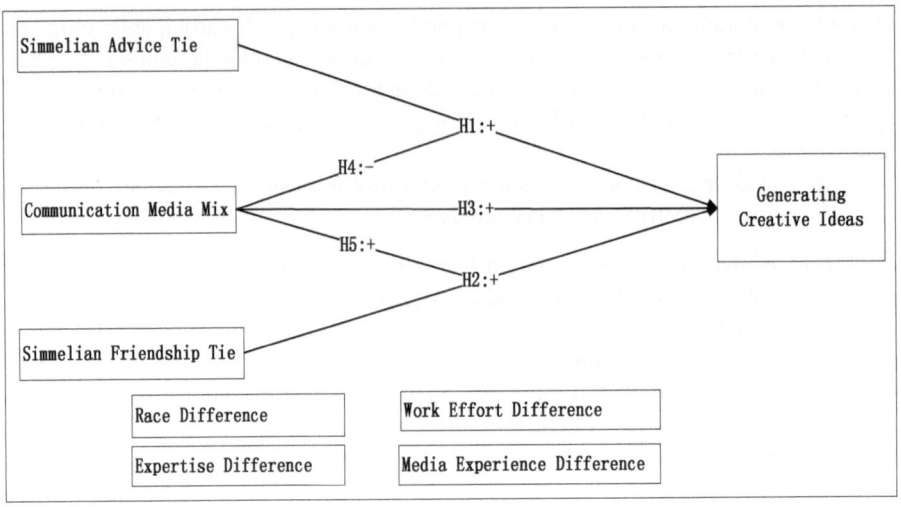

Fig. 1. Research Model

4   Methodology

4.1   Research Setting

The study, which involved knowledge-intensive teamwork, was conducted in a university course from an academic institution. The students participated in teamwork. Preliminary interviews with the instructors, observation, and existing documentation of the course confirmed that the teamwork would suffer from a lack of creative ideas. Since students were not constantly in physical contact, but frequently communicated with each other, it was important for them to have access to multiple communication tools.

Network data was collected using a combination of classical sociometric techniques [43] in a paper-based questionnaire. First, each student was provided with a fixed roster of contacts formed by the 79 students in the study. Students were asked to select those they had "gone to" for interactions that significantly affected their teamwork. The name generator used an "information seeking" perspective to ensure consistency throughout the survey because all the relational questions would be formulated from the recipient's viewpoint. This approach did not appear to lead respondents to omit a significant number of less important ties.

Responses were received from 72 of 79 students, resulting in a 91.14% response rate, which was more than the minimum 80% participation rate needed for network studies [33]. Demographic data was collected from their class rosters. The sample included a heterogeneous mix of educational backgrounds, including students from computer science (20%), information systems (35%), social science (10%), business (20%) and engineering (15%) departments. 53% percent of them were males.

4.2   Measurements

This study utilized single-item measurements to capture network variables. The combination of roster methodology and single-item measures is found to be mainly reliable [24].

Ease of generating creative ideas captures the extent to which it is easy for each pair of individuals to generate creative ideas associated with their interactions   [38]. Instead of evaluating the number of creative ideas, we focused on the source's ease of generating creative ideas with the recipient. This measurement is consistent with previous studies on knowledge transfer at the dyadic level, which relies on the source of the dyad to assess the ease of transferring knowledge to the recipient [32].   The variables was captured by asking each respondent to rate, on a four-point Likert scale ("strongly disagree", "disagree", "agree" and "strongly agree"), his/her level of agreement with statements such as: "When I interact with this person, it is easy for me to generate novel and useful ideas." [38].

Advice and friendship ties. To measure advice tie, respondents were asked to indicate their advice exchange frequency on work-related issues with the identified source on a 4-point scale ("never", "less than once weekly", "once weekly", and "several times weekly") [42].   To obtain matrix of advice network ($\mathbf{A}$), we code $\mathbf{A}_{ij}$ as "1" in case that actor i at least exchange with actor j once a week, otherwise, we set $\mathbf{A}_{ij}$ as "0". This operation is consistent with previous researches [39]. To measure friendship tie, respondents were asked to indicate their average frequency of going out with each person for non-work activities on a 4-point scale ("never", "less than once weekly", "once weekly", and "several times weekly") [35]. Thus, we gained the matrix of friendship network ($\mathbf{F}$). A reciprocated relation existed only if person i connected to person j, and vice versa. This gives us the raw advice matrix ($\mathbf{R}^{A}$) and friendship matrix ($\mathbf{R}^{F}$). A hypergraph matrix illustrating every instance in which a respondent was tied to every other respondent was derived from the raw dyadic matrix obtained from the survey. We then derived the Simmelian advice matrix ($\mathbf{A}^{S}$) and Simmelian friendship matrix ($\mathbf{F}^{S}$) [22].

Simmelian advice tie ($\mathbf{A}^{S}$). $\mathbf{A}^{S}_{ij}$ =1, indicating the advice tie between respondent i and respondent j is Simmelian. Otherwise, $\mathbf{A}^{S}_{ij}$ =0, meaning that respondent i and respondent j is not Simmelian-tied.

Simmelian friendship tie ($\mathbf{F}^{S}$). $\mathbf{F}^{S}_{ij}$ =1, indicating the friendship tie between respondent i and respondent j is Simmelia. Otherwise, $\mathbf{F}^{S}_{ij}$ =0, meaning that respondent i and respondent j is not Simmelian connected.

Communication media mix ($\mathbf{M}$). Preliminary interviews showed that email and collaborative tool (i.e., Google Documents) are also frequently used for communication and information exchange, in addition to face-to-face meeting. Given the prevailing communication options in class, the communication media mix score was calculated by looking at the ratio of mediated interaction to face-to-face interaction with sources of each recipient. Each respondent was asked to indicate the use frequency (o=never, 1=less than once a week, 2=once a week, 3=more than once a week) of each media that they used to communicate with each identified source. The communication media included face-to-face meeting, email and Google Documents. The range of communication media mix scores (ratio of mediated/face-to-face) was 0 to 2 with a mean score of 1.03 meaning that the recipient communicated with source almost equally by mediated and face-to-face interactions. Values greater than 1 indicate the majority of communication took place via mediated communication.

Control variables. Several control variables were included in the modeling to eliminate alternative explanations. First, we control social demographic differences, culture difference, by measuring their nationality, where "1" indicate that recipient and source come from the same country while "0" not, due to that culture had been shown to influence the communication [13]. Expertise difference measures their difference in majors, where "1" means two respondents have the same expertise and "0" indicate the opposite; informational demographic difference, i.e., expertise diversity, can influence creativity [38]. We also control their differences in media experience, because existing media experience can influence individual's media choice in the communication process. To measure dyadic media experience difference, we surveyed the respondents to obtain their use frequency of email and Google Documents before enrolling this course; and then calculated the difference; higher values indicate greater difference between two respondents. Finally, because the respondents from the class have common tasks in teamwork, we control their work effort by measuring their weekly work hour in task. "work effort difference" was conceptualized to capture difference in work efforts Greater values mean higher distance between two respondent's work efforts.

4.3   Analyses Strategy

Traditional methods of regression analysis are inappropriate because dyads do not constitute independent observations, and would result in high levels of autocorrelation in the regression results [8]. For this reason, we applied the multinominal logistic regression quadratic assignment procedure (MRQAP) [4] provided in UCINET 6 [5] to analyze the data. The MRQAP regression has been shown to yield unbiased parameter estimates regardless of the degree of autocorrelation. These estimates can be interpreted in the same way as those obtained from standard regressions [21]. Significance levels for correlations and regressions were based on distributions generated from 5, 000 random permutations.

5   Empirical Results

5.1   Preliminary Analyses

Network studies do not usually assess the measurement model as model variables are measured as single items and each network question addresses specific individuals in a network. Table 1 provides the descriptive and correlation statistics for all variables used in our study.

Table 1 includes minimum, maximum, mean, and standard deviation of variable values for the sample in the survey data. Results of QAP correlations show significant correlations of ease of generating creative ideas with key independent variables – Simmelian friendship tie (0.228. p<.05) and Simmelian advice tie (0.334,p<.01). Additionally, the high significant level of correlation between variables is due to the interdependence of network variables, resulting from the non independent network observations [42].

Table 1. Descriptive statistics and correlations

		Min	Max	Mean	S.D	N	1	2	3	4	5	6	7
1	WD	0	18	3.300	4.038	587	-						
2	MD	0	4	0.937	0.749	586	-0.058	-					
3	CD	0	1	0.629	0.484	587	-0.001	-0.022	-				
4	ED	0	1	0.626	0.484	586	-0.097	-0.023	0.094	-			
5	SF	0	1	0.133	0.339	587	-0.007	-0.027	0.176	0.220	-		
6	SA	0	1	0.187	0.390	587	-0.107	-0.053	0.026	0.028	0.301	-	
7	CM	0	2	1.026	0.537	587	-0.028	-0.068	0.099	0.030	-0.109	0.164	-
8	EI	1	4	2.739	0.757	586	-0.086	-0.046	0.016	0.186	0.228*	0.334*	0.113

(EI: Ease of generating creative ideas, SA: Simmelian advice tie, SF: Simmelian friendship tie, CM: communication media mix, ED: expertise difference, MD: media experience difference, CD: culture difference, WD: work effort difference, *=p<0.05, **=p<0.01)

5.2   Hypothesized Model

The results of MRQAP are displayed in table 2. The hypothesized models seem to provide an acceptable fit to the data with a R2 of 0.164, with adjusted R2 of 0.163. To plot the interaction effects, all predictors are standardized and the interactive terms are the product of standardized independent variables and moderator following Aiken et al. [1].

Hypothesis H1 is supported (b=0.534, p<0.01) from model 2. The recipient is more likely to generate useful and novel ideas in the interaction when he/she and the source share common-third worker(s). It can be seen from table 2 that hypothesis H2 is supported (b=0.275, p<0.01) from model 2. The result means that the recipient is more likely to generate useful and novel ideas in the interaction with source when s/he and the source share common-third friend(s). Regard of H3, regress of model 2 shows it is supported (b=0.146, p<0.01). This finding presents that recipient who engage in proportionally more mediated communication with source will be easier to generate creative ideas, comparing to recipient who engages in proportionally more face-to-face interaction.

Regard to the interaction effects, testing results are shown in model 3. H4 is supported (b=-0.340, p<0.01). Recipient who shares common-third coworker(s) and engages in proportionally more mediated communication with source will be less likely to generate creative ideas, comparing to those who engage in proportionally more face-to-face communication. From figure 2 of interaction plotting, it can be seen that the marginal effect of Simmelian advice tie on ease of generating creative ideas is stronger when the communication media mix is low than that when it is high, because the slop of the low communication media mix line is greater than that of the high one.

Hypothesis H5 is also supported (b=191, p<0.05) from model 3. Recipient who shares common-third friend(s) and engages in proportionally more mediated communication with source will be more likely to generate creative ideas, comparing to those who engage in proportionally more face-to-face communication. It can be seen from figure 3 that the marginal effect of Simmelian friendship tie on ease of generating creative ideas is stronger when the communication media mix is high than that when it is low, because the slop of the high communication media mix line is greater than that of the low one.

We are interested to found that there was a significantly negative relationship between work effort difference and ease of generating creative ideas from model 1, meaning that recipient and source who spent more time together will be easier to generate creative ideas. However, media experience difference will hinder recipient's ease of generating creative ideas from model 1.   The result reveals that similarity of media used between will help to generate creative ideas, probably diminishing the communication obstacles. Model 1 also showed there is a significantly positive relationship between expertise difference and ease of generating creative ideas from model 1. The result confirms that knowledge diversity could help to generate creative ideas. However, we did not any find significant relationship between culture difference and ease of generating creative ideas.

Table 2. MRQAP on generating creative ideas

Control Variables	Model 1	Model 2	Model 3
Intercept	2.655	2.377	2.341
Work effort difference	-0.014**	-0.008**	-0.006*
Media experience difference	-0.046**	-0.023*	-0.026*
Cultureace difference	-0.006	-0.035	-0.031
Expertise difference	0.282**	0.232**	0.235**
Main Effects			
Simmelian advice		0.534**	0.923**
Simmelian friendship		0.275**	0.061
Communication media mix		0.146**	0.178**
Interaction Effects			
SA*CM			-0.340**
SF*CM			0.191*
R^2	0.042	0.160	0.164
Adjusted R^2	0.042	0.159	0.163

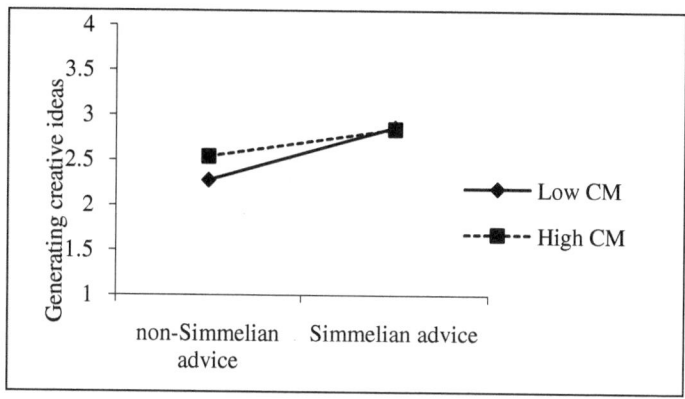

Fig. 2. Interaction effect of Simmelian advice tie with communication media mix

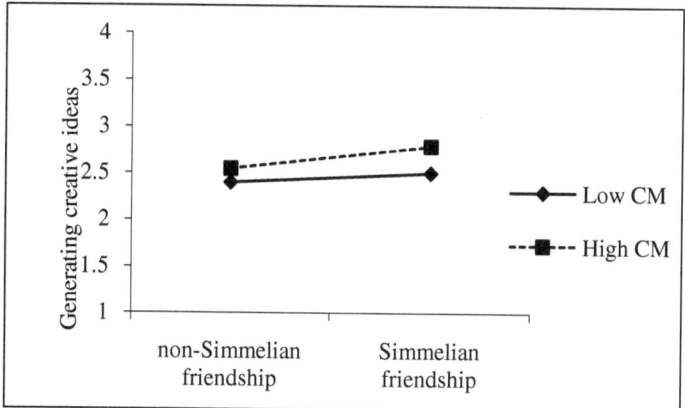

Fig. 3. Interaction effect of Simmelian friendship tie with communication media mix

6   Discussion

In this study, we examined the relationships among Simmelian advice tie, Simmelian friendship tie and communication media mix on generating creative ideas. The results clearly demonstrate the importance of looking at both the direct and indirect effects of communication media mix on ease of generating creative ideas. When the ratio of mediated communication to face-to-face communication is high, there is an overall positive impact on generating creative ideas. There is a clear, significant impact of common-third part on the interaction between recipient and source both in advice and friendship networks. However, our results present that Simmelian advice tie engaging in more face-to-face communication will be easier to generate creative ideas; while high ratio of communication media mix will strengthen the impact of Simmelian friendship tie on ease of generating creative ideas.

The formation of a shared understanding is promoted by the increased stability among the parties involved in advice network [41]. When a dyad shares common-third worker(s) that strengthens the collaborative environment around them in advice network, it improves the conditions to generate creative ideas between individuals within the dyads [12, 28]. For Simmelian friendship tie, strong friendship influences shared values [18], and enhances open communication [19], due to the emotional attachment [6] that are intrinsic to the tie. The presence of common-third friend(s) can enhance the shared value and open communication between friends, and these factors are associated with the fostering of a collaborative environment favorable to generate creative ideas [28].

Engaging in more proportionally mediated communication is useful for recipient to generate creative ideas when interacting with source. Humans process information differently when it arrives in diverse forms [30]; it is important to use multiple communication media. The total amount of possible communication activity expands along with use of multiple communication media, allowing all participants more air time. The increase in possible communication combined with the potential to generate creative ideas to arise from mediated communication ambiguity, suggest that more mediated communication is better for generating creative ideas. Mediated communication is conducive to creativity because it prevents distraction from face-to-face communication. CAT predicts that more miscommunications may arise when using mediated communication. And this communication ambiguity actually induces creative thinking

Teamwork interaction in non-face-to-face communication is less likely than those who in face-to-face communication to exchange private and relational information at work [26]. This decrease in the amount and type of information shared may hinder the ability of individuals to generate creative ideas, as knowledge diversity is useful to trigger creative ideas generation [38]. As CAT proposes, it is important to see visual cues when explaining something novel using language to be better able to share in face-to-face communication. Thus, engaging in more proportionally face-to-face communication can enhance the impact of Simmelian advice tie on ease of generating creative ideas.

However, close friends are less comfortable when expressing views that are different from others. Additionally, friends can rely on multiple communication media to interact and exchange with each other, due to the geographic and time issues. This discomfort and inconvenience may be lessened when communicating in ways that do not highlight differences, such as in a computer-mediated environment where the recipient and source do not see each other [10]. Therefore, a recipient in more proportionally mediated communication with source in friendship network is more likely to generate creative ideas.

6.1   Theoretical Implications

Our study contributed to the existing literature on creativity by calling attention to dyadic perspective in social network structures. This study emphasized the importance of studying social network phenomenon in organizations from the fundamental unit of networks (i.e., dyad), because social interactions within dyads are different as reflected by ties. Diverse knowledge was important for generating creative ideas and shared interests, but the presence of common-third party provided more conducive conditions (social support, extrinsic and intrinsic motivations) for accessing diverse knowledge sources [41].

Our research also made an important contribution to research on individual performance by showing that Simmelian ties could introduce motivations to share, as well as integrate and reconcile heterogeneous knowledge sets which were often taken for granted. Our research reveals that strong tie (i.e., Simmelian ties) can also trigger generation of creative ideas by enhancing the process of interaction inside; further analysis also confirmed this finding by treating tie strength as an predictor. This makes a complementary discussion to the debate of "strength of weak tie theory".

Last but not least, this study explores two theories, CAT and DCT, and their relevance for generating creative ideas. It is argued that the ambiguity of information received via mediated exchange may actually be helpful if the interaction is to generate creative ideas. Furthermore, DCT suggest that people learn and remember things differently depending on how the information was conveyed to them. Our study is one of the first to look at the impact of the combination of different communication media.

6.2   Practical Implications

The findings suggested important practical implications. On one hand, this study provided organizational managers with specific guidelines on how to form and structure a team with Simmelian advice and Simmelian friendship ties in work environment, cultivating collaborative environment for solving problems. Practitioners are encouraged to form cliques in both advice and friendship networks. Organizations should arrange out-work activities for employees to form their friendship network, specifically for R&D department.

The result suggests that mediated communication is equally important, and possible more so in facilitating to generate creative ideas than face-to-face communication. Teams with individuals, who only connected in advice network, should encourage team members to participate in face-to-face meeting for problem solving as much as possible; on the other hand, individuals could use mediated communication tools to interact with their friends for information to solve challenges. However, for those who are both in advice and friendship networks, it is contingent on the timing to implement different communication media. It is reasonable to assume that it is preferred to attend face-to-face meeting at work, while using mediated communication tool to interact with each other when out of work.

6.3   Future Work

This research sought to address the limitations in existing studies by examining dyadic interactions that might be more likely to trigger the generation of novel and useful ideas. However, this research is not without limitations.

In the future research, we would analyze both subjective (e.g., self-reports of network relationships) and objective measures (e.g., logs of email exchanges, product evaluation). Also, we conducted our study in academic organization by using a university course; future work should move the research context to a business organization. However, our results provided some evidences of the roles of Simmelian ties and the main effects of ties and communication media on ease of generating creative ideas, which shed insights on the innovation process in digital collaborations. Finally, it strongly recommends distinguishing effects of different communication tools in advice network and friendship network.

7   Conclusion

This paper aims to enhance our understanding of the generative aspect of creativity by examining it at the dyadic level. We tried to answer the question-- why some dyadic interactions are more likely than others to trigger the generation of novel and useful ideas. The insights generated by this work complement what we have learned from previous studies on creativity as a social phenomenon [e.g., 7, 17, 28]. However, instead of focusing on how the aggregated communication patterns of an individual contribute to his/her ability to produce creative outcomes such as new artifacts (or new proposals or patents), this paper acknowledges that not all dyadic relationships (even for the same individual) are equally good catalysts in the generation of useful and novel ideas, and thus examines precisely how attributes of a specific dyadic interaction affect the generation of creative ideas emanating from it.

References

1. Aiken, L.S., West, S.G., Reno, R.R.: Multiple regression: Testing and interpreting interactions. Sage Publications, Inc. (1991)
2. Allen, T.J.: Managing the flow of technology. MIT Press (1977)
3. Amabile, T.: Creativity in Context. West View Press, Inc, Boulder (1996)
4. Baker, F.B., Hubert, L.J.: The analysis of social interaction data. Sociological Methods & Research 9(3), 339 (1981)
5. Borgatti, S.P., Everett, M.G., Freeman, L.C.: UCINET for Windows: Software for social network analysis. Harvard Analytic Technologies 6 (2002)
6. Brass, D.J.: Power in organizations: A social network perspective. Research in Politics and Society 4, 295–323 (1992)
7. Burt, R.S.: Structural holes and good ideas. The American Journal of Sociology 110(2), 349–399 (2004)
8. Carley, K.M., Krackhardt, D.: Cognitive inconsistencies and non-symmetric friendship. Social Networks 18(1), 1–27 (1996)
9. Carlile, P.R.: Transferring, translating, and transforming: An integrative framework for managing knowledge across boundaries. Organization Science 15(5), 555–568 (2004)
10. Carlson, J.R., Zmud, R.W.: Channel expansion theory and the experiential nature of media richness perceptions. Academy of Management Journal, 153–170 (1999)
11. Clark, J.M., Paivio, A.: Dual coding theory and education. Educational Psychology Review 3(3), 149–210 (1991)
12. Coleman, J.S.: Foundations of social theory. Cambridge Belknap Press (1990)
13. Cummings, J.N.: Work Groups, Structural Diversity, and Knowledge Sharing in a Global Organization. Management Science 50(3), 352–364 (2004)

14. Dennis, A.R., Fuller, R.M., Valacich, J.S.: Media, tasks, and communication processes: A theory of media synchronicity. MIS Quarterly 32(3), 575–600 (2008)
15. Dennis, A.R., Wixom, B.H., Vandenberg, R.J.: Understanding fit and appropriation effects in group support systems via meta-analysis. MIS Quarterly, 167–193 (2001)
16. Fleming, L., Mingo, S., Chen, D.: Brokerage and collaborative creativity. Administrative Science Quarterly 52, 443–475 (2007)
17. Fleming, L., Waguespack, D.M.: Brokerage, boundary spanning, and leadership in open innovation communities. Organization Science 18(2), 165–180 (2007)
18. Gibbons, D.E.: Friendship and advice networks in the context of changing professional values. Administrative Science Quarterly 49, 238–262 (2004)
19. Jehn, K.A., Shah, P.P.: Interpersonal relationships and task performance: An examination of mediation processes in friendship and acquaintance groups. Journal of Personality and Social Psychology 72(4), 775 (1997)
20. Kock, N.: Media naturalness and compensatory encoding: the burden of electronic media obstacles is on senders. Decision Support Systems 44(1), 175–187 (2007)
21. Krackhardt, D.: Simmelian tie: super strong and sticky. In: Kramer, R.M., Neale, M.A. (eds.) Power and Influence in Organizations, pp. 21–38. Sage, CA (1998)
22. Krackhardt, D., Kilduff, M.: Structure, culture and Simmelian ties in entrepreneurial firms. Social Networks 24(3), 279–290 (2002)
23. Lipnack, J., Stamps, J.: Virtual teams: Reaching across space, time, and organizations with technology. John Wiley & Sons Inc. (1997)
24. Marsden, P.V.: Network data and measurement. Annual Review of Sociology 16, 435–463 (1990)
25. Massey, A.P., Montoya-Weiss, M.M.: Unraveling the temporal fabric of knowledge conversion: A model of media selection and use. MIS Quarterly 30(1), 99–114 (2006)
26. McLeod, P.L., Liker, J.K.: Electronic meeting systems: Evidence from a low structure environment. Information Systems Research 3(3), 195–223 (1992)
27. Monge, P.R., Cozzens, M.D., Contractor, N.S.: Communication and motivational predictors of the dynamics of organizational innovation. Organization Science 3(2), 250–274 (1992)
28. Obstfeld, D.: Social networks, the Tertius lungens and orientation involvement in innovation. Administrative Science Quarterly 50(1), 100–130 (2005)
29. Oldham, G.R., Cummings, A.: Employee creativity: Personal and contextual factors at work. Academy of Management Journal, 607–634 (1996)
30. Paivio, Lambert, W.: Dual coding and bilingual memory. Journal of Verbal Learning and Verbal Behavior 20(5), 532–539 (1981)
31. Perry-Smith, J.E.: Social yet creative: The role of social relationships in facilitating individual creativity. Academy of Management Journal 49(1), 85–101 (2006)
32. Reagans, R., McEvily, B.: Network Structure and Knowledge Transfer: The Effects of Cohesion and Range. Administrative Science Quarterly 48, 240–267 (2003)
33. Scott, J.: Social network analysis: a handbook, 2nd edn. Sage Publications (2000)
34. Shah, P.P.: Network destruction: The structural implications of downsizing. The Academy of Management Journal 43(1), 101–112 (2000)
35. Shah, P.P.: Who are employees' social referents? Using a network perspective to determine referent others. The Academy of Management Journal 41(3), 249–268 (1998)
36. Simmel, G., Wolff, K.H.: The Sociology of Georg Simmel. Free Pr. (1950)
37. Simonton, D.K.: Scientific Genius: A Psychology of Science. Cambridge University Press (1988)

38. Sosa, M.E.: Where Do Creative Interactions Come From? The Role of Tie Content and Social Networks. Organization Science 22(1), 1–21 (2011)
39. Sykes, T., Venkatesh, V., Gosain, S.: Model of acceptance with peer support: A social network perspective to understand individual-level system use. MIS Quarterly 33(2), 371–393 (2009)
40. Thatcher, S., Brown, S.A.: Individual creativity in teams: The importance of communication media mix. Decision Support Systems 49(3), 290–300 (2010)
41. Tortoriello, M., Krackhardt, D.: Activating cross-boundary knowledge: the role of simmelian ties in the generation of innovations. The Academy of Management Journal (AMJ) 53(1), 167–181 (2010)
42. Umphress, E.E., Labianca, G., Brass, D.J., Kass, E., Scholten, L.: The role of instrumental and expressive social ties in employees' perceptions of organizational justice. Organization Science 14(6), 738–753 (2003)
43. Wasserman, S., Faust, K.: Social network analysis: methods and applications. Cambridge University Press (1994)
44. Weisband, S.P., Schneider, S.K., Connolly, T.: Computer-mediated communication and social information: Status salience and status differences. Academy of Management Journal, 1124–1151 (1995)

Cultural Challenges in Information Systems Innovation: The Need for Differentiation Studies

Carl Lawrence and Markku Oivo

Department of Information Processing Science, University of Oulu,
P.O. Box 3000, Oulu 90014, Finland

Abstract. Information technology (IT) innovations have been vital to the success of organizations seeking to improve efficiency and productivity. IT's global diffusion has however raised serious questions about its neutral application across cultures and contexts. This paper synthesizes a sample of the literature to conceptualize the key cultural challenges in IS innovation as, differentiation, externality, compatibility, embeddeness. The study shows that the adoption decision is challenged by differentiation, and the adoption phase exhibits issues of externality. During implementation, compatibility is the key challenge of innovators and the assimilation literature revealed that embeddeness was the cultural challenge that phase. The synthesis also revealed that the comprehension phase where adoption decisions are made was lacking significant study. The paper proposes two opportunities for research and examples of research methods that can be use to investigate pre-adoption phenomena.

Keywords: Innovation, culture, differentiation, comprehension, methods.

1 Introduction

Information technology (IT) is a significant investment for any organization, thus extracting the most value from these innovations is vital, and can be highly rewarding (Rau & Bye, 2003). As a key resource for business in a new competitive age, IT innovations enable the complex interactions that are required to support our global economy (M. Barrett, Jarvenpaa, Silva, & Walsham, 2003). IT has become a symbol of progress throughout the world, driving greater global interactions. Information systems (IS) researchers view mitigating the challenges of innovating with IT as imperative to participating in, and reaping the benefits of our new globally connected economy (Mustonen-Ollila & Lyytinen, 2004).

Many organizations do not possess the technical expertise to develop new IT innovations, thus they are more likely to adopt them. Thus, IS innovation is the adoption of IT innovations for use in unique ways and the term has normally been restricted to early adopters (B. Swanson, 1994; E. B. Swanson, 2010). While many studies have focused on adoption, it is not the initiation of the innovation process. Prior to adoption, the adoption decision must be made, and after adoption, the innovation needs to be implemented, and assimilated by the organization. The benefits of innovation adoption can only truly be realized when it has been integrated into the activities of the organization's value chain (Armstrong & Sambamurthy, 1999).

A. Bhattacherjee and B. Fitzgerald (Eds.): Future of ICT Research, IFIP AICT 389, pp. 177–192, 2012.
© IFIP International Federation for Information Processing 2012

The importance of IT in our global society should not allow for the naive assumptions that innovations will exhibit the same productive attributes in organizations and individuals existing in culturally distant contexts (Ein-Dor, Segev, & Orgad, 1993; Kaye & Little, 1996; Vodanovich, Sundaram, & Myers, 2010; Wagner & Newell, 2004). Globalization has generated significant research interest in culture and IS, as organizations, seeking to keep pace with a growing competitive marketplace, are motived to adopt the latest innovations at a more rapid rate, ignoring potential pitfalls (M. Barrett et al., 2003; Hanseth & Braa, 2000; Leidner, 2010). Adoption and the resulting diffusion of IT innovations can adversely affect an organization's culture, often leading to reduced productivity (Vasst & Walsham, 2005). The dynamic, transformative, and sometimes unpredictable nature of culture presents many challenges to IS innovation, as it is seen as a key mediating factor (L. Harvey & M.D. Myers, 1995).

It has thus become increasingly important for researchers to address cultural challenges facing organizations when innovating with IT, in order to provide understanding and solutions. Our research question in this paper is thus, *what are the cultural challenges facing organizations when they are innovating with IT?* To answer this question this paper draws on the rich literary stream on IS innovation and culture. Using Swanson and Ramiller's (2004) IS innovation process framework, the paper extracts and synthesizing a sample of this literature and conceptualizes four challenges –differentiation, externality, incompatibility, and embeddedness. The lack of research investigating comprehension motivated the provision of opportunities for research in this area.

The paper proceeds by providing a brief background on the research on IS innovation and culture, where the IS innovation process and cultural conceptualizations are exposed. Next, a sample of the extant literature on culture and IS innovation is synthesized to identify the challenges. This is followed by a theoretical discussion on the differentiation challenge and opportunities for future research.

2   Culture and IS Innovation

The terms "IT and IS innovation" and "IT and IS innovations" are concepts that are intrinsically intertwined and are used liberally throughout the IS discipline. In this paper, the distinction is made based on coverage. The selected term "IS innovation," was introduced and defined by Swanson (1994) as "innovation in the organizational application of digital computer and communications technologies," more commonly known as IT. Other studies have used IT innovation to describe a similar process (King et al., 1994; Wang & Ramiller, 2009). The selected term "IT innovations" thus refers to both technical, process, and product innovations[1] (Fichman, 2004; B. Swanson, 1994). Enterprise resource planning (ERP), Microsoft Office, and Agile methodology would all be considered as examples of IT innovations. Henceforth, the terms "IS innovation" and "IT innovations" are used where appropriate. Consequently, IS

---

[1] Swanson (2004) provides a typology of six types of IT innovations.

innovation research is fundamentally concerned with "understanding the factors that facilitate or inhibit the adoption and diffusion of emerging IT-based processes or products within a population of potential adopters" (Fichman, 2004).

Culture has emerged as a cardinal research stream in IS, which can be attributed to the phenomenon of globalization. Barrett et al. (2003) describe globalization as a "process of social change, with many manifestations and connected to issues of self identity," "traditional ways of life affected by common cultural goods and global markets having common techniques of discipline," and "interdependence and diversity in economic, political and social environments". As the catalyst for the growth in cultural studies in IS, globalization has forced re-conceptualizations of culture and IT innovations. The impact has been an increase in studies challenging previously held assumptions regarding technology adoption and diffusion.

Much of the research on IS innovation has been focused on adoption and implementation. Since the 1980s, adoption, and implementation studies have been a mainstay in IS research. While re-conceptualization of these studies into a IS innovation framework did not occur until the early 1990s, there was an assumption that these studies were part of a larger process (Lucas, Swanson, & Zmud, 2007; B. Swanson, 1994). Empirical research on multiple phases of the IS innovation process requires significant time and resources. Longitudinal studies were typically required to cover all phases of the innovation process. While there have been some that have investigated multiple phases (Kim & Malhotra, 2005; Mustonen-Ollila & Lyytinen, 2004; Wagner & Newell, 2004), generally, studies have only tackled one or two phases. However, what the research stream does not provide is a clear picture of culture's mediating effect on IS innovation and its individual phases.

The attention to culture in this research stream emerged from the social constructionist viewpoint, which situates IT innovations in the context of their design and development (Kaptelinin & Nardi, 2006; Pinch, 2008; Pinch & Bijker, 1984) and thus users of IT will view the same IT innovation in different ways (Orlikowski & Gash, 1994). The focus on cultural research here is due to increased interaction between cultures due to globalization. According to Walsham (2002), culture diversity in itself is not a problem in cultural interaction. It is only when this diversity produces conflict that cultural diversity is cast in a negative light.

While Walsham's (2002) conceptualization of culture as "shared symbols, norms and values in a social collective" is a sufficient definition[2], by adding the underlying philosophical perspective, a deeper understanding is given to this very complex phenomenon. Moving beyond definitions, culture can be seen as conceptualized based on perspective. In IS research, the positivist paradigm has dominated early research that has given way to a healthy dose of interpretivism. Thus, have conceptualizations of culture moved beyond static characteristics to theories of emergence, construction, and evolution? Previously, IS studies on culture drew

---

[2] This is not a reflection of the perspective of Walsham, an influential figure in IS research on culture.

on Hofstede's dimensions of national culture (Hofstede, 2004). The major critics of Hofstede's cultural dimensions state that they do not take into consideration the complexity of culture in our modern world, nor do they provide explanations for creation, recreation, emergence, or destruction (Myers & Tan, 2003). The complexity of culture often leads to the avoidance of detail definitions and conceptualizations of culture also leading to an unclear picture of the cultural challenges facing organizations innovating with IT.

3   Cultural Challenges in IS Innovation

The framework for the literature review is based on the IS innovation process in organizations, defined by Swanson and Ramiller (2004). This includes the phases, comprehension, adoption, implementation, and assimilation. For synthesis, the sample publications need to provide a range of studies with a tight focus. The articles had to conform to the following criteria: (1) all articles chosen had to be empirical studies; (2) they had to study IS innovation in one or more organizations; (3) they had to develop a descriptive, explanatory, or predictive theory; and (4) they had to specifically implicate culture as having an impact on IS innovation. A literature search of the listed journals from 1999 to 2011 found 27 articles matching these criteria. The literature was first organized by situating each study in one of the four innovation process areas. It became apparent that studies on cultural in the comprehension phase were lacking in our sample, thus additional searching was carried out and theoretical support was added to conceptualize the cultural challenge. Table 1 displays the articles on each theme, and the major points.

3.1   Differentiation

The decision to adopt an innovation can be viewed as "a temporal sequence of steps through which an individual passes from initial knowledge of an innovation to forming a favorable or unfavorable attitude toward it, to a decision to adopt or reject it, to putting the innovation to use, and to finally seeking reinforcement of the adoption decision made" (Karahanna, Straub, & Chervany, 1999). During this process, conceptualized by Swanson (2004) as comprehension, potential adopters seek knowledge and attempt to make sense of IT innovations by accessing the discourses of the IT community. Fastidiousness in this phase varies and typically is reduced to a "me too" approach. Bandwagon phenomena in IS innovation has inspired research that has questioned this "mindless" innovative behavior. Riding the technology bandwagon suggests that an organization adopts a "follow the leader" strategy that exhibits limited reasoning when selecting technologies for adoption (E. B. Swanson & Ramiller, 2004). While this strategy may prove successful for some, the emerging research on culture and IS innovation questions mindless adoption.

Studies in this area do not always explicitly state that they are contributing to the comprehension phase, such as studies dealing with IT fashion (Baskerville & Myers, 2009; Wang, 2010a, 2010b). Some studies have explicitly tried to address aspects of comprehension by providing sensitizing frameworks (Lawrence & Beltran, 2010) and methods of analyzing IT discourse though a cultural lens (Lawrence & Rodriguez, 2012). However the existing research gives us sufficient theoretical knowledge to theorize the challenge of differentiation. IT innovators must thus possess contextually differentiated reasoning in order to select the appropriate IT for their organization (E. B. Swanson, 2010; E. B. Swanson & Ramiller, 2004). Contextually differentiated reasoning directly addresses the issue of the "bandwagon phenomenon" (E. B. Swanson & Ramiller, 2004; Walden & Browne, 2009). The phenomenon exposes mimicry in IT adoption trends. Organizations will adopt technologies simply based on best practice or technology fashion (Baskerville & Myers, 2009; Wang & Ramiller, 2009). When innovators access IT community discourse, they are bombarded with rhetoric promoting the adoption of IT innovations. Thus, contextually differentiated reasoning gives the innovator the ability to identify if the use context fits with their organizational culture and goals. The challenge, thus, for innovators in our multi-cultural world is to also differentiate IT innovations based on culture.

These IT community discourses do not develop randomly, but are products of loosely coupled collaborations called organizing visions. Organizing visions are said to be comprised of inter-organizational communities of heterogeneous networks who have varying interests in a particular IT innovation, but who collectively create, and employ an organizing vision (B. Swanson & Ramiller, 1997). Organizing visions are often grandiose and exaggerated beliefs of how IT should be applied. An organizing vision provides the functions of interpretation, legitimating, and mobilization. The aim is to provide a context of use of the IT innovation by giving social accounts of its potential applications. The next step is to legitimize the adoption of the innovation by linking the innovation with contemporary business issues, and with established and respected organizations, and people. Finally, organizing vision mobilizes market forces to develop and promote it throughout the community (Ramiller & Swanson, 2003).

The process of comprehension is essentially a boundary-spanning process (E. B. Swanson & Ramiller, 2004). Globalization has produced a multiplicity of boundaries due to greater interaction and specialization (Lindgren, Andersson, & Henfridsson, 2008). Within boundaries, knowledge tends to be homogenous and stagnant (Kimble, Grenier, & Goglio-Primard, 2010). Thus, to acquire knowledge of something that exists outside one's own organizational context, one must reach across organizational boundaries. Linking two or more groups separated by institutions, location, hierarchy, or function, facilitates boundary-spanning in organizational contexts (Kimble et al., 2010).

Table 1. Cultural Challenges in IS Innovation Research

Challenges	Articles	Key Issues
Differentiation	(Theoretically supported) Swanson and Ramiller (2004) Baskerville & Myers (2009)	Contextually differentiated reasoning
	Wang & Ramiller (2009) Lawrence & Rodriguez (2012)	Boundary-spanning
	Wang (2010a, 2010b)	Knowledge sharing and learning
Externality	Barrett (1999) Ishman et al. (2001) Hsiao (2003) Wagner and Newell (2004)	Acknowledging and understanding cultural differences between groups
	McCoy et al. (2007) Igira (2008) Bunker et al. (2007) Walsh et al. (2010) Kietzmann (2008)	Understanding what cultural differences will impact IT innovation
Incompatibility	Krumbholz et al. (2000) Walsham (2002) Boersma and Kingma (2005)	Understanding what cultural fit is
	Iivari and Huisman (2007) Silva and Hirschheim (2007) Strong and Volkoff (2010)	How should it fit and how to make it fit
	Abraham and Junglas (2011) Rivard et al. (2011) Ravishankar et al. (2011)	Cultural fit is not always a possibility
Embeddedness	Macredie and Sandom (1999) Walsham and Sahay (1999) Tai and Phelps (2000) Reimers (2004) Horton and Wood-Harper (2006)	Organizational cultural change requires negotiation between key stakeholders
	Canessa and Riolo (2006) Avgerou and McGrath (2007) Wainwright and Waring (2007) Van Akkeren and Rowlands (2007) Baptista (2009)	Gaining cultural legitimacy for innovation choices Presenting the IT artifact as appropriate for the culture

3.2   Externality

Introduction of external cultural elements including IT innovations have always been associated with change. Studies on this theme elaborate on the externality of IT artifacts, and the associated knowledge, and practices. The challenge is generally related to a lack of understanding and taken-for-granted assumptions about IT and culture. This theme involves research articles that stress differences in culture at national, organizational, and user levels.

Wagner and Newell's (2004) study investigated the issue of best practices in the IT industry. Their study revealed that organizations are made up of many endemic cultures, thus best practices presented by vendor organizations do not necessarily apply to adopting organizations and the endemic cultures that exist within them.

McCoy et al. (2007) warned against the underlying assumptions that IS theories developed and tested in a Western context would apply across cultures. In their study, they showed that applying TAM across cultures revealed inconsistent results. Contemporary conceptualizations of culture go beyond those of national and even organizational levels, thus understanding user-level cultural phenomena has also been investigated. In Kietzmann's (2008) study of two organizations collaborating to innovate with IT, she found that the two organizational contexts differed in their motivations to engage in the project. Without the development of an explicit shared vision, both organizations attempted to fulfill their own personal interests in the collaboration, leading to contradictions, and poor participation. Walsh et al. (2010) developed an IT user profile that would essentially be useful in identifying or creating customized applications for user groups within the organization. Their study was motivated by pre-packaged software adoption that is common practice in organizations. The externality of IT artifacts is emphasized in these studies because prior literature saw IT artifacts as neutral and not embedded with any cultural elements. These studies draw our attention to differences in cultural groups at different levels, and how their values, practices, and knowledge impact how we view and use IT. Barrett's (1999) longitudinal study found that cultural assumptions held by key stakeholders explained low levels of technology adoption in the organization. How managers view culture has a determining factor on what technology they chose to implement and how it is implemented.

Ingira's (2008) study sought to understand situated culture and its implications for IS innovation in a healthcare organization. Using activity theory, Igira provided an explanation of situated culture as activity systems representing user work practices. Culture itself was seen as embedded in activities that continuously transform over time with the introduction of new elements such as IT. The study drew attention to the persistence of cultural elements embedded in work practices. Any introduction of new elements into existing systems would create contradictions that would have to be resolved before value could be achieved. Hsiao's (2003) study further highlighted deep cultural issues such as values, fear, and trust. The study showed that cultural values related to how trust was achieved were embedded in external IT innovations. The study encouraged sensitivity to embedded cultural beliefs, as they would discourage technology use.

3.3   Incompatibility

Incompatibility is the most practical explanation for conflict in IS innovation. Incompatibilities in cultural values, beliefs, practices, governance, etc. have been cited in articles included in this theme. This theme is dominated by articles that study the implementation phase of IS innovation, as innovators encounter cultural incompatibilities only when the IT innovations have already been adopted.

Silva and Hirschheim (2007) also saw that long-standing organizational cultures are embedded with structures that pose issues to IT implementation. The changes to organizational structure in order to implement IT innovations will face resistance. Of all the cultural elements deemed necessary for compatibility, values appear to be the most difficult to conceptualize, but have been found to cause the most cultural conflict. Krumbholz et al. (2000) saw that national culture minimally impacted the influence on IT implementation, but that incompatibility of core values based on organizational culture was a factor in the innovation process.

Misfits of culture and other organizational elements are a focal area that still has many challenges. Strong and Volkoff (2010) investigated technology fit in three organizations. They found that organizational culture fit was a key misfit domain. Ravishankar et al. (2011) tackled the issue of alignment in their study of a knowledge-management system implementation. They saw that the subculture level was a key element for technology alignment. When organizations understand the necessity of technology fit with subcultures in the organization, the innovation process is more successful. Similarly, Iivari and Huisman's (2007) study showed that a fit with organizational structure was an important technology fit dimension. Essentially, the cultural elements of IT through associated practices would compete with existing organizational practices when implemented. Thus, if organizational structures aligned to those of the IT innovation, a smoother transition could be made.

Boersman and Kingma's (2005) study indicates that transformation of the organization is often inevitable in large-scale IT implementations such as ERP, involving a transformation of both the organization, and the IT innovation. Their study showed that incompatibility is generally accepted and that transformation is necessary on both sides to achieve fit. Abraham and Junglas (2011) studied how the transformation of an organization with the implementations of IT can be positive. IT was not directly implicated in all the transformations but was seen as a catalyst. The resulting transformations, however, enabled easier implementation and assimilation. Macredie and Sandom's (1999) study showed that local improvisations were correlated to customer satisfaction during IT implementation. In cases where IT was adopted in a traditional hierarchical organization, local improvisations created improved implementation success. The study does, however, suggest that the IT innovation itself had to be adoptable.

Organizations need to change and organizational leadership is the orchestrator of change. In studies where there were apparent cultural differences (e.g.Walsham, 2002; Walsham & Sahay, 1999) it was necessary to understand culture, but also leadership in cultural transformation. Particularly in cases of extreme cultural difference, technology fit and compatibility may be out of reach. Thus, organizational leaders must identify ways of reshaping their organizational cultures to take advantage of the necessary technological advancements essential for competitiveness. From this theme, the research shows that understanding cultural compatibility is key, but it may be impractical in many cases. Transformation of both the organization and its IT is thus essential to IS innovation success.

3.4   Embeddedness

For many organizations, a perfect fit is an illusion; thus, the agents charged with integrating IT into the organization's value chain are faced with the issue of conflict that is not only related to incompatibility, but also to unanticipated cultural resistance. Kai's (2004) study showed that while early adoption may prove successful, institutionalizing IT in cross-cultural settings reveals roadblocks related to culture. This theme addresses studies that go beyond implementation and look at the assimilation of IT into the organization. The sources of resistance and conflict in assimilation have to do with changing deeply embedded cultural elements.

Tai and Phelps (2000) studied chief executives' ability to overcome cultural resistance when innovating with IT. The study showed that the ability for chief executives to build a corporate culture to overcome resistance to technology was based on their perceptions of the IT vision, organizational IS issues, and IT support for knowledge management. The ability of senior leadership to understand the potential cultural challenges is key in mitigating cultural resistance. Canessa and Riolo (2006) studied how different implementations of computer-mediated communication would strengthen or dilute organizational culture, leading to differences in communication effectiveness. In their study, IT was shown to be able to have a direct impact on the resilience of culture over time. Keith and Harper (2006) conducted a longitudinal study of three police departments in the United Kingdom (UK). They concluded that the innovation process was a social activity involving constant social negotiations in the selection, implementation, and use of IT. Baptista (2009) studied the institutionalization of an intranet in a UK organization. The study found that the process of institutionalization is a product of ongoing negotiations of goals that present the IT artifact as the correct solution for the organization.

While improved productivity is generally the goal of IS innovation, embedded organizational culture has been shown to negate value due to a lack of assimilation. Avgerou and McGrath (2007) conducted a longitudinal study of IT innovation where power and authority over knowledge played a critical role in implementation failure, and where changes in governmental regimes continually changed the focus, and direction of IT in the organization. Wainwright and Waring (2007) studied how IT diffusion in organizations with strong professional cultures and ridged organizational controls posed problems for IT assimilation. Uprooting existing embedded organizational cultures is a challenge for innovators. Van Akkeren and Rowlands (2007) studied the assimilation of IT and its impact on organizational culture. The results showed that culture associated with IT through professional groups resulted in conflict. Professional groups such as those in the healthcare industry develop their own best practices.

3.5   Cultural Challenge Domino Effect

Using a sample of the research on culture and IS innovation this paper conceptualized four cultural challenges that align with the four phases of IS innovation as defined by Swanson and Ramiller (2004). Shown in Table 2 the challenges not only show alignment but also reveal a domino effect. When these cultural challenges go unaddressed the negative effect ripples through the other phases. During comprehension the cultural challenge of differentiation requires organizations to use a cultural lens when making the adoption decision. This will allow them to understand cultural and contextual differences between their organizational and the IT's organizing vision. Not addressing this challenge would show cultural naivety from lack of learning about IT not just technically but socially.

Table 2. Cultural challenge waterfall

Comprehension	Adoption	Implementation	Assimilation
Cultural Naivety			
	Cultural Apathy		
		Cultural Resistance	
			Cultural Dissonance
Differentiation	Externality	Incompatibility	Embeddedness

That naïve decision will be compounded when adoption occurs and the organization is challenged by the externality of the IT innovation. Cultural apathy at this stage ignores the externality of the IT innovation and results in cultural resistance during implemented due to the challenge of incompatibility. Continuing to ignore culture means that during assimilation the embedded culture never assimilates the IT innovation resulting in dissonance. Addressing these challenges in a timely manner by phase would provide a smoother innovation process in culturally challenging environments.

4   The Differentiation Challenge: Opportunities for Research

As we move to a more globally interconnected world, adoption of innovations without due consideration of the cultural contexts has been shown to be unwise. In the comprehension phase, the innovator must cross organizational boundaries to learn about the purpose, benefits, and technical features of an IT innovation in order to derive solutions, or identify opportunities. This type of learning is collaborative and rests on mutual understanding (B. Swanson & Ramiller, 1997; Wang & Ramiller, 2009). This paper proposes two opportunities for research to understand how we can mitigate the cultural challenge of differentiation in IS innovation.

4.1   Learning about IT across Cultural Boundaries

Cultural differences embedded in organizational and national contexts are sometimes better understood at the micro-level. Walsham (2002) proposes micro-level analysis as a better way to understand cross-cultural working. At this level, one can reveal and learn more about cultural dynamics. Working to develop new technologies to appease everyone in cross-cultural settings is challenging, and issues ranging from different perspectives on needs, different work practices, and use of IT tools may arise in multicultural projects.

Within organizations, knowledge sharing occurs naturally through interaction, and organized formal and informal gatherings (Kimble et al., 2010). Knowledge sharing with the external environment is problematic often due to reluctance and contextual understanding. "Learning about" occurs during the comprehension and early adoption phases of innovation. It involves searching and exploring IT innovations. Learning about or learning without doing enables learning without actual engagement with the innovation (Wang & Ramiller, 2009).

Ethnomethodological methods can be leveraged in this area as they have helped sociologists uncover taken-for-granted social norms and practices that are used in social interaction (See, Garfinkel, 1967, p 35). An offshoot of this approach used to investigate the specific context of talk-in-interaction is conversational analysis (L. Harvey & M. D. Myers, 1995). Created by Harvey Sacks, conversational analysis provides us with a method particularly suited to studying interaction through discourse. This interaction is considered as institutional talk by conversational analysts—focus interaction enacted to achieve institutional objectives (Heritage & Clayman, 2010). Conversational analysis exposes shared methods in interaction that can reveal successful and effective collaboration methods for comprehending IT innovations.

4.2   Cultural Sense-Making of IT Innovations

In the comprehension phase of IS innovation, boundary-spanning is also performed as a sense-making activity in order to perceive correctly peripheral information, internal or external to the organization (Lindgren et al., 2008; E. B. Swanson & Ramiller, 2004). The goal of contextually differentiated reasoning, as in other complex negotiations of meaning, is achieving mutual agreement and shared understanding. Sense-makers use retrospective accounts to make sense of new phenomenon (Weick, 1995, p. 4). These accounts are derived from diverse members of collaborative groups. Sense-making is grounded in individual and group activity (Weick, 1995, p. 5). We could view organizing vision as the product of collective sense-making. Sense-making is an iterative process, where individuals and groups form and reform assumptions and beliefs based on experiences.

As both a predecessor and successor activity to interpretation, sense-making involves the construction of the artifact to be interpreted, and translations of these interpretations into meaning (Weick, 1995, p. 8). Innovators seeking out IT innovations for adoption must interpret the discourses of IT in order to understanding its use context. It is thus through the awareness derived from previous experiences, either through the individual's, or group's experience, or that which has been learned through pervious sense-making activities, that the problem is framed. Comprehending an IT innovation that was designed and developed in an external context presents the challenge of using the innovator's previous experiences and background to make sense and derive the context of use of the innovation.

There are thus opportunities for deconstructing IS discourse though use of various discourse analysis methods to uncover cultural patterns. A common research method also shows potential when investigating comprehension. Content analysis is a research method for making inferences from text using a set of procedures. The study of text can reveal "cultural patterns of groups, institutions, or societies" (Weber 1980, p. 10). Krippendorff (2004) promotes the use of content analysis to expose social realities that "are too complex to be accessible otherwise." This method can be used to identify various cultural elements in symbolic systems that represent IT innovations. Content analysis, and other discourse methods, have been used to study IS innovation discourse at the field level (Tsui, Wang, Fleischmann, Oard, & Sayeed, 2009).

5   Conclusion

In this paper we set out to better understand the cultural challenges facing innovators with IT in organizations. Through a synthesis of a sample of the literature, the paper revealed four cultural challenges correlating with IS innovation phase defined by Swanson and Remiller (2004). In the often ignore comprehension phase differentiation was theorized as the cultural challenge. In the adoption phase externality was the cultural challenge and during implementation we exposed that compatibility arose as the challenge for innovators and in the assimilation phase embeddeness was revealed as the cultural challenge. Additionally the study revealed that the challenges created a domino effect that would create and compound future challenges. The review also revealed that the comprehension phase where key adoption decisions are make was lacking in the research stream and provided opportunities for future research.

The study is limited by its conceptual nature but provides an important understanding and direction for research on IS innovation and culture. During comprehension organizations need to cross organizational and cultural boundaries to makes sense and learn about IT innovations. This requires knowledge to be put into context and greater understanding of cultural elements embedded in IT innovations. The paper draws attention to an under researched area of comprehension in IS innovation that is important for further investigation. The application of new and traditional research methods are recommended to investigate pre-adoption activities often ignored by IS innovation research.

References

Abraham, C., Junglas, I.: From cacophony to harmony: A case study about the IS implementation process as an opportunity for organizational transformation at Sentara Healthcare. The Journal of Strategic Information Systems 20(2), 177–197 (2011)

Armstrong, C., Sambamurthy, V.: Information Technology Assimilation in Firms: The Influence of Senior Leadership and IT Infrastructures. Information Systems Research 10(4), 304–327 (1999)

Avgerou, C., McGrath, K.: Power, Rationality, and the Art of Living Through Socio-Technical Change. MIS Quarterly 31(2), 295–315 (2007)

Baptista, J.: Institutionalisation as a process of interplay between technology and its organizational context of use. Journal of Information Technology 24(4), 305–319 (2009)

Barrett, M., Jarvenpaa, S., Silva, L., Walsham, G.: ICTs, Globalization and Local Diversity. Communications of the Association for Information Systems 11(1), 486–497 (2003)

Barrett, M.I.: Challenges of EDI adoption for electronic trading in the London Insurance Market. European Journal of Information Systems 8(1), 1–15 (1999)

Baskerville, R., Myers, M.: Fashion on waves in information systems research and practice. MIS Quarterly 33(4), 647–662 (2009)

Boersma, K., Kingma, S.: From means to ends: The transformation of ERP in a manufacturing company. Journal of Strategic Information Systems 14(2), 197–219 (2005)

Canessa, E., Riolo, R.L.: An agent-based model of the impact of computer-mediated communication on organizational culture and performance: an example of the application of complex systems analysis tools to the study of CIS. Journal of Information Technology 21(4), 272 (2006)

Ein-Dor, P., Segev, E., Orgad, M.: The effect of national culture on IS: Implications for international information systems. Journal of Global Information Management 1(1), 33–44 (1993)

Fichman, R.: Going Beyond the Dominant Paradigm for Information Technology Innovation Research: Emerging Concepts and Methods. Journal of the Association for Information Systems 5(8), 314–355 (2004)

Garfinkel, H.: Studies in ethnomethodology. Blackwell Publishing Ltd., Malden MA (1967)

Hanseth, O., Braa, K.: Globalization and 'Risk Society'. In: Ciborra, C.U. (ed.) From Control to Drift, p. 3. Oxford University Press, Oxford (2000)

Harvey, L., Myers, M.D.: Scholarship and practice: the contribution of ethnographic research methods to bridging the gap. Information Technology & People 8(3), 13–27 (1995)

Harvey, L., Myers, M.D.: Scholarship and practice: the contribution of ethnographic research methods to bridging the gap. Information Technology & People 8(3), 13–27 (1995)

Heritage, J., Clayman, S.: Dimensions of Institutional Talk. In: Talk in Action: Interactions, Identities and Institutions, pp. 34–50. Wiley-Blackwell, Oxford (2010)

Hofstede, G.: Cultures and Organizations: Software of the Mind. McGraw-Hill (2004)

Hsiao, R.-L.: Technology Fears: Distrust and Cultural Persistence in Electronic Marketplace Adoption. The Journal of Strategic Information Systems (12), 169–199 (2003)

Igira, F.T.: The situatedness of work practices and organizational culture: implications for information systems innovation uptake. Journal of Information Technology 23(2), 79 (2008)

Iivari, J., Huisman, M.: The Rellationship between Organizational Culture and the Deployment of Systems Development Methodologies. MIS Quarterly 31(1), 35 (2007)

Kai, R.: GEARBOX (China) Ltd.: will the company's ERP system support its ambitious growth strategy? Journal of Information Technology 19(2), 140 (2004)

Kaptelinin, V., Nardi, B.: Artifacts, Agents, and (A)symmetry. In: Acting with Technology - Activity Theory and Interaction Design, pp. 237–252, 210. MIT Press (2006)

Karahanna, E., Straub, D.W., Chervany, N.: Information Technology Adoption across Time: A Cross-Sectional Comparison of Pre-Adoption and Post-Adoption Beliefs. MIS Quarterly 23(2), 183–213 (1999)

Kaye, R., Little, S.: Global business and cross-cultural information systems: Technical and institutional dimensions of diffusion. Information Technology & People 9(3), 30–54 (1996)

Keith, S.H., Trevor, A.W.-H.: The shaping of I.T. trajectories: evidence from the U.K. public sector. European Journal of Information Systems 15(2), 214 (2006)

Kietzmann, J.: Interactive innovation of technology for mobile work. European Journal of Information Systems 2008(3), 305–320 (2008)

Kim, S., Malhotra, N.K.: A longitudinal model of continued IS use: an integrative view of four mechanisms underlying post-adoption phenomena. Management Science 51(5), 741–755 (2005)

Kimble, C., Grenier, C., Goglio-Primard, K.: Innovation and knowledge sharing across professional boundaries: Political interplay between boundary objects and brookers. International Journal of Information Management 30, 437–444 (2010)

King, J.L., Gurbaxani, V., Kraemer, K.L., McFarlan, W.F., Raman, K.S., Yap, C.S.: Institutional Factors in Information Technology Innovation. Information Systems Research 5(2), 139–169 (1994)

Krippendorff, K.: Content Analysis: An Introduction to its Methodology, 2nd edn. Sage, Thousand Oaks (2004)

Krumbholz, M., Galliers, J., Coulianos, N., Maiden, N.A.M.: Implementing enterprise resource planning packages in different corporate and national cultures. Journal of Information Technology 15(4), 267 (2000)

Lawrence, C.A., Beltran, F.: Caveat Emptor: Cultural Assumptions in Information Technology Innovation. Paper Presented at the Proceeding of the 16th Americas Conference on Information Systems, AMCIS 2010 (2010)

Lawrence, C.A., Rodriguez, P.: The Interpretation and Legitimization of Values in Agile's Organizing Vision. Paper Presented at the Proceedings of the European Conference on Information Systems, ECIS 2012 (2000/2012)

Leidner, D.E.: Globalization, culture, and information: Towards global knowledge transparency. The Journal of Strategic Information Systems 19(2), 69–77 (2010), doi:10.1016/j.jsis.2010.02.006

Lindgren, R., Andersson, M., Henfridsson, O.: Multi-contextuality in Boundary-Spanning practices. Information Systems Journal 18, 641 (2008)

Lucas, H.C.J., Swanson, E.B., Zmud, R.: Implementation, Innovation, and Related Themes Over The Years In Information Systems Research. Journal of the Association for Information Systems 8(4), 205–211 (2007)

Macredie, R.D., Sandom, C.: IT-enabled change: Evaluating an improvisational perspective. European Journal of Information Systems 8(4), 247 (1999)

Mustonen-Ollila, E., Lyytinen, K.: How organizations adopt information system process innovations: a longitudinal analysis. European Journal of Information Systems 13(1), 35–51 (2004)

Myers, M., Tan, F.: Beyond models of national culture in information systems research, 14–29 (2003) doi:citeulike-article-id:3752890

Orlikowski, W.J., Gash, D.C.: Technological frames: making sense of information technology in organizations. ACM Trans. Inf. Syst. 12(2), 174–207 (1994), doi:10.1145/196734.196745

Pinch, T.: Technology and institutions: living in a material world. Theory and Society 37(5), 461–483 (2008) doi:citeulike-article-id:3440325

Pinch, T., Bijker, W.: The Social Construction of Facts and Artefacts: or How the Sociology of Science and the Sociology of Technology might Benefit Each Other. Social Studies of Science 14(3), 399–441 (1984) doi:citeulike-article-id:3997929

Ramiller, N., Swanson, B.: Organizing Visions for Information Technology and the I.S. Executive Response. Journal of Management Information Systems 20(1), 13–50 (2003)

Rau, S.E., Bye, B.S.: ARE YOU GETTING VALUE FROM YOUR IT? Journal of Business Strategy 16, 15 (2003)

Ravishankar, M., Pan, S., Leidner, D.: Examining the Strategic Alignment and Implementation Success of a KMS: A Subculture-Based Multilevel Analysis. Information Systems Research 22, 39 (2011)

Scott, M., Dennis, F.G., William, R.K.: Applying TAM across cultures: the need for caution. European Journal of Information Systems 16(1), 81 (2007)

Silva, L., Hirschheim, R.: Fighting Against Windmills: Strategic Information Systems and Organizational Deep Structures. MIS Quarterly 31(2), 327–354 (2007)

Strong, D., Volkoff, O.: Understanding Organization-Enterprise System Fit: A Path to Theorizing the Information Technology Artifact. MIS Quarterly 34(4), 731 (2010)

Swanson, B.: Information systems innovation among organizations. Management Science 40(9), 1069–1092 (1994)

Swanson, B., Ramiller, N.: The Organizing Vision in Information Systems Innovation. Organization Science 8(5), 458–474 (1997)

Swanson, E.B.: Consultancies and capabilities in innovating with IT. Journal of Strategic Information Systems 19(1), 17–27 (2010)

Swanson, E.B., Ramiller, N.C.: Innovating mindfully with information technology. MIS Quarterly: Management Information Systems 28(4), 553–583 (2004)

Tai, L.A., Phelps, R.: CEO and CIO perceptions of information systems strategy: Evidence from Hong Kong. European Journal of Information Systems 9(3), 163 (2000)

Tsui, C.-J., Wang, P., Fleischmann, K.R., Oard, D.W., Sayeed, A.B.: Understanding IT Innovations Through Computational Analysis of Discourse. In: Paper Presented at the International Conference on Information Systems (2009)

Van Akkeren, J., Rowlands, B.: An epidemic of pain in an Australian radiology practice. European Journal of Information Systems 16(6), 695 (2007)

Vasst, E., Walsham, G.: Representations and Actions: the transformation of work practices with IT use. Information and Organization 2005(15), 65–89 (2005)

Vodanovich, S., Sundaram, D., Myers, M.: Digital Natives and Ubiquitous Information Systems. Information Systems Research 21(4), 711–723 (2010)

Wagner, E.L., Newell, S.: 'Best' for whom?: the tension between 'best practice' ERP packages and diverse epistemic cultures in a university context. The Journal of Strategic Information Systems 13(4), 305–328 (2004), doi:10.1016/j.jsis.2004.11.002

Wainwright, D.W., Waring, T.S.: The application and adaptation of a diffusion of innovation framework for information systems research in NHS general medical practice. Journal of Information Technology 22(1), 44 (2007)

Walden, E., Browne, G.: Sequential Adoption Theory: A Theory for Understanding Herding Behavior in Early doption of Novel Technologies. Journal of the Association for Information Systems 10(1), 31–62 (2009)

Walsh, I., Kefi, H., Baskerville, R.: Managing culture creep: Toward a strategic model of user IT culture. The Journal of Strategic Information Systems 19(4), 257–280 (2010), doi:10.1016/j.jsis.2010.09.002

Walsham, G.: Cross-Cultural Software Production and Use: A Structurational Analysis. MIS Quarterly 26(4), 359–380 (2002)

Walsham, G., Sahay, S.: GIS for District-Level Administration in India: Problems and Opportunities. MIS Quarterly 23(1), 39–66 (1999)

Wang, P.: Chasing the Hottest IT: Effects of Information Technology Fashion on Organizations. MIS Quarterly 34(1), 65–85 (2010a)

Wang, P.: The Surprising Impact of Fashions in Information Technology. Sloan Management Review 51(4), 14–17 (2010b)

Wang, P., Ramiller, N.C.: Community Learning in Information Technology Innovation. MIS Quarterly 33(4), 709 (2009)

Weick, K.E.: Sensemaking in Organizations. Sage, Thousand Oaks (1995)

Track V

Innovative Trends
in Information Systems Research

Digital Artifacts as Institutional Attractors: A Systems Biology Perspective on Change in Organizational Routines[*]

SungYong Um[1], Youngjin Yoo[1], Nicholas Berente[2] , and Kalle Lyytinen[3]

[1] Fox School of Business, Temple University, 1810 North 13th Street, Philadelphia, Pennsylvania 19122
{sungyong.um,youngjin.yoo}@temple.edu
[2] Terry College of Business, University of Georgia, Athens, Georgia 30602
berente@uga.edu
[3] Department of Information Systems, Case Western Reserve University, 10900 Euclid Avenue, Cleveland, Ohio 44106
kalle@case.edu

Abstract. Digital artifacts have become fundamental elements of organizational change. Such change is not frictionless, since routines and associated structures are deeply embedded- or institutionalized. Though, organizational institutionalism has been traditionally concerned with stability and change in routines and underlying structures, it has so far meagerly theorized the role of digital artifacts in balancing stability and change. To address this gap, we draw on systems biology to understand how introduction of new digital artifacts can influence routines in organizations. In particular, we approach digital artifacts as institutional attractors and examine the role of such attractors within gene regulatory networks. In this view institutional attractors become endogenous to sociomaterial systems and are keys to simultaneously promoting stability and inducing change. Just as attractors are implicated in changes to established gene regulatory networks within cells, so too are digital artifacts implicated in the efforts of institutional entrepreneurs to bring about change to organizational routines (behaviors). Based upon this analogous reasoning we outline elements of a research agenda and conclude with a discussion of methodological directions to deal with digitally induced endogenous sociomaterial change.

Keywords: Digital Artifact, Institutional attractor, Institutional change, Systems biology.

---

[*] This paper is based on work supported, in part, by the National Science Foundation under grants *VOSS-0943157* and *VOSS-0943010*. Any opinions, findings, and conclusions or recommendations expressed in this material are those of the author(s) and do not necessarily reflect the views of the National Science Foundation.

A. Bhattacherjee and B. Fitzgerald (Eds.): Future of ICT Research, IFIP AICT 389, pp. 195–209, 2012.

1   Introduction

Striking a balance between change and stability has been one of the fundamental concerns of contemporary organizational thinking (Farjoun 2010). "Organizational institutionalism" (Powell & DiMaggio 1991; Greenwood et al 2008) has a long and rich tradition of heeding to the simultaneous interplay of stability and change. On one hand, organizational actors internalize and continually reproduce established routines in their institutionalized practices thus shaping identities and erecting cultures (Berger & Luckman 1966; Zucker 1977). Being institutionalized, these routines are difficult to change. On the other hand, organizational actors are under constant pressure to comply with new regulations and normative demands that arise in society that drive change in their routines (DiMaggio & Powell 1983; Scott 2008). So, organizational actors face constant dilemma of reinventing their organizations without fully divorcing themselves from the institutional logics in which they are deeply embedded.

This 'structurational' (Giddens 1984; Bourdieu 1977) position underlies the bulk of recent thinking on institutional change and institutional entrepreneurship (Powell & DiMaggio 1991; Seo & Creed 2002). As a result, organizational institutionalism is one of the most robust theoretical positions for understanding organizational stability and change (Farjoun 2010). However, institutionalism has largely ignored the role of digital artifacts in this process (Jones and Karsten 2008). In fact, Orlikowski and Scott (2008) note that in organizational research, "technology is largely missing in action." Digital artifacts can be defined generally as software-based information technology (IT) that has the capability to mediate and present semiotic relationships (Bailey et al. 2012). Therefore digital artifacts are not comprised primarily of matter but signs. Yet, their existence is not entirely defined in the conceptual domain as their behaviors are founded on material properties of some substrata (such as silicon) and these material features influence their use and applicability. Being sign based digital artifacts are unique in that they are editable, interactive, open, and distributed (Kallinikos et al. 2011; Leonardi 2010). This lack of interest has become recently increasingly problematic, because digital artifacts are deeply embedded in contemporary organizational practices (Baxter & Berente 2010; Gaskin et al 2011) and constitute essential elements of change in organizational practices (Yoo et al 2006; Zammuto et al 2007).

Institutional theory generally characterizes digital technologies in terms of exogenous forces for change. They can be triggers for social change (Barley 1986); a form of structure that (weakly) enables and constrains new routines (DeSanctis & Poole 1994); or as carriers of institutional scripts (Scott 2008). In each of these institutionalist conceptualizations, digital artifacts remain exogenous to the practices and go under-theorized and researched. This exogenous characterization of digital artifacts stands also in stark contrast to recent calls to attend to concrete technologies-in-practice (Orlikowski 2000; Leonardi & Barley 2008) where digital artifacts are viewed as endogenous to the practices. Yet, this thinking has not been reconciled within the dominant institutional discourse.

In this paper we begin to take some steps reconcile this insight of digital artifacts as endogenous to organizational routines with scholarship on institutional change. In so doing, we draw on recent models of systems biology (Kauffman 1993; Crombach & Hogeweg 2008). Because the field of systems biology is concerned with conditions of endogenously triggered probabilistic (and often chaotic) change, it provides an appropriate analogue for investigating organizational change (Kitano 2002). The way the systems biology field combines the study of sequence patterns (described by proteins) with the study of networks (genes) (Kauffman 1993) is quite similar to task faced by an institutional theorist grappling with the way the role of digital artifacts in institutional change. The presence of simultaneous change and stability is enabled through the interactions of digital artifacts with organizational structures (networks) and routines of actions (sequences) (Contractor et al 2011; Pentland et al 2008).

In systems biology, a gene regulatory network offers the main explanation for how the same DNA sequence can produce variety of differently functioning cells and their mutations. In particular, genetic regulatory networks coordinate how genes are activated in cells. This perspective is based on the notion of attractors which 'tip' the activation of genes to specific trajectories and lead to changes in cell behaviors. An attractor, a type of 'rogue' or 'heterogeneous' gene, triggers a mutation of a gene structure, and the structure then stabilizes around that attractor. In viewing organizational change as a highly dynamic process, conceptualizing digital artifacts as attractors offers a powerful way of accounting for endogenous change in organizations. Therefore, rooted in this analogue of genetic regulators, we conceive of digital artifacts as institutional attractors. Institutional attractors initiate shake ups in organizational routines and catalyze configurations of how 'social' and 'technological' elements become meshed in organizational routines.

The idea of an institutional attractor combines two distinct elements of digital artifacts that simultaneously explain both the generativity of that artifact in a particular context (Avital et al 2009) and the regularities it expresses across contexts (Robey & Boudreau 1999). Generativity is defined here as the capacity of digital artifacts to trigger unprompted changes driven by varied and uncoordinated behaviors (Zittrain 2006). Institutional attractors in the form of digital artifacts within organizational networks can thus enable generativity that leads to unprompted changes in activity by forming unexpected connections between actors and activities. Thereby generative artifacts become new attractors that can contribute to the explication of change both symbolically and materially (Leonardi & Barley 2008) in ways that create different practices. The attractors can also be enacted in ways that are consistent with existing pluralistic logics thus reinforcing institutions (Berente & Yoo 2012). The generativity can thus reinforce certain elements of institutional structures, while at the same time bringing about new practices that can result in a maelstrom of changes in the institutional order over time. In an organizational context, an institutional attractor can be an artifact whose affordances are enacted by organizational actors in order to bring about either change or stability in organizational routines in a manner consistent with particular institutional logics. The idea of attractors places the focus on complex, chaotic and probabilistic changes enabled by various local interactions with the digital artifacts and broader institutional elements.

The goal of this paper is to introduce the idea of digital artifacts as institutional attractors and discuss the consequences of such approach in the study of organizational change enabled by digitalization. First, we will review the literature on institutional change and the ways organizational institutionalism has accounted for digital artifacts. Second, we introduce the idea of gene regulatory networks and discuss how they can be used to explain endogenous organizational change. Then we combine these two streams and analyze the digital artifact as an institutional attractor. We conclude with a discussion on the implications of this perspective on research into organizational change – particularly the recent work on sociomateriality and sociomaterial routines.

2   Institutional Change and Digital Artifacts

An institution is a reproduced pattern of activity that is both objectified and internalized by actors in a given context (Berger & Luckman 1967; Jepperson 1991). Institutions are objectified when their representations have meaning (i.e. the institution has a name like "marriage," "army" or "handshake"). An institution is internalized when it is chronically reproduced by actors enacting established scripts through their practices (Giddens 1984). Thus actors reinforce existing institutions with their actions, leading to stability (Zucker 1977). However, as institutions are reinforced in certain contexts, at the same time, they are diffused to other contexts, bringing about change to those other contexts (DiMaggio & Powell 1983). Thus, institutional analysis is centrally concerned with the both stability and change.

Organizational institutionalism is concerned with stability in that it emphasizes the way established institutions are difficult to change (Zucker 1977). When a pattern of action is well-established, alternative patterns of action may be less legitimate or deemed inappropriate (Selznik 1996). Legitimate courses of action enable access to resources and often protect the actor from external scrutiny. Therefore, actors may enact established, legitimate institutions no matter how poorly they are served by the institutions (DiMaggio & Powell 1983; Meyer & Rowan 1977). Further, it requires effort to create new courses of action, and actors economize by enacting ready-made scripts and typifications that come complete with social meaning (Goffman 1969). Finally, much of human activity is unreflected-upon and actors enact institutions habitually (Giddens 1984).

At the same time, organizational institutionalism is concerned with change in that it emphasizes the way institutions diffuse across a field and put pressure on organizational actors to change existing patterns of activity to be isomorphic with others in the field (DiMaggio & Powell 1983). Different contexts are different, and actors must continually translate existing institutional scripts into novel, idiosyncratic environments – resulting in change and bifurcation of those institutions over time (Czarniawska & Sevon 1996). Further, situated actions and accidents can lead to unintended consequences that result in change to the existing institutional order (Giddens 1984). In addition, society is institutionally plural (Kratz & Block 2008) in that it is comprised of multiple levels of institutions whose guiding logics may be more or less congruent with each other (Friedland & Alford 1991; Thornton & Ocasio 2008). As the salience of logics ebb and flow across contexts, and as contradictory institutions collide, the result is change to institutions over time (Seo & Creed 2002). Institutional entrepreneurs reflectively draw upon logics different than those established in a given domain to bring about change to that domain (Garud et al 2002). Institutional entrepreneurs can thus mobilize various resources such as structures and technological standards in order to change the very institution in which they are deeply embedded (Rao 2000, Garud et al. 2002).

While it is generally understood that institutional entrepreneurs can play significant roles in bringing about changes in organizations, not every individual action leads to a large change. We still lack a clear theoretical understanding when and how actions taken by institutional entrepreneurs lead to large-scale organizational changes. This, in particular, is an important question for information systems scholars as digital technology is often introduced as a potential catalyst for organizational change (Teece 1995). For example, Garud and associates (2002) show that a technological standard can define how heterogeneous product components are combined together to work in an integrated system within an existing institutional space.

There are three broad ways that institutional theory characterizes digital technologies and their role in change. The first and classic response is to bypass deterministic thinking about technology induced change and looks at digital artifacts as "triggers" structural social change (Barley 1986). In this conception, IT artifacts becomes a change catalyst, but the change itself happens idiosyncratically in the social domain – outside the world of technologies. In another, more recent conception, digital artifacts can act as a form of structure that 'softly-deterministically' brings about change in agent's behaviors when augmented with complementary practices (DeSanctis & Poole 1994). Finally, digital artifacts can be considered to be "carriers" of institutions – in that they symbolically represent institutional change and embody scripts for new patterns of action (Scott 2008). Organizational actors can then adopt, resist, or loosely couple their practices from those scripts implied by particular digital artifacts based upon the (in)congruence of multiple and competing institutional logics (Berente & Yoo 2012). In each conceptualization, digital artifacts are exogenous factors that cause an institutional change. As a result, technology and institutional entrepreneur's actions are kept   separate (Orlikowski 2008).

What we need is an evolutionary perspective that embraces digital technology and actions by organizational actors as institutional entrepreneurs endogenously. In this way we can understand how certain changes emerge within organizations that lead to large-scale institutional reconfigurations (Van de Ven and Poole 1995). As organizations always inhabit contested fields (Dunn & Jones 2010), these changes will only emerge from multiple events and related elements that sometimes complement, and other times compete with one another (Berente & Yoo 2012). Therefore, a theoretical perspective that explores how organizational actors can skillfully deploy digital technology to bring about large-scale change in organizations must embrace the multiplicity of competing logics and heterogeneity of elements involved with the change. Further, this perspective should also conceptualize digital technologies as endogenous to the existing practice – simultaneously generative and stable - not as external forces for change. In this paper, we therefore propose a systems biology perspective inspired by the recent developments to address this gap in the literature.

3   System Biology on Change and Stability

An organization is comprised of various actors interacting with one another. Each actor engages in a series of actions over time and space. A change in an activity by an actor requires the actor to be adaptive to feedback from the activity. Change in the activity can influence other actors and their activities which, in turn, interact with that actor. Through this feedback, a change of an activity is occasionally amplified and can lead to the emergence of a new set of activities by a group of interconnected actors. Furthermore, the outcome of such an emergent process can often lead to unexpected and unintended consequences that can affect organizations and institutions. However, existing theories fail to offer precisely how the unexpected and novel ideas stem out from such network of actors and tools. Furthermore, a large-scale institutional change rarely occurs when new technology-enabled change is introduced. Instead, new institutional orders emerge in a much more sporadic and chaotic fashion (Boland et al. 2007).

To account for this observation we adopt a systems biology perspective (Kauffman 1993, Kitano 2002). Systems biology is an attempt to systematically understand how the biological system exhibits structural stability and generativity (endogenous change) at the same time. One of the key fundamental questions that systems biology is trying to answer is how the same DNA sequence can produce many different cells that provide different functions. And, how can a single cell's behavior be affected by another cell? A systems biology perspective provides two important concepts that offers insights on how a biological system maintain a stability and generativity at the same time: gene regulatory networks and attractor.

A gene regulatory network is a collection of DNA segments (genes) in a cell that interact with each other as to govern the rate at which genes are expressed in the cell. A gene provides both structure through DNA sequences and dynamisms by regulating cellular behaviors. A gene is a segment of DNA that contains the basic genetic information of cellular behaviors to produce different proteins. Each gene has its own unique genetic information. Therefore, a gene forms the basic unit by which genetic information is inherited from one generation to another. At the same time, a gene provides another vital function as it sends instructions to produce proteins that become the basic building blocks of observed characteristics of organisms. In this process, genes are networked with other genes as they interact together to express particular functions of cells. The cell regulates each gene function, because all the genes in the network that form the phenotype function (observed characteristics) at the same time are used to express the cell behavior (Kauffman 1993). Therefore, a change in a gene triggers a sequence of changes in other genes that eventually lead to the changes in the behavior of the cells.

In this process, a gene regulatory network plays an essential role in determining how different genes are expressed and thus produce proteins. A gene regulatory network is based on a binary function of a gene that indicates "on" if an activity is expressed and "off" if an activity is inhibited within the system. It can express a dynamic network, determining if the gene function is related to prior activity of an element in the network. Kauffman (1993) also proposes that gene regulatory networks are well-defined ensembles having both structural and behavioral features at the same time. They are based on the collective order of genes in the system. Thus, from a gene regulatory network perspective, the generativity of an organism can be understood when genes react to the environmental change by mutating.

Another important concept from a systems biology perspective is attractor (Kauffman 1993). An attractor is an element that drives a certain trajectory of change from the interaction with other elements, thus disrupting the stability of a system. Kauffman(1993) argues that an attractor can be introduced into or generated by a gene regulatory network as the system of a cell that is deterministic and repeats the recurrent state cycle. When a set of attractors are generated by the system, they can constitute a basis of attractors that can become an alternative pattern of activities in the system. To be generative, the cell system needs an attractor that coordinates the behaviors other genes in reaction to the stimulus. Therefore, an attractor in the system is a 'rogue' gene that instigates the increase of internal energy in the system (Aldana 2002). Once an attractor instigates changes in a cell system, the impact of stimulation is transferred to the other genes in the cell system. The energy transferred to others can amplify the perturbation of other genes that can in turn lead to unexpected change. Corresponding to such amplification, change can be differentiated in order to express the function as the genes are inter-dependent with one another. The expression in the gene regulatory system depends on which gene is expressed and which gene is inhibited (Crombach and Hogeweg 2008). The expressed genes form a new gene regulatory network to determine the cell behaviors stemming from their functional interdependency.

4   Systems Biology Perspective on Institutional Change

Inspired by the model of systems biology, we propose a new theoretical perspective anchored on institutionalism to understand changes enabled by new digital artifacts. We first conceptualize institutionalized domain of organizations to be established configurations of sociomaterial practices that involve routines of activities performed by individual actors and the repetitive patterns of interactions among actors (and also, their routines). As early as 1950, Eric Trist (1950) argued that organizations comprise of nested socio-technical systems consisting of human and technological elements "intertwined in a complex web of mutual causality" (p.13). A routine is "a repetitive, recognizable pattern of interdependent actions, involving multiple actors" (Feldman and Pentland 2003, pg. 96). More recently, Pentland et al. (2011) argues that actions in an organization are distributed over time and space, thus forming a network of activities. As such, routines that involve multiple actors performing different actions can be modeled as a system of actions. To be more precise, we see institutionalized practices as an equivalent of a cell system and individual routines as individual genes. A routine is further made up of individual actions and tools that are used in those actions. The performative aspect of institutionalized practices then is regulated in the way that individual routines are expressed or inhibited in an organization or a project, just like behaviors of a cell are regulated by gene expressions through a gene regulatory network.

Once we conceptualize institutionalized practices as a kind of gene regulatory network, it allows us to model the generativity resulting from the introduction of digital artifacts by treating these artifacts as attractors. That is, the modified (or mutated) routines resulting from a newly adapted digital tool as a part of it can cause a systemic change in organizations, in the same way a change in a singular rogue gene can bring about changes in a cell system. The recombinatorial nature of organizational processes from the modified routines can also create multiple connections among distributed practices. Such recombination of routines for institutionalized practiecs is possible, because of the presence of multiple actors, who have multiple views and objectives in performing those practices (Pentland and Feldman 2007). This multiplicity makes the routine system generative. During the generative process, any action (technology-in-practice) can become an attractor that can change the overall organizational process in multiple directions, whereby other actions are changed to varying degrees depending on the degree of stimulus created by the 'gene'.

This way of conceptualizing sociomaterial routines and the role of digital artifacts allows us ask a number of questions that we were not able to answer in the past. First, we are able to locate precise micro mechanisms by which an endogenous change in digital-artifacts-supported-actions by individuals in organization bring about a larger systemic change in institutionalized practices. Scholars have explored the process of such institutional entrepreneurship using varying rich metaphors such as "path creation" (Garud and Karnoe 2001) or "wakes of innovations" (Boland et al. 2007). Yet, we still do not know exactly how an action taken by an organizational actor can lead to a larger scale institutional change. Longitudinal empirical studies based on such theoretical view can provide us detailed accounts of how such processes take place. Thus, the first research question that we propose is:

Research Question 1: What are the micro mechanisms by which individual endougeous actions enacting new digital artifacts instigate larger institutional change?

We can also explore why certain routines become more generative than others, causing wider range of institutional changes. In systems biology, some attractors are more effective at transforming a system, while other attractors are not. The size of such perturbation of an attractor in a cell affects the degree of impact on another genes. The answer to this question will let us know the reasons for differential attractor impact within a cell. When an attractor starts an activity, a certain amount of counter energy is generated to maintain a state of equilibrium (Pregogine and Stengers 1984, Kauffman 1993). As the activity of an attractor increases, the tension between the attractor and the other genes increases. The tension remains until an attractor's energy leaps over a certain critical threshold. Then the energy dissipates to the other genes throughout the system. Thus, a new order of genes is established by expressing and inhibiting genes to achieve a new equilibrium given the increased energy. The determination of which attractor is more effective can be derived from the degree of energy needed to overcome the tension. If an attractor cannot overcome the tension, the impact is limited only to the nearby genes, which will be reordered to meet the original status quo.

Similarly, each organization shares a level of isomorphism across an institutional field, with its pervasive, or dominant, institutional logic (Thornton & Ocasio 2008). This isomorphism is expressed in a certain set of rules that govern the organization's responses to make them fit to its resources. Each organization has therefore a certain institutional resistance that obstructs the interrelated components to be involved in change (Zucker 1977). Put it in a systems biology language, an established order of a 'gene regulatory network' directly resists the creation of novel actions. If a routine does not have potential for enough impact on other actors interconnected with it, it will not carry 'enough energy' to amplify the change among other actors. If a routine reaches sufficient energy level to overcome the conflict with the other actors, the new action will lead to broader change among the existing order leading to a larger systemic change. Unlike the systems in nature, however, the destabilization of institutionalized practices does not directly lead to a state of non-equilibrium. Routines have sedimentary traits in that the existing order is layered in practices within an institution (Seo and Creed 2002). Consequently, a dominant institutional logic in a field cannot account for every situation. In such cases, alternative, even contradictory, logics may be drawn upon by actors (Berente & Yoo 2012). This lead to the following research question:

Research Question 2: What are the conditions under which the introduction of digital artifacts will modify existing action, or introduce a new action, within existing routines that leads to larger systemic change in the routine system?

Finally, our conceptualization invites us to explore co-evolution of digital artifacts, actions, routines and institutional order at the same time. While new genes such as digitally enabled new actions embedded in artifacts work as instructions to produce proteins that determine observable behaviors of cell systems, genes also carry genetic information over generations. This is how digital artifacts achieve their power to institutionalize existing order. In that process, however, 'digital' genes constantly mutate and recombine bringing changes to the observable traits of organizations. Like a gene's interaction with other genes, a single cell interacts all the time with other cells in an organism. For example, intercellular substances, the substances in which tissue cells are embedded, continuously interact with other cells to balance the metabolic work. The attractor can amplify the impact through the connection of other cells that causes them to show homogenized features within the organism. Once the attractor affects the other cells, the dynamic interactions among the cells are determined by the level of impact that an attractor and the feedback have on other genes and cells. The impact of change is related to the attractors' possibility to be reacted to by other cells (Kauffman 1993). The attractors thus have a similar nature in other cells so that the impact of the original attractor can stimulate to perturb the status quo. This happens in reactions that instigate genes near them to change the cells' expression by spontaneously organizing the order. In this regard the gene network enables the cells to sporadically respond to possible attractors spread across various cells on the impact of an attractor. This process amplifies the activity of an attractor to others by broadening the scope of change extensively.

Similarly, a gene regulatory network approach to routines allow us to model co-evolutionary patterns of digital artifacts, actions, routines, and institutional orders. March (1996) argued that an activity of an actor can affect the actions of others through network structures that impact the dynamics of change. In other words, the actions within an organizational process cannot only be confined to a single boundary, but can reach out to other parts of the organization and outside to other organizations that interact with the focal organization (Orlikowiski and Scott 2008). Similar to the sporadic responses of genes through a network, this expansive activity needs to be understood in a broad sense. The impact of action variation is not only confined within an organization but should be examined across organizations. How an organization can be changed through the impact of other actors is related to the evolution of organizational learning in institutional fields. Actions, which can impact the others, have also exogenous features linked through networks across the organizations. This idea is aligned with that of Pentland and associates (2011) who suggest that an atypical action leading to the change of routine shows typically exogenous characteristics. Zucker (1977) argues that all the interconnected components in organizations are not resistant to change, but accept it as legitimate if it is 'institutionally' necessary (i.e. legitimate and viewed to have positive impacts). However, if the change is consistent with a legitimate, alternative institutional logic, actors may adopt changes if they represent valuable improvements (Powell 1991; Seo & Creed 2002). This leads us to propose the research question:

Research Question 3: What are the underlying patterns of co-evolution of digital artifacts, individual actions, routines and institutional orders?

5   Discussion

Consistent with the emerging intuition in information systems research that rejects to treat digital artifacts as exogenous factors, (Leonardi & Barley 2008), digital artifacts are to be understood being embedded into routines and institutionalized practices (Orlikowski 2008). However, institutional views of organizations typically conceive technologies as exogenous to practice (if they conceive of them at all). So, the purpose of this paper is to explore how we can conceive of digital artifacts in an institutional approach whereby those artifacts are endogenous to institutionalized practice. In characterizing organizations as dynamic, evolutionary systems, we draw on systems biology to characterize institutional routines as gene regulatory networks and technologies-in-practice as institutional attractors. Digital artifacts as institutional attractors emerge from within an institutional practice: they are not foreign objects introduced from without, but internal reactions to either endogenous or exogenous shifts and thus drawn from within – motivated, anchored, and embedded in practice (Baxter & Berente 2010). The digital artifacts are reinvented in practice and generate derivative innovations around that then become institutionalized. Even if digital artifacts are forced from outside of practice – the practice can loosely couple from these artifacts (Berente & Yoo 2012) and reinvent them over time (Bourdieu & Robey 2005). An institutional attractor is consistent with a particular institutional logic that is available in a pluralistic field (Dunn & Jones 2010). On one hand this attractor generates change to salient practices that were previously consistent with an alternative logic, while on the other hand the attractor aids stabilizing and reinforcing the logic consistent with the attractor. From a systems biology standpoint, an institutional logic is expressed through a gene regulatory network–established patterns by which different routines interact with one another.

This view of digital artifacts as institutional attractors has implications methodologically. Historically researchers have looked to understand social change through either a structural lens or a sequential lens. Structural analysis involves cross-sectional analysis of relationships between elements of social systems – what Sandberg & Tsoukas (2011) refer to as "entity-based approaches." This could involve variance theories of relationships between latent factors (Van de Ven 2007), or social network analyses of relationships between social actors (Monge & Contractor 2003). In either case, change is accounted for by contingency variables and comparison of cross-sectional structures. An alternative way of viewing social activity is by expressly attending to temporal elements of activities – as processes described by patterns of events (Van de Ven & Poole 1995) or sequences of activities (Abbott 1995). These methods capture patterns of change, but do so at the expense of rich contextual attention (Pentland & Feldman 2007). Emerging sociomaterial approaches are adding cross-sectional context to sequence approaches (Pentland et al 2012; Gaskin et al 2011), or adding temporal elements to multimodal networks (resulting in "multidimensional" networks, see Contractor et al 2011).

Essentially we need to combine "zooming in" to practice and "zooming out" to regularities across practices (Sandberg & Tsoukas 2011; Latour 2010). By thinking of digital artifacts as institutional attractors, we enable this zooming in and out using the multilevel device of an institutional logic (Friedland & Alford 1991). Institutional attractors embedded in practice work to co-constitute the stabilization and change associated with those practices in a way consistent with particular logics that are rooted in society's broader institutions (Berente & Yoo 2012).

By drawing on a systems biology perspective, our approach also offers ways to utilize contemporary computational techniques that are often used to analyze large-scale genetic information. Our approach necessitates new forms of methodological tools and analytical frameworks that simultaneously consider both sequential and structural data. Combined with increasingly available digital trace data from organizations, we can explore how seemingly chaotic and random changes of sociomaterial routines in organizations emerge from recombinations of relatively small set of abstract genetic elements. Recently, scholars offer an idea of computational social science that combines the availability of 'big data' from digital archives and computational network science (Lazer et al. 2009). Our view suggests an alternative approach to computational social science that focuses on the genetics and evolution; one that embraces both sequence analysis and network analysis simultaneously.

6   Conclusion

IFIP 8.2 has historically been a venue for novel theoretical combinations and alternative research methodologies (Boland & Lyytinen 2004). In this paper we look to draw on and extend this tradition by juxtaposing concepts from system biology and organizational institutionalism. In doing so we look to add one perspective in the emerging movement in IS research to go beyond idiosyncratic local practices, while not falling victim to decontextualized universal generalities (Leonardi & Barley 2008; Pollock & Williams 2009). This paper argues for an evolutionary view of how an activity can lead endogenous changes to routines within an organization through networks of influence. Here in particular, the digital artifact can become a tool that both stabilizes patterns of action and at the same time generates changes in organizational routines through diverse enactments of various scales. This view implies a combined sociomaterial routine and multidimensional network view of organizational practice which would call for combined sequence and network methods that include digital artifacts as key actants – a theoretical foundation for some of the emerging methodological innovations of recent years (Contractor et al 2011; Pentland et al 2008; Gaskin et al 2011). It is our hope that this initial step can provide the scaffolding for future researchers to explore and extend theoretically and with novel methodological applications.

References

Aldana, M.: Dynamics of Boolean networks with scale-free topology. Arxiv preprint cond-mat/0209571 (2002)

Avital, M., Boland, R.J., et al.: Introduction to designing information and organizations with a positive lens. Information and Organization 19(3), 153–161 (2009)

Bailey, D.E., Leonardi, P.M., et al.: The lure of the virtual. Organization Science 23(5), 1485–1504 (2012)

Baxter, R.J., Berente, N.: The process of embedding new information technology artifacts into innovative design practices. Information and Organization 20(3), 133–155 (2010)

Barley, S.R.: Technology as an occasion for structuring: Evidence from observations of CT scanners and the social order of radiology departments. Administrative Science Quarterly, 78–108 (1986)

Berger, P.L., Luckmann, T.: The Social Construction of Reality (1966)

Boland, R., Lyytinen, K.: Information systems research as design: Identity, process, and narrative. Information Systems Research, 53–68 (2004)

Boland, R.J., Lyytinen, K., et al.: Wakes of innovation in project networks: the case of digital 3-D representations in architecture, engineering, and construction. Organization Science 18(4), 631–647 (2007)

Bourdieu, P.: The economics of linguistic exchanges. Social Science Information 16(6), 645–668 (1977)

Boudreau, M.C., Robey, D.: Enacting integrated information technology: A human agency perspective. Organization Science 16(1), 3–18 (2005)

Berente, N., Yoo, Y.: Institutional Contradictions and Loose Coupling: Postimplementation of NASA's Enterprise Information System. Information Systems Research (2012)

Contractor, N., Monge, P.R., et al.: Multidimensional networks and the dynamics of sociomateriality: Bringing technology inside the network. International Journal of Communication 5, 682–720 (2011)

Crombach, A., Hogeweg, P.: Evolution of evolvability in gene regulatory networks. PLoS Computational Biology 4(7), e1000112 (2008)

Czarniawska-Joerges, B., Sevón, G.: Translating organizational change. de Gruyter (1996)

DeSanctis, G., Poole, M.S.: Capturing the complexity in advanced technology use: Adaptive structuration theory. Organization Science, 121–147 (1994)

DiMaggio, P.J., Powell, W.W.: The iron cage revisited: Institutional isomorphism and collective rationality in organizational fields. American Sociological Review, 147–160 (1983)

DiMaggio, P.J.: Interest and agency in institutional theory. Institutional Patterns and Organizations, 3–21 (1988)

Dunn, M.B., Jones, C.: Institutional logics and institutional pluralism: The contestation of care and science logics in medical education, 1967–2005. Administrative Science Quarterly 55(1), 114–149 (2010)

Farjoun, M.: Beyond dualism: Stability and change as a duality. The Academy of Management Review (AMR) 35(2), 202–225 (2010)

Feldman, M.S., Pentland, B.T.: Reconceptualizing organizational routines as a source of flexibility and change. Administrative Science Quarterly 48(1), 94–118 (2003)

Friedland, R., Alford, R.R., et al.: The new institutionalism in organizational analysis. The New Institutionalism in Organizational Analysis (1991)

Gaskin, J., Thummadi, B.V., et al.: Digital Technology and the Variation in Design Routines: A Sequence Analysis of Four Design Processes1 (2011)

Garud, R., Karnøe, P.: Path creation as a process of mindful deviation. Path Dependence and Creation 138 (2001)

Garud, R., Jain, S., et al.: Institutional entrepreneurship in the sponsorship of common technological standards: The case of Sun Microsystems and Java. Academy of Management Journal, 196–214 (2002)

Garud, R., Karnøe, P.: Path creation as a process of mindful deviation. Path Dependence and Creation 138 (2001)

Giddens, A.: The constitution of society: Outline of the theory of structuration. Univ. of California Press (1984)

Goffman, E.: Strategic interaction. University of Pennsylvania Press (1969)

Greenwood, R., Oliver, C., et al.: Organizational Institutionalism. Sage, Los Angelos (2008)

Jepperson, R.L.: Institutions, institutional effects, and institutionalism. The New Institutionalism in Organizational Analysis 6, 143–163 (1991)

Jones, M.R., Karsten, H.: Giddens's structuration theory and information systems research. Mis Quarterly 32(1), 127–157 (2008)

Kauffman, S.A.: The origins of order. Oxford University Press, New York (1993)

Kallinikos, J., Mariátegui, J.C.: Video as digital object: production and distribution of video content in the internet media ecosystem. The Information Society 27(5), 281–294 (2011)

Kitano, H.: Systems biology: a brief overview. Science 295(5560), 1662–1664 (2002)

Kraatz, M.S., Block, E.S.: Organizational implications of institutional pluralism. The Sage Handbook of Organizational Institutionalism 840 (2008)

Lazer, D., Pentland, A.S., et al.: Life in the network: the coming age of computational social science. Science (New York, NY) 323(5915), 721 (2009)

Leonardi, P.M., Barley, S.R.: Materiality and change: Challenges to building better theory about technology and organizing. Information and Organization 18(3), 159–176 (2008)

Leonardi, P.: When flexible routines meet flexible technologies: Affordance, constraint, and the imbrication of human and material agencies. Mis Quarterly 35(1), 147–167 (2011)

March, J.G.: Continuity and change in theories of organizational action. Administrative Science Quarterly, 278–287 (1996)

Meyer, J.W., Rowan, B.: Institutionalized organizations: Formal structure as myth and ceremony. American Journal of Sociology, 340–363 (1977)

Monge, P.R., Contractor, N.S.: Theories of communication networks. Oxford University Press, USA (2003)

Orlikowski, W.J.: Using Technology and Constituting Structures: A Practice Lens for Studying Technology in Organizations. Organization Science 11(4), 405 (2000)

Orlikowski, W.J., Scott, S.V.: 10 Sociomateriality: Challenging the Separation of Technology, Work and Organization. The Academy of Management Annals 2(1), 433–474 (2008)

Orlikowski, W.J.: Using technology and constituting structures: A practice lens for studying technology in organizations. Resources, Co-Evolution and Artifacts, 255–305 (2008)

Pentland, B.T., Feldman, M.S.: Organizational routines as a unit of analysis. Industrial and Corporate Change 14(5), 793–815 (2005)

Pentland, B.T., Feldman, M.S.: Narrative networks: Patterns of technology and organization. Organization Science 18(5), 781–795 (2007)

Pentland, B.T., Feldman, M.S.: Designing routines: On the folly of designing artifacts, while hoping for patterns of action. Information and Organization 18(4), 235–250 (2008)

Pentland, B.T., Hærem, T., et al.: The (N) Ever-Changing World: Stability and Change in Organizational Routines. Organization Science 22(6), 1369–1383 (2011)

Pentland, B.T., Feldman, M.S., et al.: Dynamics of organizational routines: a generative model. Journal of Management Studies (2012)

Pollock, N., Williams, R.: The sociology of a market analysis tool: How industry analysts sort vendors and organize markets. Information and Organization 19(2), 129–151 (2009)

Powell, W.W., DiMaggio, P.J.: The new institutionalism in organizational analysis. University of Chicago Press (1991)

Progogine, I., Stengers, I.: Order out of chaos: Man's new dialogue with nature. Fontana, London (1984)

Rao, H., Morrill, C., et al.: Power plays: How social movements and collective action create new organizational forms. Research in Organizational Behavior 22, 237–282 (2000)

Robey, D., Boudreau, M.C.: Accounting for the contradictory organizational consequences of information technology: Theoretical directions and methodological implications. Information Systems Research 10(2), 167 (1999)

Sandberg, J., Tsoukas, H.: Grasping the logic of practice: Theorizing through practical rationality. The Academy of Management Review (AMR) 36(2), 338–360 (2011)

Scott, W.R.: Institutions and Organizations. Sage, Thousand Oaks (2001)

Scott, W.R.: Lords of the dance: Professionals as institutional agents. Organization Studies 29(2), 219–238 (2008)

Selznick, P.: Institutionalism "old" and "new". Administrative Science Quarterly, 270–277 (1996)

Seo, M.G., Creed, W.E.D.: Institutional contradictions, praxis, and institutional change: A dialectical perspective. Academy of Management Review, 222–247 (2002)

Teece, D.J.: Profiting from technological innovation: Implications for integration, collaboration, licensing and public policy. Research Policy 15(6), 285–305 (1986)

Thornton, P., Ocasio, W., et al.: The handbook of organizational institutionalism. Sage (2008)

Trist, E.: The relations of social and technical systems in coal-mining. British Psychological Society, Industrial Section (1950)

Van de Ven, A.H., Poole, M.S.: Explaining development and change in organizations. Academy of Management Review, 510–540 (1995)

Van de Ven, A.H.: Engaged scholarship: A guide for organizational and social research. OUP Oxford (2007)

Yoo, Y., Henfridsson, O., et al.: Research Commentary—The New Organizing Logic of Digital Innovation: An Agenda for Information Systems Research. Information Systems Research 21(4), 724–735 (2010)

Yoo, Y., Boland Jr, R.J., et al.: From organization design to organization designing. Organization Science, 215–229 (2006)

Zammuto, R.F., Griffith, T.L., et al.: Information technology and the changing fabric of organization. Organization Science 18(5), 749–762 (2007)

Zittrain, J.L.: The generative internet. Harvard Law Review, 1974–2040 (2006)

Zucker, L.G.: The role of institutionalization in cultural persistence. American Sociological Review, 726–743 (1977)

Amazon Mechanical Turk: A Research Tool for Organizations and Information Systems Scholars

Kevin Crowston

Syracuse University School of Information Studies
348 Hinds Hall, Syracuse, NY 13210 USA
crowston@syr.edu

Abstract. Amazon Mechanical Turk (AMT), a system for crowdsourcing work, has been used in many academic fields to support research and could be similarly useful for information systems research. This paper briefly describes the functioning of the AMT system and presents a simple typology of research data collected using AMT. For each kind of data, it discusses potential threats to reliability and validity and possible ways to address those threats. The paper concludes with a brief discussion of possible applications of AMT to research on organizations and information systems.

Keywords: Amazon Mechanical Turk, crowd sourcing, research methods.

1   Introduction

The crowdsourcing system Amazon Mechanical Turk (AMT) was initially invented to support Amazon's business processes, but has since been used for research in disciplines such as natural language processing [e.g., 1, 2], machine learning [e.g., 3, 4] and human computer interaction [e.g., 5, 6]. There has been some social science use, e.g., in political science [e.g., 7] and psychology [e.g., 8]. However, AMT does not yet seem commonly used in information systems (IS) (one exception is Conley [9], who used AMT to code some of her data). To introduce AMT to IS researchers, I briefly explain how AMT works and present a simple typology of different applications of AMT to research. I then discuss concerns about reliability and validity of data generated by AMT for these different kinds of research. I conclude with suggestions for applying AMT to research on organizations and IS in particular.

AMT is a "marketplace for work that requires human intelligence" [10]. It provides a web-based system to dispatch tasks to a pool of human workers, known colloquially as Turkers. As such, it is an example of crowdsourcing, defined as outsourcing a function to a large by undefined group of people via an open call [11]. AMT is not the only crowdsourcing system, but it is well developed, commonly used and has the most information available to assess its suitability for research, hence our focus on it in this paper. In contrast to other systems for crowdsourcing, such as InnoCentive, the tasks on AMT are typically small (i.e., a few minutes to perform rather than days or weeks), and payments are low (on the order of a few cents).

A. Bhattacherjee and B. Fitzgerald (Eds.): Future of ICT Research, IFIP AICT 389, pp. 210–221, 2012.
© IFIP International Federation for Information Processing 2012

As a background to our discussion of research uses of AMT, we first briefly walk through the steps involved in using the system. Interested readers may wish to consult Mason & Suri's [12] paper on using AMT for behavioural research.

The unit of work done on AMT is called a human intelligence task (HIT). A HIT may be carried out entirely on Amazon's system, e.g., for a survey, or may refer the Turker to another website for more complicated tasks, e.g., an on-line experiment. The most common HITs on AMT are tasks such as transcription, content generation or classification of images for companies, mirroring the original purpose for Amazon [13]. Research tasks are a small part of the total volume of HITs: they add novelty for Turkers but are not an important concern for Amazon.

Most HITs offer very small payments. Ipeirotis [13] reports that "25 percent of the HITs created on Mechanical Turk have a price tag of just US$0.01, 70 percent have a reward of $0.05 or less, and 90 percent pay less than $0.10" (p. 19). The payment offered is expected to roughly reflect the difficulty of the task; if desired, a bonus can be paid above the base amount. Horton & Chilton [14] estimated the reservation hourly wage ("the minimum wage a worker is willing to accept... for performing some task") to be about US$1.40/hour (p. 2). The actual pay offered seems to be somewhat higher: Ipeirotis [13] reports an average pay of US$4.80/hour for tasks (high enough that Turkers in low-wage countries can earn a living from AMT). Higher pay may motivate Turkers to work on tasks more quickly, though Buhrmester et al. [8] found that even tasks that paid lowest amount (US$0.01) did eventually attract some Turkers, apparently without reducing data quality. Contrariwise, a too high payment (e.g., more than US$1) is viewed by Turkers as signalling a bogus task [15]. Amazon charges 10% on top of the amount paid to the Turker.

The creator of a HIT determines the number of Turkers wanted and how many times an individual Turker can respond. For example, a survey should allow a Turker to respond only once, while a classification task might require 3 different responses for each item but allow the same Turker to classify multiple items. AMT enables some limited screening of Turkers. HITs can be restricted to Turkers in particular countries, which may be helpful for cross-cultural studies. A HIT may require that Turkers be prequalified, e.g., by requiring acceptable answers on prescreening questions before taking a survey or doing an experiment. Turkers with less than a given percentage of satisfactorily completed tasks can be blocked. Turkers who have completed a previous HIT can be invited to a new one, e.g., for a panel survey.

Once a HIT is released, it goes into long list of available HITs: on the order of 100,000 HITs may be available at a time [15]. Amazon presents a browsing interface with hundreds of pages of HITs, as well as a simple search interface. Chilton *et al.* [15] found that the first page of HITs has the highest "click through" rate and that most Turkers use the "recently posted" and "largest number of HITs" sort orders (the later to be able to repeat a HIT). Research work is likely to be prominent only with the first sort order. HITs are typically completed very quickly, within a day or two. However, if a HIT is not completed within that time frame, it may be delayed for a long time since it will disappear from first few pages of the recent post list [13].

Results provided by Amazon include answers to the questions posed, an ID that allows tracking results from same Turker and time spent on the task. After reviewing results, a poster can choose to not pay or to block a particular Turker from future tasks, e.g., if the work done is of low quality. The possibility that they might not get paid leads to questions among Turkers about the honesty of new posters. Turkers talk amongst themselves on a variety of web forums, so a reputation for not paying (or contrary) will spread [16].

The AMT system offers many potential benefits for research. First, the cost of recruiting subjects is much lower than alternatives [7], e.g., US$0.50 per subject rather than a $10 gift card. Second, Amazon handles all payments and Turkers are anonymous to researchers. Third, the large pool makes it easy to recruit a diverse set of subjects and to get multiple subjects to participate at same time, e.g., for group experiments [12]. Finally, work is typically done within hours or days [13].

However, AMT has significant limitations as a research environment. Since the work is being done remotely, the researcher has no control over the physical environment (e.g., what setting or what kind of computer and monitor) or even the web environment (e.g., which browser). There are only basic features for selecting and filtering participants. It is difficult to know how well Turkers understand a task or how hard the Turker will concentrate on it. There are only a few very limited ways to follow up with a Turker after a task (e.g. sending a bonus or a payment rejection with a message); the only possibility for debriefing is to include questions in the HIT [17]. These limitations mean that certain kinds of studies will not be not feasible (e.g., these limits seem to pose significant challenges for interpretivist research). And of course, the novelty of the system creates concerns about the reliability and validity of the data, which we discuss in the following section.

2   Research Data from Amazon Mechanical Turk

Considering the subject of the data collection, we suggest that there are three general ways to use AMT to collect research data (as shown in Figure 1):

1) to collect data about Turkers,
2) to use Turkers to collect data about some research stimulus, or
3) to collect data about the Turkers' reactions to some stimulus.

Published papers using AMT generally examine only a single mode of data collection, without being explicit about how the characteristics of the task affect the outcomes. However, it is useful to distinguish these modes, as the nature of the different data collected raise unique reliability

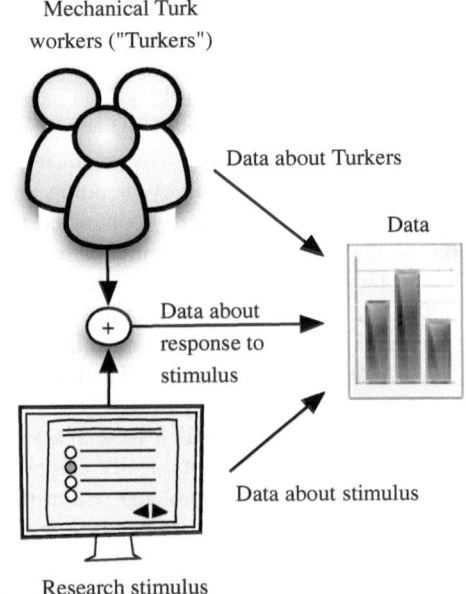

Fig. 1. Three modes of data collection using AMT

and validity concerns with different possible remedies. For each mode, we consider reliability (i.e., random error in the data), internal validity (i.e., bias in the data) and external validity (i.e., the possibility to generalize from the data).

2.1   Data about Turkers

The first possibility is to use AMT where the data to be collected are about the Turkers themselves, e.g., using Turkers as subjects for a survey or psychological test [e.g., 5, 16]. In this case, an individual Turker will respond only once to a HIT. However, the same Turker might take part in different HITs, e.g., for repeated runs of an experiment. If multiple responses are undesirable, they can be removed from analysis or prevented in the implementation of the HIT.

Reliability of the data collected can be addressed as in other survey designs, e.g., by including multiple items for each construct (though this approach is more appropriate for positivist than for interpretivist research approaches). A more difficult concern is the internal validity of the data, i.e., if the respondents reply truthfully rather than simply making up data. Mason & Suri [12] reported that only a small percentage of respondents to their survey seem to be falsifying demographic data, and report similar results from other researchers. However, others have found that a few Turkers—referred to as spammers [12]—will try to do a HIT as quickly as possible without attention to the instructions or will even game the system, e.g., by quickly submitting many erroneous answers [4, 6]. A one-time survey offers a limited opportunity for spam, but as surveys can be quick to fill out (especially if one skips reading the questions), the possibility needs to be guarded against.

A simple spam detection approach is to look at the time taken to perform the task (e.g., a survey answered in a minute) or at the pattern of responses (e.g., all questions answered with the same option). A survey can include a check question to determine if respondents are actually reading the questions. For example, Paolacci et al. [16] included the question, "While watching the television, have you ever had a fatal heart attack?", using a six-point scale ("Never" to "Often") identical to that used for other questions. Any survey that was not answered "Never" was discarded. They observed about the same failure rate on this check question (on the order of 5%) in AMT as with other subject pools (students and Internet pools).

A second concern about using AMT to recruit subjects is the question of external validity. Clearly, using AMT is not a substitute for surveying members of an organization, but Turkers might be taken as representative of the general population of Internet users more specifically. There has been research on the demographics of the population of Turkers that addresses this question, revealing that Turkers in fact differ somewhat from the reported averages for Internet users in general [18]. Overall, Turkers were younger than average Internet users. The self-reported education was higher than average, but income lower. Most were single and without children. Furthermore, there are differences within the pool of Turkers, with resulting variability in other capabilities, e.g., the level of English ability [3]. Ipeirotis [18] reported finding Turkers from 66 countries, but 46% of Turkers were US-based and 34% Indian (the two currencies in which Amazon offers payment). US Turkers were about 2/3 female, while Indian Turkers were about 70% male [18]. Money was an important factor for all Turkers, but US Turkers generally viewed AMT as a secondary source of income, while for many Indians it was a primary source of income. The importance of a monetary incentive for participation could be a contaminating factor for studies of motivation or related phenomena, though this problem also affects studies done with other paid subject pools.

Despite these differences, the Turker population may not be appreciably less representative of the Internet or general population than other commonly-used subject pools, such as college students or subjects recruited on the Internet. Buhrmester et al. [8] noted that the AMT sample is likely to be more diverse than the others. Berinsky et al. [7] found that a sample of AMT respondents was at least as representative, if not better than convenience samples or student samples and was most similar to a probability Internet survey. The sample was different from a face-to-face probability sample of US participants, but was described as not "wildly distorted" (p. 12).

Finally, in this case, the Turkers are human subjects for the research, so the rules and ethical principles that govern human subjects research apply, e.g., the requirement for obtaining informed consent before starting the research task and balancing risks and benefits of the research. It seems likely though that the risks of participating in an AMT HIT would be minimal. Indeed, use of AMT might reduce some risks, e.g., the anonymity of the system would reduce the risk of inadvertent disclosure of private data, which may be beneficial for human subjects review [16]. An issue to consider is if the use of AMT shifts the burden of the research to a vulnerable group, i.e., to those willing to work for the low pay offered. As always, careful consideration of the risks and benefits of the research is needed.

2.2   Data about a Research Stimulus

A second possibility for AMT research is that the researcher is studying some collection of objects that need humans to provide data about them. We refer these objects generically as research stimuli; an individual Turker may work on many stimuli. In this case, we assume that the data of interest are inherent in the stimuli (i.e., different individuals are not expected to have different interpretations) and require observation with minimal interpretation. (These assumptions are more characteristic of a positivist research approach.)

This case describes many uses of AMT for research. For example, Kaisser & Lowe [2] had Turkers read documents known to contain the answer to a question; the Turkers identified the specific sentence in the document that included the answer. Wang, Kraut, & Levine [19] had Turkers code discussion forum messages for whether they offered information or emotional support. Sorokin & Forsyth [4] had Turkers annotate images to locate people.

A first issue with this mode of data collection is reliability (i.e., random errors in the data). Researchers have identified a variety of approaches to resolve this issue. First, tasks must be carefully designed, since Turkers have only the training offered in the HIT. For example, Sorokin & Forsyth [4] explored four alternative task designs to identifying people in pictures to determine which could be done most reliably. A second strategy is to require a qualification task to ensure that subjects understand the task and can (and will) do it [5]. Rashtchian et al. [3] reported that pre-screening Turkers led to the highest improvement in quality on an image annotation task.

A third common strategy is to use replication, i.e., instead of doing content analysis with a few trained analysts, use more untrained workers, pooling data to obtain a consensus for each stimulus. Snow et al. [1] found that combining judgments from about five Turkers on factors such as "emotions expressed, the relative timing of events referred to in the text, word similarity, word sense disambiguation, and linguistic entailment or implication" [19] gave results similar to experts.

Finally, Turkers can be used to validate work done by other Turkers, i.e., create a HIT that presents the prior task and its responses and asks Turkers to judge whether the response is appropriate for the task. However, researchers suggest that it is more effective to use other strategies to ensure higher initial reliability rather than trying to filter out bad work after the fact [3].

The second issue is internal validity, i.e., does the data that non-trained Turkers can extract really represent what the researcher wants to study? To guard against inadvertent bias requires careful design of the stimulus and instructions (as in any research setting). Sprouse [17] obtained essentially identical results from an AMT experiment and a laboratory experiment on a linguistic judgement task, suggesting that AMT experiments can provide valid data.

Spam is a more significant issue in this mode of data collection, since a Turker can work on multiple tasks. Ipeirotis, Provost, & Wang [20] estimated that 30% of the responses to a task they posted were provided by spammers; the spammers were a small number of the total, but posted many bogus responses. Therefore, the HIT must be designed to deter and enable detection of spammers. As Kittur et al. [6] put it, the task should be designed "such that completing it accurately and in good faith requires as much or less effort than non-obvious random or malicious completion." (p. 456).

The strategies used for the previous mode can be used in this case as well, i.e., checking the timing and pattern of responses or asking a question that demonstrates that workers are paying attention to the task. Another simple approach to spam detection is to include a few stimuli with known correct answers ("gold standard" data); responses to these stimuli can be used to check the quality of a Turker's work. Responses from multiple Turkers can be compared to detect Turkers who are outliers. For example, Sprouse [17] plotted the distributions of data from different Turkers and rejected those that were significantly different from the others (about 14.2% of the total responses). Ipeirotis, Provost, & Wang [20] developed a more sophisticated model for detecting quality of Turkers on a classification task that requires 5 labels per object and 20-30 objects per Turker.

Finally, because the data are not about the Turkers themselves, the issue of representativeness and external validity of Turkers as a sample does not arise (though there may be issues concerning the representativeness of the sample of stimuli). A further consequence is that the ethical concerns regarding the use of human subjects in research do not apply. Instead, the Turkers can be seen as out-sourced employees, raising a different set of concerns about the fairness of such employment [e.g., 21]. One concern might be about the quality of the job offered, though as noted above, the typical wage offered is low only by the standards of developed countries; it is considerably more than the average in most developing countries.

2.3   Data about Reactions to a Research Stimulus

The final possibility is that the data of interest are not about the Turkers themselves nor explicit in a stimulus but rather come from interaction of people with a stimulus. It might be argued that data in mode 1 also come from an interaction with a stimulus such as a survey or test, but the difference here is that we are interested in data about the stimulus, not just the Turker. For example, a common research use of AMT is to recruit users for tests of IT systems in order to get usage data and user feedback [e.g., 6]. The goal of the study may be to compare different stimuli or to determine how members of different groups react to the same stimulus (e.g., which kinds of users find a particular system harder to use). In these cases, subjects' responses to the stimulus are expected to be different, rather than simply reflecting an underlying truth inherent in the stimulus as in mode 2. As a result, this mode of data collection presents the most challenging issues for both validity and reliability.

Validating subjective data for reliability is inherently difficult. Some of the techniques from the other modes may carry over. As in mode 1, it may be possible to use multiple items per construct to assess reliability. As in mode 2, careful task design and prequalification of Turkers will be useful. However, since many different answers could plausibly be correct [6], it is not possible to use "gold standard" data, to spot check results or to use replication to arrive at a consensus. These limitations would seem to limit the usefulness of AMT for interpretivist research in particular.

Spam continues to be a possible threat to internal validity. One approach is to include a few questions that can be used to check that the work required for the task is actually being performed, even if the work itself can not be checked. For example, Kittur et al. [6] had Turkers evaluating the quality of a Wikipedia page also report on "how many references, images, and sections the article had. In addition, users were required to provide 4-6 keywords." The answers to the first three questions were used to verify that the Turker had actually viewed the page; the answer to the last question required the Turker to carefully read the page, as required to rate quality.

This mode of data collection poses additional threats to internal validity. Berinsky et al. [7] suggested that because of concern about getting paid, conscientious Turkers may follow instructions closely, resulting in higher risk of researcher demand. For example, in evaluating a system, participants may provide positive or enthusiastic responses under the assumption that this will improve their chances of getting paid. It is also possible for an experiment that Turkers will discuss the experimental conditions in message boards or through other means [12]. However, if the experiment concludes quickly, this may not be a practical problem.

The specific demographics of Turkers raise concerns about the external validity of studies, as discussed above. However, Paolacci et al. [16] repeated three well-known psychological tests with Turkers and obtained results comparable to prior results, again suggesting that AMT results can generalize. Finally, as in the first case, since data will be collected about the Turkers, they will likely be considered human subjects in the research and so the concerns about the use and protection of human subjects apply.

To summarize, the specific recommendations made above to address concerns of reliability and validity in the three cases are presented in Table 1.

Table 1. Summary of recommendations to address reliability and validity of data from different modes of data collection

Research concern	Mode 1: Data about Turkers	Mode 2: Data about research stimulus	Mode 3: Data about interaction
Reliability (i.e., errors in responses)	Use multiple indicators per construct	Prequalify Turkers Replicate work Use AMT to validate responses	Use multiple indicators per construct Prequalify Turkers
Internal validity (i.e., biased responses)	Prevent or remove duplicate responses Consider effects of monetary compensation on research questions		Same as mode 1 Design task to minimize demand Minimize time to reduce discussion of experiment
Spam	Examine time taken to perform task Examine pattern of responses Include check questions	Same as mode 1 Include gold standard data Compare responses to detect outliers	Same as mode 1 Include objective-answer questions that demonstrate task performance
External validity (i.e., generalizability)	Not perfectly representative of Internet users, but not worse than alternatives	N/A	Same as mode 1

3   Case Study

To illustrate the application of AMT to an Information Systems research project, we present an example drawn from our own research. In this presentation, we present only how we used AMT to conduct the research; the details of the research questions, theories and the results of the study are reported elsewhere [22].

We have been conducting a design science research project to design and build a new citizen science system. In citizen science projects, members of the public are recruited to contribute to scientific investigations [23, 24]. Our project addresses a challenging problem in the life sciences: the taxonomic classification of plant, animal, and insect species from photographs. A photograph of a specimen, tagged with the date and location where it was taken, can provide valuable scientific data (e.g., on how urban sprawl impacts local ecosystems or evidence of local, regional, or global climactic shifts). To be useful though, it is necessary to know what the picture is of, expressed in scientific terms, i.e., the scientific name of the species depicted. *Citizen Sort* was developed to let members of the public view collections of pictures maintained by researchers and annotate them with data about the specimens they depict, with the goal of classifying the picture as a particular species. To motivate participation, we drew on the idea of purposeful gaming, developing *Happy Match*, a sorting and matching game that awards points and high scores for classification. To be successful, the game needs to motivate users to both play and to create quality data about the photographs.

We used AMT to conduct an initial evaluation of the game. Our study falls into the third category above: we are interested in the reactions of Turkers to the system as a kind of research stimulus (design science system evaluations would generally follow this pattern). We note that the AMT subject pool is not really appropriate to test theories about motivation, as offering payment makes it difficult to assess the effects of other motivations. However, in this preliminary evaluation our main interest was on the question of data quality (could untrained users successfully classify photographs), as well as the general usability/playability of the system. The possibility of rapid results offered by AMT seemed a good tradeoff for coverage of all research questions for this stage of the project. As well, AMT users seemed to be representative of our target population of active Internet users.

In setting up the HIT, we offered to pay participants US$0.50 for playing the game and completing a survey. To motivate good performance on the game, we offered a bonus of US$0.50 for getting a high score on any round in the game. We linked performance on the game to the survey results using a unique identifier, though a few players did not copy the identifier correctly, making their data unavailable for analysis. We offered to pay up to 100 users in each round of the study and ran two rounds in total, for a planned total of 200 participants. Because of the way AMT works, more than 100 people started each round. However, not all who started completed the task and of those who did, not all completed the survey that was necessary to be paid.

Those who accepted the AMT task were asked to accept an informed consent statement, to play *Happy Match* at least once and to then fill out the survey. The *Happy Match* system collected the number of games each player played and their score on each game. From the scores, we computed both the average score and high score. Finally, the system recorded each classifications performed by the users. For this initial evaluation, we only used photographs for which we had a professionally applied classification, enabling us to check the agreement of every user classification decision with the known data. From these data we computed each player's overall accuracy (the fraction of their classification that agreed with the expert), which we used to explore factors affecting data quality. After playing, users filled out a 28-item survey administered through AMT; these data were used to identify which users were more or less accurate as well as to explore motivational factors.

The results of our trial show both the strengths and weaknesses of the use of AMT. On the positive side, we were able to recruit a large number of users in a very short time and at low cost. For each round, we had the desired 100 responses within a day at a total cost of less than $100.00 per round. The subject pool was also much more diverse than a student pool would have been (e.g., ages ranged from 18 to 65). On the negative side, a few of the participants were apparently spammers, making little effort to play the game or to answer the survey questions; their data had to be filtered from the results. (We still paid them, as US human subjects rules require that we provide the offered compensation to any subject who starts the research.)

4   Conclusion

Prior experience with AMT suggests that with careful task design, AMT offers an interesting new capability to recruit research subjects or labour for a research project, providing useful research data. The typology presented above suggests relevant approaches. For studies of information systems and organizations, the first mode of data collection noted above is likely to be of limited use, as Turkers are likely too general a population for organizationally-focused research. Still, they may be a reasonable sample for studies of Internet use in general. Researchers could use this subject pool to examine attitudes or beliefs about technologies or specific systems. For example, a survey could be directed to users of eCommerce sites, such as Amazon, to examine attitudes or beliefs about the site's features or security.

AMT can provide a pool of workers to analyze research data, the second mode of use. It may be possible to crowdsource certain kinds of qualitative data analysis (e.g., content analysis), using the large number of Turkers to offset their minimal training. For example, researchers might use AMT to code email messages for evidence of particular kinds of group processes to explore how different kinds of participation is related to group effectiveness. A concern specific to organizational research is how to protect confidential data when its analysis is crowdsourced. However, many companies use AMT for their data, suggesting that this problem can be addressed.

Finally, studies in the third mode are likely to be particularly interesting for design science researchers, who might use AMT to recruit pilot study participants for system evaluations. As shown in the case study, the author has had some success using AMT in this way for a quick evaluation of a design science prototype. AMT could also be used for experiments by randomly assigning participants to different conditions. For example, a researcher could test the merits of an innovative interface by comparing the performance of Turkers on a task using a new and current system interface.

Acknowledgements. This research was partially supported by US NSF Grant 09–68470. The paper has benefited from helpful comments from Nathan Prestopnik and three anonymous reviewers.

References

1. Snow, R., O'Connor, B., Jurafsky, D., Ng, A.Y.: Cheap and fast—But is it good?: Evaluating non-expert annotations for natural language tasks. In: Proceedings of the Conference on Empirical Methods in Natural Language Processing, pp. 254–263. Association for Computational Linguistics (2008)
2. Kaisser, M., Lowe, J.: Creating a research collection of question answer sentence pairs with Amazon's Mechanical Turk. In: Proceedings of the Sixth International Conference on Language Resources and Evaluation, LREC 2008 (2008)
3. Rashtchian, C., Young, P., Hodosh, M., Hockenmaier, J.: Collecting image annotations using Amazon's Mechanical Turk. In: Proceedings of the NAACL HLT 2010 Workshop on Creating Speech and Language Data with Amazon's Mechanical Turk, pp. 139–147. Association for Computational Linguistics (2010)
4. Sorokin, A., Forsyth, D.: Utility data annotation with Amazon Mechanical Turk. In: Proceedings of the IEEE Computer Society Conference on Computer Vision and Pattern Recognition Workshops, pp. 1–8 (2008), doi:10.1109/CVPRW.2008.4562953
5. Heer, J., Bostock, M.: Crowdsourcing graphical perception: Using Mechanical Turk to assess visualization design. In: Proceedings of the 28th International Conference on Human Factors in Computing Systems (CHI 2010), pp. 203–212. ACM (2010), doi:10.1145/1753326.1753357
6. Kittur, A., Chi, E.H., Suh, B.: Crowdsourcing user studies with Mechanical Turk. In: Proceedings of the ACM Conference on Human-factors in Computing Systems, pp. 453–456. ACM, New York (2008)
7. Berinsky, A.J., Huber, G.A., Lenz, G.S.: Evaluating online labor markets for experimental research: Amazon.com's Mechanical Turk. Political Analysis 20, 351–368 (2012), doi:10.1093/pan/mpr057
8. Buhrmester, M., Kwang, T., Gosling, S.D.: Amazon's Mechanical Turk. Perspectives on Psychological Science 6, 3–5 (2011), doi:10.1177/1745691610393980
9. Conley, C.A.: Design for quality: The case of Open Source Software development. PhD dissertation. New York University, New York, NY (2008)
10. http://www.amazon.com/gp/help/customer/display.html?nodeId=1 6465291
11. Brabham, D.C.: Crowdsourcing as a model for problem solving: An introduction and cases. Convergence 14, 75 (2008)
12. Mason, W., Suri, S.: Conducting behavioral research on Amazon's Mechanical Turk. Behavior Research Methods 44, 1–23 (2012)
13. Ipeirotis, P.G.: Analyzing the Amazon Mechanical Turk marketplace. XRDS 17, 16–21 (2010), doi:10.1145/1869086.1869094
14. Horton, J.J., Chilton, L.B.: The labor economics of paid crowdsourcing. In: Proceedings of the 11th ACM Conference on Electronic Commerce, pp. 209–218 (2010)
15. Chilton, L.B., Horton, J.J., Miller, R.C., Azenkot, S.: Task search in a human computation market. In: Proceedings of the ACM SIGKDD Workshop on Human Computation, pp. 1–9. ACM (2010), doi:10.1145/1837885.1837889
16. Paolacci, G., Chandler, J., Ipeirotis, P.G.: Running experiments on Amazon Mechanical Turk. Judgment and Decision Making 5, 411–419 (2010)
17. Sprouse, J.: A validation of Amazon Mechanical Turk for the collection of acceptability judgments in linguistic theory. Behavior Research Methods 43, 155–167 (2011), doi:10.3758/s13428-010-0039-7

18. Ipeirotis, P.G.: Demographics of Mechanical Turk. Working Paper CEDER-10-01, New York University (2010), http://ssrn.com/abstract=1585030
19. Wang, Y.-C., Kraut, R., Levine, J.M.: To stay or leave? The relationship of emotional and informational support to commitment in online health support groups. In: Proceedings of the ACM Conference on Computer Supported Cooperative Work, pp. 833–842. ACM (2012), doi:10.1145/2145204.2145329
20. Ipeirotis, P.G., Provost, F., Wang, J.: Quality management on Amazon Mechanical Turk. In: Proceedings of the ACM SIGKDD Workshop on Human Computation, pp. 64–67. ACM (2010), doi:10.1145/1837885.1837906
21. De George, R.: Information technology, globalization and ethics. Ethics and Information Technology 8, 29–40 (2006)
22. Crowston, K., Prestopnik, N.R.: Motivation and data quality in a citizen science game: A design science evaluation. In: Proceedings of Hawai'i International Conference on System Science (2013)
23. Cohn, J.P.: Citizen science: Can volunteers do real research? BioScience 58, 192–107 (2008)
24. Wiggins, A., Crowston, K.: From conservation to crowdsourcing: A typology of citizen science. In: Proceedings of 44th Hawaii International Conference on System Sciences, pp. 1–10 (2011), doi:10.1109/HICSS.2011.207

Customization of Product Software:
Insight from an Extensive IS Literature Review

Matthias Bertram, Mario Schaarschmidt, and Harald F.O. von Kortzfleisch

University of Koblenz-Landau
{matthias.bertram,mario.schaarschmidt,
harald.von.kortzfleisch}@uni-koblenz.de

Abstract. In recent years, companies started not only to ask customers by means of market research but to integrate them into the innovation process. Within information systems (IS) research, both customization as a way to serve the uniqueness of customers (inside-out) and as a form of customer integration and value co-creation (outside-in) has been considered. However, since many software vendors have consummated the shift from being manufacturers to being service firms, in practice, customization as a service highlights the continuance of customization projects. This paper addresses the research question of how concepts of customization are distinguished in recent IS literature. By conducting an extensive review of the IS literature between 2001 and 2011 we find that future research could benefit from considering knowledge interactions in customization processes more deeply.

Keywords: Customizing, Customization, Value Co-Creation, Information Systems, Literature Review.

1   Introduction

Companies increasingly need to understand their customers' wants and needs in order to strengthen their competitive positions. Thus, in recent years companies started not only to ask customers by means of market research but to integrate them into the innovation process [1, 2]. Concurrently, since the late 1970s the co-creation of value has become a field of intense research in marketing and service science. Researchers have analyzed co-creation under many different aspects as for example: productivity gains through customer self-service (e.g., [3], [4]), customer satisfaction, quality, employee's performance and emotional responses (e.g., [5]), and the opportunity to differentiate their products and services (e.g., [6]). Thereby, customization has emerged as a concept to provide customers with tailor-made products and services.

With respect to customization, researchers further concluded that customers may not be recognized as passive receivers, but should be seen as active and knowledgeable participants in common innovation or co-creation processes ([7]). For example, Firat et al. [8] introduced the concept of customerization and stated that it enables consumers to serve as the co-producer of the product and service offering.

A. Bhattacherjee and B. Fitzgerald (Eds.): Future of ICT Research, IFIP AICT 389, pp. 222–236, 2012.

Relatedly, Ghosh et al. [9], who investigated the role of control in complex product customization, stated that success of customization is a function of the customer's knowledge. Thus, co-creation researchers assume an outside-in perspective of customization in that they focus on the integration of external resources into the innovation process.

Another stream of research pertaining to the concept of customization stems from economics and marketing. Here, researchers obtain an inside-out perspective in that they refer to customization as a way to tailor and deliver products and services according to customers' needs (e.g., [10]). They further highlight the role of mass customization as a customer specific production with near mass production efficiency and realization of economies of scales (e.g., [11], [12]).

However, the majority of articles in both areas have been written in a business-to-consumer (B2C) context, documented by the emphasis of the role of consumers and individual customers (e.g., [13], [14]). Within business-to-business (B2B) contexts, such as with the market for business software (e.g., enterprise resource planning (ERP) software), concepts such as mass customization are comparatively seldom because (1) buyers markets usually consist of only a few firms and (2) products are generally more complex than in B2C scenarios [9].

Given the importance of customization for an entire service industry (i.e. customization of business software such as SAP R/3) along with the scarce focus on integrative research studies in this field, a thorough analysis and synthesis of the concept is needed to promote future research. Against this background, the central research question of this paper is: How does current academic IS literature differ in definitions and applications of customization approaches in B2B scenarios? To answer this question, we conducted an extensive information systems (IS) literature review concerning the past decade. We draw on two different sources of academic IS literature: major journal papers including the IS senior scholars' basket of journals and conference proceedings.

The remainder of the paper is organized as follows. Section 2 provides a closer look at concepts and ideas of customization in the context of software products and exposes existing concepts and terms of customizing and (mass) customization. Section 3 describes the underlying research design including data collection, data analysis and results. In section 4, an interpretation of the results and a critical discussion is provided. The paper closes with a conclusions and implications for further research and practice.

2   Related Work

2.1   Concepts of Product Software

According to Sawyer [16] the concept of "make one, sell many" is common to all product software. He states that product software and tailor-made software can be distinguished by three major differences: First, while tailor-made software is oriented towards one customer, product software is market-oriented. Second, there are much more conditions for using a software product according to the hardware and software platform than for a tailor-made software which usually runs under one platform. And finally, with software products, the vendor usually retains the ownership of the software, while with tailor-made software all the corresponding artifacts (source code, documentation, etc.) are entirely sold to the customer.

From Xu and Brinkkemper's [17] perspective the process for developing product software consists of four development operations, Analysis of Requirements, Development, Delivery and Implementations Service. Each operation results in a stock or an IT artifact: Design Specification (D), Source Code (S), Delivered Software (P) and Running System (R). The biggest difference to the development process of tailor-made software is that due to the number of customers and changing (business) re-quirements product software is almost never finished. With reference to other devel-opment processes such as eXtreme Programming, Scrum or the Rational Unified Process, Xu and Brinkkemper [17] state that the development of product software has a continual need for improvement and cannot be modeled in a sequential process.

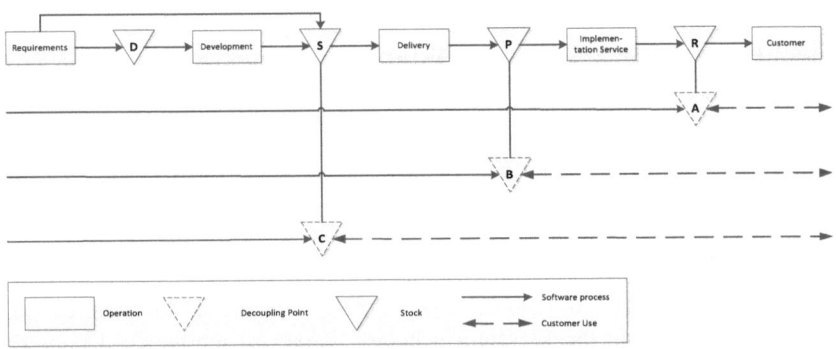

Fig. 1. Software production flow pipe-line (Source: adapted from Xu and Brinkkemper 2007)

From this perspective, product software can be classified into three categories according to the position of the decoupling point. The first category (C) is called semi-finished-products which are software products like components or libraries that is intended to be sold to other business partners. The second category (B) self-install software contains software products, which can be sold by vendor and installed by the customer without special help. The third category (A) includes software products that require professional help for implementation (i.e. customizing) into the business (Figure 1).

2.2   Customization of Product Software

In the early days of software development, when software and hardware was still closely bundled, the prices for those systems were extremely high since the market for software products was simply not existent. Usually those systems were solely developed for individual companies according to their individual needs and requirements. In the late 1960s computer manufactures started to unbundle hardware and software systems foundations as a result of an IBM initiative ([17]). As a consequence, an independent software market for business-to-business (B2B) was built where during 1980s, a new class of software vendors started to pre-built and offer software for ranges of business functions that could be delivered separately in large scales.

However, to address each customer's wants and needs, software was designed in a way that each customer could adapt certain parts without changing the source code of the software (e.g., changing a desktop background, hiding navigation, etc.). Today, global enterprise software companies such as SAP, Oracle and Microsoft generally develop product software for wider, more anonymous (B2B) markets or industries. In these cases, requirements usually are not fully specified and are worked out in implementation projects with customers. Thereby, customization in information systems can be understood as a special type of co-creation of value and late product differentiation. The economic importance of those customization projects is very high. For example IBM's total revenue in 2007 was $99B with more than 50% ($54B) resulting from consulting services including customization ([18]).

As discussed, the service of customizing complex product software has become business itself. Crucial to the existence of this service industry is that large business software requires changes at the source code level in order to be adapted to a user firm's need. In addition, as shown by Ghosh et al. [9] for mechanical industries, within software customizing projects, the project success is a function of the customer's knowledge. In particular, compared to mass customization in B2C scenarios where customers can chose colors or materials of the desired product ([19]), due to the complexity of business software, the customer usually is not able to communicate the needs in a proper way. In addition, the professional customer's needs change due to environmental turbulences and market dynamics. Consequently, the process of adapting a software product according to the professional customer's need drags on and demands several iterations. Thus, instead of communicating needs just once as in the case of mass customization in B2C contexts, customizing complex product software requires an iterative approach and is dependent on the customer's knowledge as well as his ability to communicate needs.

Based on our preliminary insights we provide the following working definition of customization for our analysis, knowing that customization in general and mass customization in particular need to be distinguished more specifically:

Customization is the process of configuring, parameterizing, or generally adopting an IS artifact to a customer's need.

3   Research Approach

According to authors such as Huff [20] or Creswell [21], one of the most well-established methods to integrate research findings and assess the cumulative knowledge within a domain is a qualitative literature review. This method allows researchers to analyze and evaluate both qualitative and quantitative literature within a research domain to draw conclusions about a state of a field. Since this method is well-established, researchers have already performed and adopted it to their needs and thereby developed several approaches to reviewing literature. For example, Huff [20] differentiates between at least four types of literature reviews: (1) survey to identify key issues and trends, (2) critical review to identify arguments, standards and potential for new contributions, (3) systematic review to expose quantitative and qualitative results across several areas of interest and (4) supportive review to generate new ideas and to resolve specific problems from existing literature. Those four differ in for example in purpose and primary and secondary sources of literature.

The research aim of this paper is to draw a coherent picture of ideas and concepts of customization in current IS literature and thereby helps to categorize existing ideas and concepts and furthermore identify potentials for future contributions to that field. Hence, according to Huff's [20] systematic of literature reviews this paper uses a critical review approach.

Since journal and conference publications are both a very accepted way to communicate research findings to the IS research community and referring to Webster and Watson [22], major IS-journals and -conferences were chosen as primary sources for the review. By adopting Jourdan et al.'s [23] research approach, we decided to split our research design into two sequential phases. The aim of the first phase was to identify relevant papers in mayor IS journals/conferences. During the second phase, an in-depth analysis of the selected papers was conducted (Figure 2).

In phase 1, we first determined the pool of journals and conference proceedings relevant to our study. For journals, we concentrated on the senior scholars' basket of journals that embrace six journals (i.e. MIS Quarterly, Information Systems Research, Journal of Management Information Systems, Journal of the Association for Information Systems, European Journal of Information Systems, Information Systems Journal) as well as on journals as recommended by Fisher et al. [24], Jourdan et al. [23], and Mustafee [25]. For conferences, we decided to include the proceedings of the International Conference on Information Systems (ICIS) and European Conference on Information Systems (ECIS). Additionally, the proceedings of the Wirtschaftsinformatik conference was included since this conference is (1) the major German speaking conference for IS research and (2) receives a higher share of design-oriented papers ([26]) what we consider important concerning our aim to provide a coherent picture of customization.

We used the ISI Web of Knowledge as well as the electronic library of the Association of Information Systems (AISel) to find potential papers for our review. We used the search functionality of each database to search titles and abstracts of the research articles using the phrases "customizing", "customizing", "customisation", and "customisation" and a publication date between 2001 and 2011. While the search engine and interface in the case of ISI Web of Knowledge was very user friendly, a little more handwork was needed in the case of the AISel because we were not able to restrict the search to the designated conferences. In the end we were able to build a superset of 84 journal articles and 23 conference proceedings for our research.

Table 1. Results after research phase 1

#	Journal	Acronym	# Articles	# Preselect
1	MIS Quarterly	MISQ	8	4
2	Information Systems Research	ISR	7	3
3	Communication of the ACM	CACM	3	2
4	Journal of Management Information Systems	JMIS	5	5
5	Management Science	MS	16	15
6	Journal of the ACM	JACM	0	0
7	European Journal of Information Systems	EJIS	9	9
8	IEEE Transactions on Software Engineering	IEEETSE	8	4
9	Information Management	I&M	4	1
10	Harvard Business Review	HBR	20	8
11	Wirtschaftsinformatik	WI	4	3
	Total Journals		**84**	**54**

#	Proceedings	Acronym	# Articles	# Preselect
1	European Conference on Information Systems	ECIS	12	6
2	International Conference on Information Systems	ICIS	5	3
3	Wirtschaftsinformatik	WIP	6	2
	Total Proceedings		**23**	**11**
	Total		**107**	**65**

As a last step in our research phase 1, based on the abstract we preselect relevant articles for our further analysis. As a code for the categorization we used a very simple A, B and C scheme, where A meant the article fits greatly our topics (i.e. customization in IS and B2B), C it doesn't fit at all and B somewhere in between the former two. Two of the three authors assigned each publication to a category based upon the reading of abstracts. If both authors came to the same conclusion, the focal publication was assigned to the chosen category. For papers that have been assigned to different categories by the authors (N=18), both authors agreed to a common category after a rigorous discussion. In the end, all articles within category A and B were considered to be relevant for this research. Finally, we ended up with a set of 54 journal papers and 11 conference papers. Table 1 summarizes the results of research phase 1.

After the pre-selection process we organized phase 2 - the in-depth analysis of the papers - as follows. Subsets of the research papers were allocated to each author; taking care that each subset consisted of papers from heterogeneous sources (i.e. a mixture of journals and conference proceedings).

For each paper in his subset each author had to identify the underlying research approach and definitions for customization concepts. We determined that each researcher had to analyze not more than three papers a week and that the findings had to be presented and discussed in weekly feedback meetings. Therefore, it was possible to organize an efficient research process which on the one hand allows a discourse on single papers and on the other hand avoided researcher fatigue.

Using this approach we were able to resolve disagreements and provide consensual results for each paper. Table 2 provides an extract of the most interesting results of research phase 2, grouped into customization as a *form of delivery* and a *form of co-creation of value*.[1]

Table 2. Extract of results after research phase 2

Author	Definition / Concept	Paper Type
Customization as form of distribution		
[27]	Computer workarounds are a post-implementation phenomenon widespread in organizations. They are commonly defined as non-compliant user behaviours vis-à-vis the intended system design, which may go so far as to bypass the formal systems entirely.	Case study
[28]	Although known primarily as a production principle [...], mass customization has also been applied to intangible products [...] focus distributive and marketing aspects when mass customizing offerings and deals.	Conceptional paper
[29]	One important question in packaged software design and consumption is determining what the software can and will do, in supporting, changing, and inhibiting desired organizational practices.	Case study (Participation)
[30]	This improvement in manufacturing flexibility allows mass customization of consumer products without significantly compromising cost efficiency. Not surprisingly, mass customization has begun to erode the domain of mass-produced standard items.	Game theory
[31]	Both [OS and COTS software] need to be customized to fit the requirements of the adopting organization. Configuration and parameterization are the approaches of choice in this case. If they are not sufficient, customization of the SW code is necessary.	Action research
[32]	The internet has increased the expectation of customers for complete customization at a nominal charge. Even before the advent of e-business, firms faced the challenge related to mass customization and high productivity variety, but this has increased immensely over the last few years.	Conceptional paper

---

[1] The entire list of journal articles and conference papers is available upon request.

Table 2. (*continued*)

[33]	Packaged enterprise software is ready-made mass product offing users a solution based design process aimed at generic customer groups in a variety of industries and geographical areas. Packaged software can be contrasted with custom-built approaches, based on the organization of the development and delivery process.	Conceptional paper (Qualitiative interviews)
[34]	Product configuration systems are useful instruments of individualization in the field of mass customization.	Experiment

Customization as co-creation

[35]	Within mass customization, customers are integrated into value creation by defining, configuring, designing, matching, or modifying their individual solution out of a list of options and pre-defined components.	Conceptual paper
[36]	In such cases, clients can either change their organizational practices to fit the software or customize the software application to fit their needs at some cost.	Hypotheses development
[37]	The goal of SPLs is to improve productivity, time-to-market, and quality of application development by leveraging the commonalities of systems within an application domain while managing their variations. SPLs package these commonalities in domain-specific platforms, which may be customized through configuration settings or code extensions.	Conceptional paper
[38]	A related stream of research has focused on the tailoring of software methods to the actual needs of the development context. Factors such as organizational issues [...], distributed teams [...], or the existence of legacy systems [...] often require the use of a different method, or at least changes to the existing method.	Interviews
[39]	Process customization or tailoring involves adapting, particularizing, or selecting certain (often standard or "best practice") software processes to fit the needs of specific organizations or projects.	Case study (Qualitative interviews)

4   Findings and Discussion

4.1   Levels of Customization

While there is a common understanding of customization as the adaption of software products, or more general IT artifacts, to specific customer's needs, the existing IS literature primarily uses concepts of customization from other disciplines. For example, the term mass customization was almost always defined in relation to industrial contexts without providing a sufficient definition in relation to characteristics of IS artifacts. Furthermore, the literature differs to a great extend in describing the level of customization since the term is used for configuration, parameterization, as well as adaption or development of existing or new source code.

Due to customer as well as vendor related reasons, the intensity of interaction in customization projects can be very high. For instance, because of a high level of innovation neither the customer nor the vendor is able to pre-estimate the effort to implement desired functionalities [29, 33]. In these cases, customization involves the customer's support to understand and change his own processes (e.g., by means of consulting services). On the vendor side, the software product's "manufacturing flexibility" or architectural agility may not be sufficient to implement the desired functionality in a standardized way and, for example, the source code has to be changed [31]. From our perception of customization in IS studies under investigation we define customization (in general) as a highly iterative form of IS implementation or adaption, where vendor and customer interactions are so intensive that it is not possible to handle them in single iterations of knowledge transfer.

> *Customization is the process of configuring, parameterizing or in general adopting an IS artifact to a customers need, in more than one iteration. In this case either the customer is NOT able to communicate his requirements in one step OR the vendors' manufacturing and distribution system is NOT capable to deliver the customized artifact in one additional step and a more intensive interaction between those two parties is necessary.*

In contrast, mass customization focuses on the efficiency aspect of customization. The term was initially introduced by Davis [41] and later defined in the work of Tseng and Jiao [12] on industrial engineering as "producing goods and services to meet individual customer's needs with near mass production efficiency". Within IS, product configuration is an instrument to implement mass customization [34]. Due to the efficiency aspect of mass customization, the customer has to have a sufficient understanding of his requirements on the one hand and the vendors' delivery system has to be flexible (and standardized) enough to integrate this requirements in the existing product. Thus, at least one iteration of knowledge transfer occurs: The customer provides his knowledge on the requirements to the vendor and the vendor reacts by delivering a customized product. With respect to IS research and regarding the efficiency aspect of mass customization, we define it as follows:

Mass customization is the process of configuring, parameterizing or generally adopting an IS artifact to a customer's need in one iteration. This happens only if the customer is able to communicate his requirements in one step and the vendor's manufacturing and distribution system is capable to deliver the customized artifact in one additional step.

4.2   Intentions of Customization

Customization as a Way to Deliver Software Products. As expected, customization seems to be a central topic in IS research. Predominantly, researchers focus on the way of how software is delivered to customers in relation to distribution economics[28, 33, 34]. Packaged software, as one incarnation of product software, has been one way to address the challenges of customization in many articles of our review. For example, Van Fenema et al. [33] described packaged software as "ready-made mass product offering users a solution based design process aimed at generic customer groups in a variety of industries and geographical areas." A more general focus is delivered by Chiasson and Green's [29] definition of packaged software, who argue that an important question in packaged software design and consumption is determining what the software can and will do, in supporting, changing, and inhibiting desired organizational practices.

In a similar vein, Sia and Soh [40] describe the package-organizational fit as the central point of interest for package customization. Regarding uncertainty in customization projects, Safadi and Faraj [27] describe workarounds as a valid way to address requirements that have not been foreseen during the development or implementation of a software package. They define this post-implementation phenomenon as a non-compliant user behavior vis-á-vis the intended system design. Although in extreme cases formal systems are entirely bypassed, workarounds are widely spread among organizations. From an architectural point of view Czarnecki et al. [37] describe software product lines as a tool "to improve productivity, time-to-market, and quality of application development by leveraging the commonalities of systems within an application domain while managing their variations" to address some of the above described challenges.

So far, a considerable stream of research addresses the way of distribution (i.e. packaging) of product software and regards customization in an "after-production"-sense. As this perspective accrued from a logic in which a product is first produced and then distributed, it corresponds with the inside-out perspective of customization in IS introduced earlier.

Customization as the Co-creation of Value. Another stream of research in IS literature addresses the development side of software as well as customer integration during the development processes in particular. For example, Piller et al. [35] state that "with in mass customization, customers are integrated into value creation by defining, configuring, designing, matching, or modifying their individual solution out of a list of options and pre-defined components". In a similar vein Xin and Levina [36] argue that clients not only customize the software to their needs, but also change organizational practices to fit the software product.

Additionally, research has focused on the tailoring of software methods to development contexts. Fitzgerald et al. [38] argue that factors such as organizational issues, distributed teams, and the existence of legacy systems require different or changed development methods. In a similar vein, Slaughter et al. [39] describe the strategy and process fit as important for the development process. From their point of view, process customization or tailoring is important to fit the needs of specific organizations or projects. This involves adapting, particularizing, or selecting certain software processes.

In summary, a considerable stream of research addresses customization as a form of co-creation of value and thus supports our notion of a distinct outside-in perspective of customization in IS.

4.3   Customization as a Service and Future Directions

As expected, IS literature has paid attention to both customization as a form to realize economies of scales by using "make one, sell many "-approaches (inside-out) as well as a way of integrating customers into the innovation process (outside-in). Surprisingly, the combination of both perspectives has somewhat been neglected by IS research. Regarding customization as understood in practice, that is, the service of customization of large business software in B2B contexts, the customer provides his knowledge in his area of expertise as well as his requirements in multiple iterations. Thus, the customer complements the vendor's knowledge at a technological and at a market level not only at a distinct point in time as, for example, with mass customization, but continuously. Because receiving formulated requirements frequently is demanding, vendors in a customization scenario must develop a particular absorptive capacity [43] to be able to benefit from external knowledge sufficiently. However, as our review shows, reciprocal knowledge flows within IS literature pertaining to customization and customizing are largely neglected.

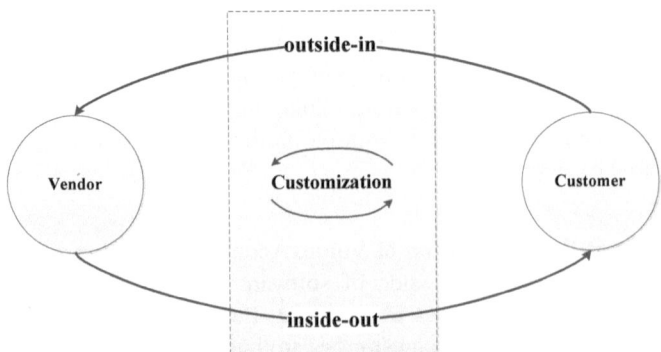

Fig. 2. Customizing as an iterative-circular process of knowledge flows

In summary, from our observation we posit that the existing literature is anemic to knowledge transfer between vendor and customer in multiple iterations which drives us to delineate future research areas. To clarify our assumptions, Figure 3 shows the reciprocal "inside-out" and "outside-in" relationship between vendor and customer. For the reason of simplicity we left intermediates such as consultants and professional services out and sub summated them under the term vendor. While our research results highlight the differences in definition and application of customization concepts in IS literature, we recognize several aspects where further research in this area is needed.

First, as our review revealed, current studies differentiate customization by the means of level (customization and mass customization) and intention (co-creation of value and product distribution). Although existing literature considers those aspects to a certain extent, it lacks research studies that integrate the accumulated body of research. For instance, while literature differentiates the level of customization regarding customization (in general) and mass customization approaches, further studies are needed investigating the influence of the underlying customization technique on those levels. So far, existing literature describes product configuration as a tool for implementing mass customization functionality. Considering our definition of customization and mass customization based on interaction efficiency, mass customization might also be implemented using other techniques such as parameterization or source code development. Additionally, further research studies are needed investigating how customization intention influences software product management and vice versa. For instance, from a vendor perspective co-creation of value projects might be valuable for the orientation of the software product. From this point of view such projects can be considered a crucial investment in software product management. Here, future research should focus on what are the drivers and barriers of those customization activities and how vendors value and balance co-creation of value and product distribution projects.

Second, as already mentioned, customization strongly depends on the interaction and the knowledge transfer between vendors and customers. Considering customization as a service, a reciprocal knowledge exchange from vendor to customer (inside-out) and customer to vendor (outside-in) can be assumed. In this area further research is needed investigating the influence of customization level and intention on characteristics and transfer of exchanged knowledge. Regarding the level of customization, we assume that due to interaction intensity with respect to tangible and intangible knowledge, customization (in general) is a richer medium of knowledge transfer than mass customization. On the other hand, within mass customization the vendor's manufacturing system has to be close to the customers' requirements to provide efficient customization functionality. In this case, we assume that the vendor has already a certain knowledge base about the topic of interest, which facilitates the exploration and assimilation of new knowledge. Here we state that future research in the context of customization should place more emphasis on knowledge characteristics and knowledge exploration, assimilation and exploitation processes.

Finally, if customization of large product software is regarded as a full service with multiple rounds of knowledge transfer between vendor and customer instead of a 'one-time-only' on-top service for software goods, several issues such as customer integration and satisfaction have to be reconsidered in relation to innovation. Here, further research is needed that (1) identifies the factors that influence the success of customization projects on both vendor and customer side, that (2) considers the reciprocal nature of knowledge transfer with regard to the tension between vendors service delivery and innovation activities (i.e. standard product development), and (3) that investigates service properties (e.g., high vs. low degree of product customization) in relation to customer outcomes.

5   Conclusion

In this article, we provided an intensive review of the literature of the past ten years on customization and customizing aspects of B2B software in the IS field. Although this timeframe partly limits the generalizability our research results, it reflects recent developments in the software markets such as the rising complexity of software system which increases the need for customization.

We found support for the notion of customization as a form of co-creation of value between vendors (also intermediates like consultants/professional services) and customers as well as for how widely spread the phenomenon is in the IS field. Similarly, we found support for an inside-out perspective of customization in that customization is understood as a form of software delivery. Furthermore, we described why the degree of customization is strongly dependent on the software product itself and the decoupling point where the customer comes into place during the development process and they criticize that many packages are not able to address important needs and expectations of organizations.

Our literature review revealed that even being an issue of interest in IS research for quite a period, concepts of customization have still not been defined sufficiently. Terms such as mass customization and customization are often used inconsistently (and sometime even interchangeably) or are provided with poor definitions referring to other disciplines. By providing definitions of customization and mass customization based on knowledge and vendor-customer interactions, we contribute to IS in general and software engineering in particular. Our research may act as a starting point for deeper and further-reaching contributions to this field of interest, regarding the tension between standardization (product software) and individualization (tailor-made software) under consideration of vendor and customer requirements. We further call for more in-depth studies that consider the role of knowledge exchange in customization of IS artifacts.

References

1. Prahalad, C.K., Ramaswamy, V.: Co-opting customer experience. Harvard Bus. Rev. 78(1), 79–88 (2000)
2. Von Hippel, E.: Democratizing Innovation. MIT Press, Cambridge (2005)

3. Czepiel, J.A.: Service encounters and service relationships: Implications for research. J. Bus. Res. 20(1), 13–21 (1990)
4. Kelley, S.W., Donnelly, J.H., Skinner, S.J.: Customer participation in service production and delivery. J. Retailing 66(3), 315–335 (1990)
5. Bendapudi, N., Leone, R.P.: Psychological implications of customer participation in co-production. J. Marketing 67(1), 14–28 (2003)
6. Song, J.H., Adams, C.R.: Differentiation through customer involvement in production or delivery. J. Consum Marketing 10(2), 4–12 (1993)
7. Nambisan, S.: Designing virtual customer environments for new product development: Toward a theory. Acad. Manage. Rev. 27(3), 392–413 (2002)
8. Firat, A.F., Dholakia, N., Venkatesh, A.: Marketing in a postmodern world. Eur. J. Marketing 29(1), 40–56 (1995)
9. Ghosh, M., Dutta, S., Stremersch, S.: Customizing Complex Products: When Should the Vendor Take Control? J. Marketing Res. 43(4), 664–679 (2006)
10. Franke, N., Keinz, P., Steger, C.: Testing the value of customization: When do customers really prefer products tailored to their preferences? J. Marketing 73(5), 103–121 (2009)
11. Kotler, P.: From mass marketing to mass customization. Strategy and Leadership 17(5), 10–47 (1989)
12. Tseng, M.M., Jiao, J.: Mass customization. In Handbook of Industrial Engineering, Technology and Operation Management, 3rd edn. Wiley, New York (2001)
13. Etgar, M.: A descriptive model of the consumer co-production process. J. Acad. Marketing Sci. 36(1), 97–108 (2008)
14. Franke, N., Schreier, M.: Product uniqueness as a driver of customer utility in mass customization. Marketing Letters 19(2), 93–107 (2007)
15. Müller, J., Krüger, J., Enderlein, S., Helmich, M., Zeier, A.: Customizing enterprise software as a service application: Back-end extension in a multi-tenancy environment. Enterprise Inform. Syst. 24(1), 66–77 (2009)
16. Sawyer, S.: A market-based perspective on information systems development. Commun. ACM 44, 97–102 (2001)
17. Xu, L., Brinkkemper, S.: Concepts of product software. Eur. J. Inform. Syst. 16(5), 531–541 (2007)
18. Spohrer, J., Maglio, P.P.: The emergence of service science: Toward systematic service innovations to accelerate co-creation of value. Prod. Oper. Manage. 17, 238–246 (2008)
19. Reichwald, R., Piller, F.T.: From mass production towards customer integration and co-production. Wirtschaftsinformatik 45(5), 515–519 (2003)
20. Huff, A.S.: Designing Research for Publications. Sage Publications, London (2008)
21. Creswell, J.W.: Research design: Qualitative, quantitative, and mixed methods approaches, 3rd edn. Sage Publication, London (2009)
22. Webster, J., Watson, R.T.: Analyzing the past to prepare for the future: Writing a literature review. MIS Quart 26(2), 8–13 (2002)
23. Jourdan, R.Z., Kelly, R., Marshall, T.E.: Business intelligence: An analysis of the literature. Inform. Syst. Manage. 25(2), 121–131 (2008)
24. Fisher, J., Shanks, G., Lamp, J.: A ranking list for information systems journals. Austral. J. Inform. Syst. 14(2), 5–18 (2007)
25. Mustafee, N.: Evolution of IS research based on literature published in two leading IS journals – EJIS and MISQ. In: Proceedings of the European Conference on Information Systems (2011), http://aisel.aisnet.org/ecis2011/228

26. Oesterle, H., Becker, J., Frank, U., Hess, T., Karagiannis, D., Krcmar, H., Loos, P., Mertens, P., Oberweis, P., Sinz, E.: Memorandum on design-oriented information systems research. Eur. J. Inform. Syst. 20, 7–20 (2010)
27. Safadi, H., Faraj, S.: The role of workarounds during an opensource electronic medical record system implementation. In: Proceedings of the International Conference on Information Systems (2010), http://aisel.aisnet.org/icis2010_submissions
28. Brocke, H., Ubernickel, F., Brenner, W.: Mass customizing IT service agreements: T owards individualized on-demand services. In: Proceedings of the European Conference on Information Systems (2010), http://aisel.aisnet.org/ecis2010/101
29. Chiasson, M.W., Green, L.W.: Questioning the IT artefact: user practices that can, could, and cannot be supported in packaged-software designs. Eur. J. Inform. Syst. 16(5), 542–554 (2007)
30. Dewan, R., Jing, B., Seidmann, A.: Product customization and price competition on the Internet. Manage. Sci. 49(8), 1055–1070 (2003)
31. Keßler, S., Alpar, P.: Do best practice frameworks fit open source software customization? In: Proceedings of the European Conference on Information Systems 2008 (2009), http://aisel.aisnet.org/ecis2008/20
32. Swaminathan, J.M., Tayur, S.R.: Models for supply chains in e-business. Manage. Sci. 49(10), 1387–1406 (2003)
33. Van Fenema, P.C., Koppius, O.R., van Baalen, P.J.: Implementing packaged enterprise software in multi-site firms: intensification of organizing and learning. Eur. J. Inform. Syst. 16(5), 584–598 (2007)
34. Weinmann, M., Robra-Bissantz, S., Witt, M., Schmidt, E.: Einflussfaktoren auf die Präferenz bei Produktkonfiguratoren - Eine empirische Studie am Beispiel der Automobilindustri. In: Proceedings of Wirtschaftinformatik 2011 (2011), http://aisel.aisnet.org/wi2011
35. Piller, F., Schubert, P., Koch, M., Möslein, K.: From mass customization to collaborative customer codesign. In: Proceedings of the European Conference on Information Systems 2004 (2004), http://aisel.aisnet.org/ecis2004/118
36. Xin, M., Levina, N.: Software-as-a service model: Elaborating client-side adoption factors. In: Proceedings of the International Conference on Information Systems (2008), http://aisel.aisnet.org/icis2008/86
37. Czarnecki, K., Antkiewicz, M., Kim, C.H.P.: Multi-level customization in application engineering - Developing mechanisms for mapping features to analysis models. Commun. ACM 49(12), 61–65 (2006)
38. Fitzgerald, B., Hartnett, G., Conboy, K.: Customizing agile methods to software practices at Intel Shannon. Eur. J. Inform. Syst. 15(2), 200–213 (2006)
39. Slaughter, S.A., Levine, L., Ramesh, B., Pries-Heje, J., Baskerville, R.: Aligning software processes with strategy. MIS Quart. 30(4), 891–918 (2006)
40. Sia, S.K., Soh, C.: An assessment of package-organisation misalignment: institutional and ontological structures. Eur. J. Inform. Syst. 16(5), 568–583 (2007)
41. Davis, S.: Future Perfect, 10th anniversary edition. Addison-Wesley Pub. Co, Harlow (1996)
42. Lakhani, K., Von Hippel, E.: How open source software works: Free user-to-user assistance. Res. Policy 32, 923–943 (2003)
43. Lichtenthaler, U.: Absorptive capacity, environmental turbulence, and the complementarity of organizational learning processes. Acad. Manage. J. 52(4), 822–846 (2009)

Author Index

Ahangama, Supunmali   143
Alam, M. Shahanoor   51
Almklov, Petter   91

Berente, Nicholas   195
Bertram, Matthias   222
Bin Mohd Shariff, Ahmed Shafeeq   3
Brooks, Laurence   51

Chang, Klarissa   160
Crowston, Kevin   210

Datta, Anindya   3, 18
Donnellan, Brian   35
Dutta, Kaushik   3, 18

Furuholt, Bjørn   68

Helfert, Markus   35
Hepsø, Vidar   91

Kajanan, Sangaralingam   3
Khan, N.I.   51

Lawrence, Carl   177
Lyytinen, Kalle   195

Monteiro, Eric   91

Østerlie, Thomas   108
Oivo, Markku   177

Poo, Danny Chiang Choon   143

Schaarschmidt, Mario   222
Schultze, Ulrike   79
Sein, Maung Kyaw   68
Shaikh, Maha   123
Sjöström, Jonas   35

Um, SungYong   195

von Kortzfleisch, Harald F.O.   222

Wu, Yi   160

Xu, Xiaoying   18

Yoo, Youngjin   195